Asian Mergers and Acquisitions

Asian Mergers and Acquisitions

Riding the Wave

VIKRAM CHAKRAVARTY
CHUA SOON GHEE

WILEY

John Wiley & Sons Singapore Pte. Ltd.

Other Wiley Editorial Offices

John Wiley & Sons, 111 River Street, Hoboken, NJ 07030, USA

John Wiley & Sons, The Atrium, Southern Gate, Chichester, West Sussex, PO19 8SQ, United Kingdom

John Wiley & Sons (Canada) Ltd., 5353 Dundas Street West, Suite 400, Toronto, Ontario, M9B 6HB, Canada

John Wiley & Sons Australia Ltd., 42 McDougall Street, Milton, Queensland 4064, Australia

Wiley-VCH, Boschstrasse 12, D-69469 Weinheim, Germany

ISBN 978-1-118-24709-9 (Hardcover)
ISBN 978-1-118-24712-9 (ePDF)
ISBN 978-1-118-24711-2 (Mobi)
ISBN 978-1-118-24710-5 (ePub)

Typeset in 10/13 pt. Photina-Regular by MPS Limited, Chennai, India.
Printed in Singapore by Markono Print Media Pte Ltd

10 9 8 7 6 5 4 3 2 1

Contents

Foreword

ASIA CAN BE A tricky place to do business. With its multitude of cultures and languages coupled with the fragmented nature of its markets and the diversity of its customers, the risks here are incredibly varied. The potential pitfalls are many, whether for a company intending to expand into Asia or an Asian company that is hungry for growth via acquisitions. Having run Asian businesses for several Western companies in the past decade, I have had direct experience with the challenges of operating in the region and, in particular, doing deals.

Yet it is hard to imagine a multinational corporation that would not have "expansion in Asia" somewhere near the top of its list of priorities. Indeed, after the significant downturn in most Western markets, Asia is the only sustainable growth story. Besides being the home of manufacturing for most of the world's products, domestic demand in Asia has also seen a step increase as urbanization grows and more Asians get wealthier. This presents the perfect environment for game-changing acquisitions.

With all of these aspects in mind, this excellent and accessible guide to mergers and acquisitions (M&A) in Asia by Vikram Chakravarty and Chua Soon Ghee is timely, essential reading for anyone either within Asia considering growth through acquisition or outside Asia wondering how best to get in. With the distinction of being the first book on the subject over the past six to seven years, coinciding with a time when Asia has been on the rise, this book is a practical "thought map" to guide your M&A strategy for the region, punctuated with well-placed case studies that offer a quick grasp of the key issues.

In the first part of the book, the authors make the case for how a wave of Asian M&A will define the next decade and how companies that ride this wave will emerge bigger and bolder than ever before. Statistics, examples, case studies, and market comparisons give weight to this proposal. In the second part, the authors go on to identify what it takes to win in Asia and give a step-by-step guide on how companies can get it right. Years of consultancy experience, coupled with high-quality analysis, have resulted in conclusions that are compelling and include insights that corporations will do well to consider and adopt.

The authors take the opportunity to share their extensive analysis of emerging prospects for M&A in the government-dominated sectors of Asia. Their insights into the need for more acquisitions in these sectors, both where it is appropriate and where it never will be, give both executives of state-owned enterprises and those seeking to do business with them a great basis for where their strategies should be pitched.

As Vikram and Soon Ghee point out, A.T. Kearney research has shown that fewer than half of all M&As are successful and only 25 percent of mergers in Asia deliver on their value promise. However, the right combination can reap great rewards. As leader of the global integration of Dyno Nobel following its 2005 acquisition by Orica, I know firsthand how significant value can be created if a company can get its integration and synergy delivery right. Techniques such as the 100-day plan and establishment of a clean room described in the book have been found to be critical in expediting the entire integration process. Readers will be able to relate to issues around leadership and management structure, communication challenges, seamless transfer of customers, cultural integration and the like. The difficult subject of managing cultural differences is explained in depth. Identifying and managing all of these issues and many others is essential in a good M&A implementation strategy and is dealt with in an excellent manner, with real-life examples and innovative suggestions on how to avoid pitfalls and accelerate value capture. Research has also shown that most of the value of an integration exercise needs to be captured in the first 12 months, failing which it becomes an uphill task to deliver the promised benefits. The preparation and planning described in the book are therefore vital to success.

Vikram and Soon Ghee's message is clear. The time for M&A in Asia is now. Asian companies have gained stature and confidence, and dealing with them from both within Asia and outside requires unique skills and techniques. This book provides the insights necessary to help achieve that winning combination, an understanding of why M&A in Asia is different, and then strategies for leveraging those differences to add value and opportunity to your deals. It is a compelling read, and I recommend it to anyone considering M&A in Asia. Enjoy the book and equip yourself to achieve outstanding, value-creating deals.

Sanjay Dayal
Chief Executive, Asia
BlueScope Steel Ltd.

Preface

WE DID NOT START OUT wanting to write a book about Asian M&A. For the past decade or so we have been mulling over how to improve the competitiveness of Asian companies. After having seen the onslaught of Western multinational corporations in the late 1990s, Asian companies have risen in their global ranking and prominence. Indeed, there is a large number of firms that are now global household names, listed on U.S. or U.K. stock exchanges and increasingly featured in business school case studies.

In our opinion, many of these firms have achieved global excellence despite the poor industry structures in their home markets—where there is deep fragmentation, low differentiation, poor management practices, and the inevitable copycat strategies and price-based competition. To win, many Asian champions have had to expand abroad, acquiring established firms and building from there.

We see M&A as a critical driver of industry structure and future competitiveness in this region. However, mergers and acquisitions have been slow to come to Asia. Though deal activity is heating up in Asia, the industry endgames are still far away and dealmaking is still in its infancy. We expect the coming decade to be critical for Asian M&A and therefore the competitiveness of Asian industry. The Asian M&A story is expected to unfold rather differently, and perhaps unpredictably, from the patterns established in the developed markets of the West.

This book attempts to lay out the best ways to think about M&A and the associated industry consolidation, and explains how to make M&A work for Asian companies in their drive to become regional and global champions.

Vikram Chakravarty
Chua Soon Ghee

Acknowledgments

WRITING A BOOK IS hard work, and it could not have been done without the help and support of many colleagues and friends, especially those from our Southeast Asia unit. We would like to thank everyone who has contributed in ways large and small to our book, especially the following:

- We could not have written this book without Cris Prystay, who helped us craft it and put our thoughts into words, and Vu Kim Ngan, who was tireless in doing much of the research, as well as Patricia Sibo, T. Govindasamy, Janice Tan, Gerald Hoe, Jaron Tay, Francine Tan, Bai Zhiyong, and Akrit Soin, who helped out in one way or another in research, graphics, editing, and proofreading.
- We leveraged prior A.T. Kearney white papers, articles, and presentations for the book. Special mention goes to Jürgen Rothenbücher, who is one of our firm's leading thinkers on M&A and who has written extensively on the topic. There are also many others who have written on ideas we have touched on in this book. They include Joerg Schrottke, Naveen Menon, Martin Handschuh, Badri Veeraghanta, Mui-Fong Goh, Sumit Chandra, Sandra Niewiem, Sebastian Declercq, Phil Dunne, Simon Mezger, Christian Hagen, Pablo Moliner, Marcy Beitle, Arjun Sethi, Jessica Milesko, Alyson Potenza, Chee Wee Gan, Jeffrey Perry, Thomas Herd, Karambir Anand, Jian Li, Francesco Cigala, Kiran Karunakaran, Jason Miller, Tejal Thakkar, Abha Thakkar, Tammy Ku, Adam Qaiser, Rizal Paramarta, and Navin Nathani.
- A few partners and consultants have contributed time and energy to patiently expand on some of the ideas and examples we have incorporated in the book. Besides Chee Wee, Badri, and Karambir, whom we have mentioned above, we would also like to thank Yasushi Kubokawa, Akifumi Hirao, and Saurine Doshi for their contributions.

▪ Special thanks goes to Nick Melchior, who gave us the opportunity to work with a prestigious publishing firm, and Joon Ooi, who as unit head of Southeast Asia gave us unqualified support for the work.

Finally, this book is a deep collaboration between two authors who have worked closely over the past decade. We would like to give thanks to the large number of business leaders whom we have interacted with over the past decade, and who have helped us understand the world of business and the true essence of competitiveness.

1

Asia Rewrites the M&A Rules

C ONSOLIDATION FOLLOWS A FAIRLY predictable pattern in developed economies in the West: Big fish eat little fish in the domestic market, and a small handful gains dominance of the pond. These dominant players start looking for targets abroad after they've built might and muscle at home. Domestic consolidation precedes global mergers and acquisitions (M&A).

Nobody, however, told that to India's Tata Tea.

In February 2000, Tata bought Tetley Tea, a 160-year-old British company and one of the world's best-known tea brands, for $431 million. Tata Tea, a relatively young company, was one of many players in India's large, diverse tea sector that had yet to go through consolidation. That didn't stop Tata from heading overseas or homing in on much bigger prey. Tetley Tea was three times the size of Tata.

Asian companies are rewriting the rules on M&A. Small Asian players are buying large Western brands. Asian companies that compete in crowded, fragmented domestic markets are snapping up competitors over the border instead of in their own backyard. Waves of consolidation are sweeping through Asia, but it won't play out in a textbook fashion. The reasons Asian companies undertake M&A are different, the way they approach M&A is different, and the way Asia's consolidation story will play out will be different, too.

DEAL ACTIVITY IS ON THE RISE IN AN ASCENDANT ASIA

The plot of this particular story is starting to thicken. Asian companies emerged from the 2008 global financial crisis and entered the 2011 slowdown in a stronger financial position than many of their Western peers; they're relatively cash rich and hungry for acquisitions. Strong Asian currencies are giving these companies plenty of firepower as is the legion of investment banks competing to grow their loan books in Asia, one of the few growth markets around. Numerous sectors in the region's emerging markets, meanwhile, are ripe for

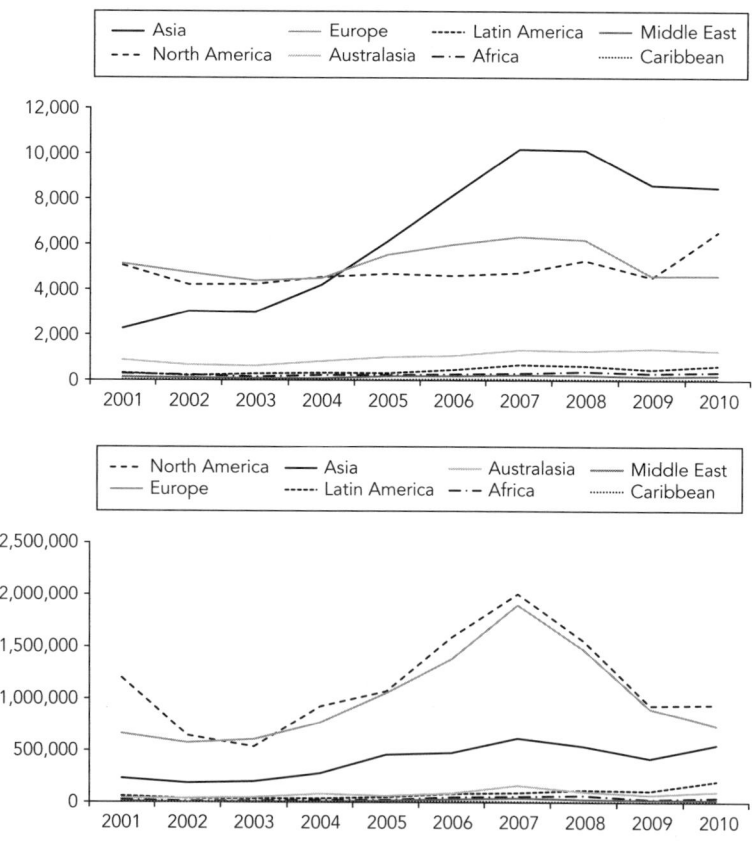

FIGURE 1.1 Global M&A Deals by Volume (top graph) and Value (bottom graph, in USD millions)
Source: Dealogic.

consolidation. Western companies, anxious to tap one of the world's strongest bastions of growth, want to get skin in the game. These multiple drivers are all playing out in the numbers.

Asia Pacific was the most active deal region in 2010, reporting over 8,300 mergers or acquisitions that involved an Asian company as the buyer or seller, according to Dealogic (see Figure 1.1). That figure outstrips Europe and North America by volume. North America and Europe account for more global M&A deals by value, but Asia is trending upward at a time when those two markets are declining. Asia nearly tripled the value of deals between 2001 and 2010, from $230 billion to $552 billion, and more importantly, it has increased its share of the world's M&A pie. Back in 2001, Asia's share of global M&A was one-fifth of North America's and one-third of Europe's share. By 2010, the picture was markedly different: Asia's share was about half of North America's share and slightly more than half of Europe's share, according to Dealogic.

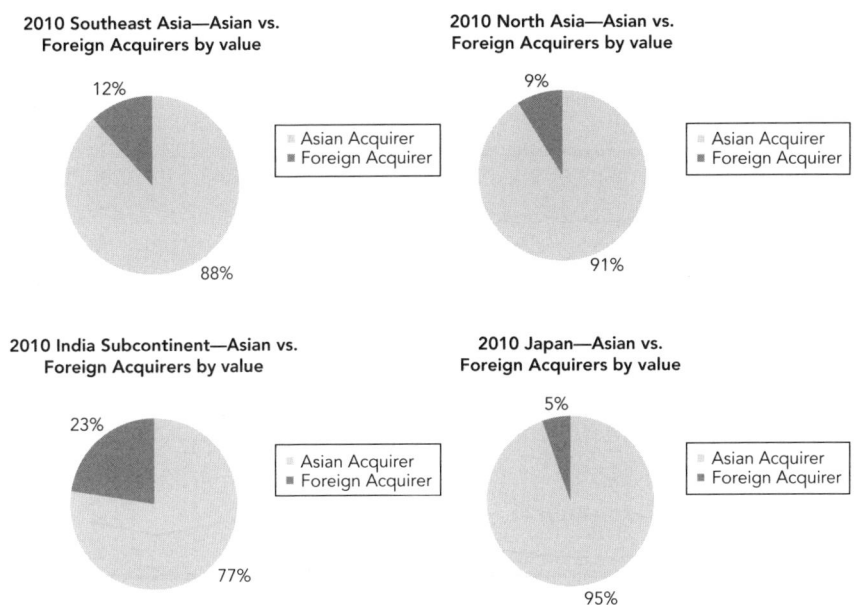

FIGURE 1.2 Asian versus Foreign Acquirers in 2010, by Value: Southeast Asia, North Asia, Indian Subcontinent, and Japan
Source: Dealogic.

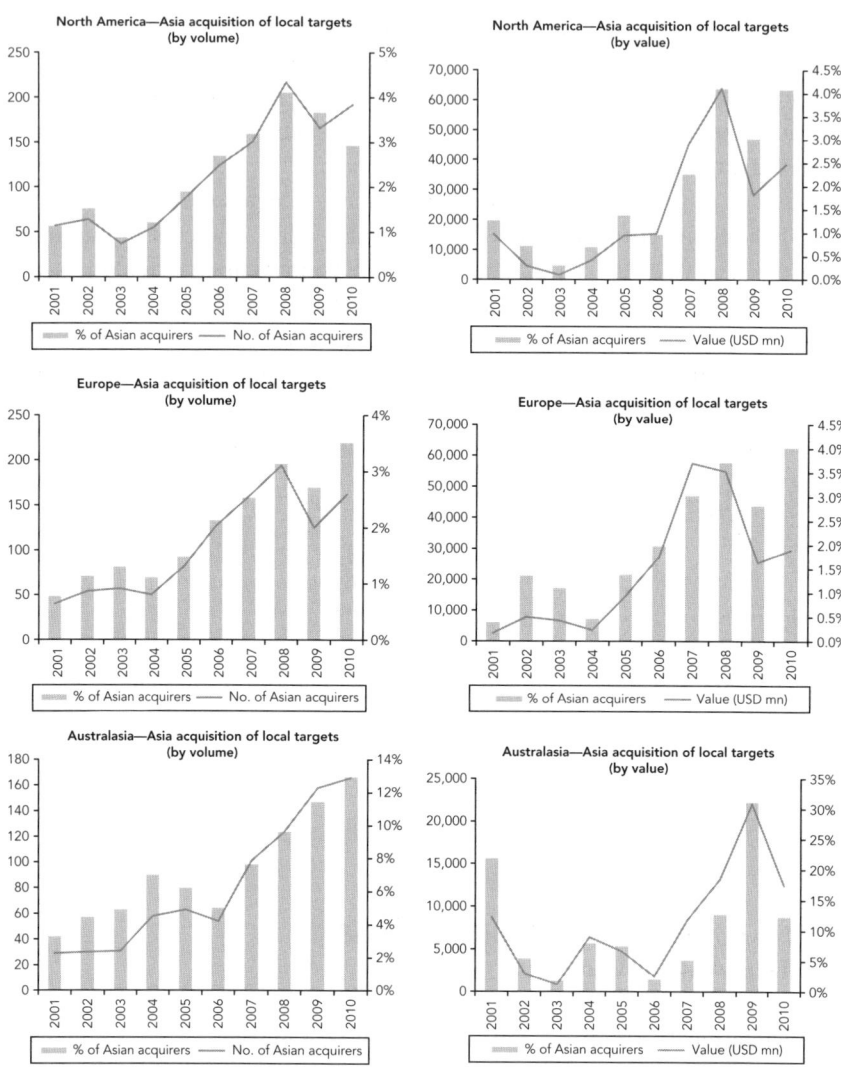

FIGURE 1.3 Asian Acquisitions of Foreign Targets (by volume and value): North America, Europe, and Australasia
Source: Dealogic.

China and India are fueling this growth, with a growing appetite for acquisitions. China chalked up $112 billion worth of in-country deals in 2010, up 120 percent from 2007. India's M&A streak was equally hot. The value of deals done in India grew by 198 percent to $45 billion. The number of in-country deals doubled in both markets during that same period.

Pull these numbers apart, and the story gets more interesting. Asian companies are driving most of the region's M&A boom, inside and outside Asia. They're snapping up domestic competitors, regional companies, and global brand names in Western markets faster than ever before. Asian companies are pouring into Europe and North America.

Asian acquirers accounted for 91 percent of deals done in North Asia in 2010, 88 percent of deals in Southeast Asia, and 77 percent in the Indian subcontinent (see Figure 1.2). The number of Asian companies making acquisitions in North America more than trebled between 2001 and 2010 and quadrupled in Europe in the same period (see Figure 1.3). They're having a huge impact, too. India's Tata, which also owns Jaguar Land Rover and Corus Steel, employs 40,000 workers and is now the United Kingdom's largest industrial manufacturer, according to *The Economist*. (For more on Tata, see Tata Tea Leads Global Acquisition Charge, in Chapter 3.)

Mergers and acquisitions are going to dominate Asia's business landscape over the next decade. Every company interested in Asia needs to understand how this will play out in their particular industry. Asian companies, meanwhile, need to invest more time developing a solid game plan. Deal activity may be picking up steam, but Asian companies are relative novices when it comes to M&A. Many Asian companies don't plan for it, and few executives have much merger expertise. We believe Asian companies that understand why M&A in Asia is different—and figure out how to capitalize on that—will emerge as champions of their industries. In Chapters 5, 6, and 7, we've created an M&A primer for Asian executives on how to plan and execute a successful integration.

NATURAL PROGRESSION IN M&A, THE ASIAN WAY

Consolidation is a natural consequence of free market forces. Companies acquire local competitors when markets get crowded, growth slows, and margins sag. In Asia, certain barriers remain that impede and redirect the natural forces and currents of a free market flow. Government-linked companies dominate certain sectors and often resist consolidation; some industries in certain countries, meanwhile, remain protected, like Malaysia's oil, China's steel, and India's retailing industry. We focus on this trend in Chapter 4, and talk about how Asia's public sector could revitalize itself through M&A. Family-run companies also have a strong presence across Asia, and they don't always make decisions based on financial reasons alone. Many have rejected good acquisition offers to hang on to control.

More cross-border M&A activity is occurring in developing Asia than analysts would expect, given the stage of development of the region's economies. The classic call would be long on local consolidation and short on cross-border activity in the region's more fragmented industries. These made-in-Asia barriers, however, are driving acquisitive companies over the border or overseas earlier than you'd expect in a textbook consolidation wave.

It's not just push—there's plenty of pull. Asian companies are moving fast to acquire regional or global competitors to gain access to new markets, new technologies, new brands, more resources, and better research and development capability. These companies want to use their capital to catapult up the value chain, in double time. We examine this trend in detail in Chapter 3.

Asia is also home to a diverse and fragmented set of consumer markets, which gives another twist to the consolidation story. Income levels are all over the map, with a wide range of affordability. A wide variety of ethnicities, languages, and cultures impacts consumer tastes and preferences. What customers in one country might need and want differs among the provinces, never mind among consumers in the country next door.

This particular scenario will redefine the outcomes of Asia's merger endgame. In the West, a small handful of large companies dominate a market after various rounds of consolidation. Two or three big players will typically command a 60 to 70 percent share. Free market advocates argue that industries naturally settle into a situation where an optimum number of sizeable players command control, earning economies of scale that allow them to thrive and pass the best prices on to consumers.

Asia's fragmented markets will give rise to series of sub-segments at different price points within each market. Coca-Cola, for example, might dominate a national soft drinks market, but local soft drinks that cost less and come in flavors that appeal to local tastes will dominate specific segments. Local companies with strong consumer insight will have the edge in segmented markets like this. Industries, meanwhile, will not be dominated by an "optimum" number of large companies. Consolidation will play out along these segmented lines, giving rise to what we call "local optima," meaning small clusters of local champions that will dominate different price points or subcategories. We go into depth on this in Chapter 2. Asian companies that can start planning now, while their industry is still in the nascent stage, can make tactical moves that will put them ahead of the curve before the industry matures.

Asia's industrial and consumer sectors, along with energy and mining, are the hottest deal sectors (see Figure 1.4). Asia's energy sector chalked up a whopping $70 billion worth of M&A deals in 2010, according to Mergermarket.

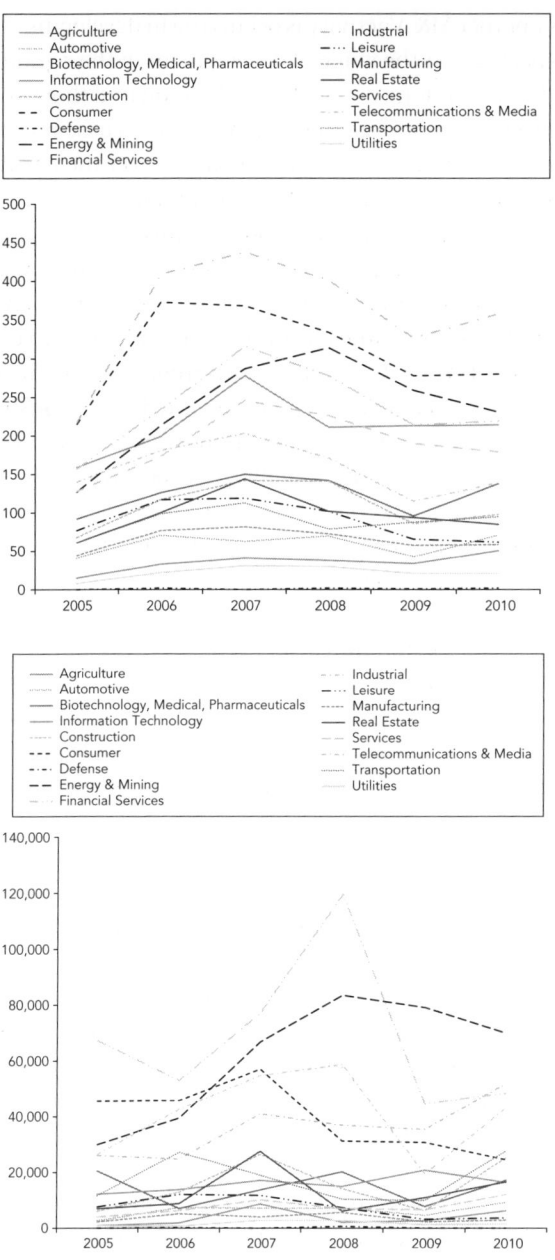

FIGURE 1.4 Asia M&A Deals by Sector, by Volume (top graph) and Value (bottom graph, in USD millions)
Source: Dealogic.

The industrial and financial services sectors were the second most active by value. The consumer sector was the second most active by volume, a signal that Asia's developing markets are starting to mature and smaller players will increasingly be subsumed as margins start to fall.

 ## TOMORROW'S WINNERS ARE MOVING FAST, TODAY

All of these factors equate to one conclusion: Now is the time for deal making.

Many Asian industries are in the developing stages, but consolidation is right around the corner. Executives who anticipate what's ahead are better placed to steer their companies in the right direction. Companies who ignore the road signs risk being swallowed by more forward-thinking peers.

There are risks. The vast majority of M&A fail to deliver the originally anticipated value. That's typically due to poor planning, poor execution, and cultural clashes between staff from different companies and countries. We provide practical tools on how to troubleshoot these problems before they crop up in our M&A "primer" section, starting in Chapter 5. Cultural clashes can trip up a merger at the starting gate: Asian executives need to understand this critical, but often overlooked, issue before they start snapping up companies in the West. Chapter 8 provides insights, examples, and useful tools to help acquirers navigate this potential minefield.

The ongoing volatility in global markets creates opportunity. Asia weathered the 2008–2009 global financial crisis well, and the IMF and World Bank tipped it as the engine that would power the world out of recession. When consumption from Western markets dropped off, Asian consumers stepped up to the plate and the region's economies ticked along on the back of strong domestic demand. Asian companies saw opportunity and took it. The level of M&A activity in Asia stayed constant between 2008 and 2010 even as Europe and North America fell off a cliff, as illustrated in Figure 1.1.

Then came a second wave of bad news. In the last half of 2011, the twin specter of a double-dip recession in the U.S. and the European debt crisis roiled global markets. Economists scrambled to revise global forecasts downward. The volume of global M&A deals dropped by about 20 percent in the second half of 2011 compared with the first half. The pace of deal making slowed in Asia, too, but in a less dramatic way: Deal activity in Asia dropped by less than 10 percent.

Our view is that bleak economic scenarios present opportunities to strong companies, who make use of this volatile time to bolster their standing in their respective industries and to orchestrate "game changing" initiatives. We believe strong companies must actively seek out opportunities to consolidate their industries and gain market share, acquire new technologies and know-how, strengthen their competitive advantage, and position themselves to take advantage of an improving economy. M&A is the ideal mode for such opportunities: It's a buyer's market and companies acting now are likely to emerge as winners when the upswing comes. Timing is everything.

CHAPTER TWO

Asian Companies Are Poised to Triumph in the Merger Endgame

One of the primary themes of Western mergers and acquisitions (M&A) is the inexorable drive toward consolidation. Indeed merger endgame theories seem to suggest a single optimum of a handful of companies dominating an industry. In Asia, there will be room for multiple "local optima" since significant fragmentation exists between markets and customers. This requires companies to make a decision about which markets and customers they wish to serve and how to drive consolidation at that level. Early analysis shows different industries will have varied outcomes.

W E BELIEVE THAT A number of Asian industries will undergo a wave of consolidation over the next few years. We also believe that Asian companies and brands will emerge as national and as regional champions in this formative merger endgame.

Consolidation follows a predictable path as industries develop and mature. In Western markets like the United States and Europe, a handful of companies tend to dominate an industry as it reaches maturity, first nationally, then regionally within its continent, and then across the Western world, and finally, globally. In Asia, consolidation will play out differently. Asia's markets are fragmented in many critical ways: regionally, culturally, linguistically and, most importantly, economically. The disparity makes it tough for companies such as Vodafone, a telecommunications company that has a 20 to 40 percent market share in 13 European countries, to replicate that success in Asia.

Consolidation is inevitable, but key Asian industries will merge along segmental lines. Companies that come to dominate each segment will be those that understand it best. For example, after the industry consolidates, two or three soft drink brands might not dominate a country such as India, or an entire region; instead, champions will dominate a specific price point or segment within the soft drink market. Insights into local tastes, preferences, and purchasing power will be critical.

This paves the way for Asian national players with a strong connection to local consumers and a solid plan in place to ride the incoming waves of consolidation and emerge triumphant in Asia's merger endgame.

THE DRIVE TOWARD CONSOLIDATION

Industry consolidation is inevitable. Two key facts of business life are behind this truism. The first is economies of scale: A larger company that produces a high volume of goods has lower costs per unit. The second is this: Big fish eat smaller fish. Companies can gain market share and score other corporate wins, some of which are psychological, by acquiring smaller competitors. The inevitable quest for lower costs and the intrinsic urge to consume competitors drive consolidation. Consolidation helps improve industry economics, which is beneficial after a period of intense competition.

The level of fixed costs associated with an industry will impact the number of players operating in that particular space. The higher the fixed costs, the more concentrated an industry will be. High fixed costs are a major barrier to entry for new players. Companies that have made those core investments and generated the cash needed to sustain ongoing high-cost capital expenditure plans have a head start. For example, the automotive, steel, chemicals, and pharmaceutical industries all have high fixed costs and are concentrated, even on a global scale.

The inevitable push toward consolidation and concentration should be factored into any company's long-term business plan. Every strategic move should be made with the merger endgame in mind. The endgame for a particular industry could be five years from now—or 15. Either way, companies need to plan for it today.

A.T. Kearney conducted long-term research a few years ago on high-value M&A. The conclusions were remarkable: Though M&A activity can seem chaotic, consolidation follows a set of laws and can be predicted. The research, which included more than 25,000 companies in 24 industries and 53 countries, found that all industries consolidate and follow a similar course.

Each industry passes through three stages: opening, scale, and dominance. During the opening phase, a few pioneers dominate a nascent industry. The level of concentration is high because only a handful of players have entered this space. As time goes on, the opening phase is marked by increasing fragmentation as more competitors pile into the industry. The market is ripe and wide open, and there's room for many competitors to grow organically to meet untapped demand. A number of factors contribute to this stage, including deregulation and the creation of a new business or industry. Consider, for example, the myriad budget airline operators that emerged in Thailand and Indonesia after Malaysia-based AirAsia, the region's first low-cost carrier, proved this fledgling business model could work in Southeast Asia. Meanwhile, deregulation of Asia's telecommunications industry ended the era of government monopolies and opened the floodgates to a slew of competitors. As mobile phones became more affordable and widespread, more rivals came on the scene, limited only by the number of licenses the regulators handed out.

Toward the end of the opening phase, the market becomes saturated, profit margins start to shrink, and earnings growth begins to slow. The market becomes less fragmented, and size starts to matter. As competitors grow, they begin to reduce costs by achieving economies of scale. Their larger size can prevent hostile takeovers. The smaller companies, who can't achieve scale, become takeover targets.

The next phase is about building scale. As the industry consolidates, the concentration increases. The more aggressive companies acquire more small fish, and the less competitive are subsumed. In time, the number of players drop dramatically.

The industry enters the dominance phase. A handful of companies lead the sector and together command the majority of the market share. The dominant players strive to solidify and reinforce their hard-won position. They have reached a size that puts them out of reach of hostile takeovers. At this point, the industry hits equilibrium. Mergers and acquisitions become a rarity, and antitrust laws block further consolidation. At this stage, M&A is about the selective exchange of business units to strengthen core competencies and clean up the company's portfolio.

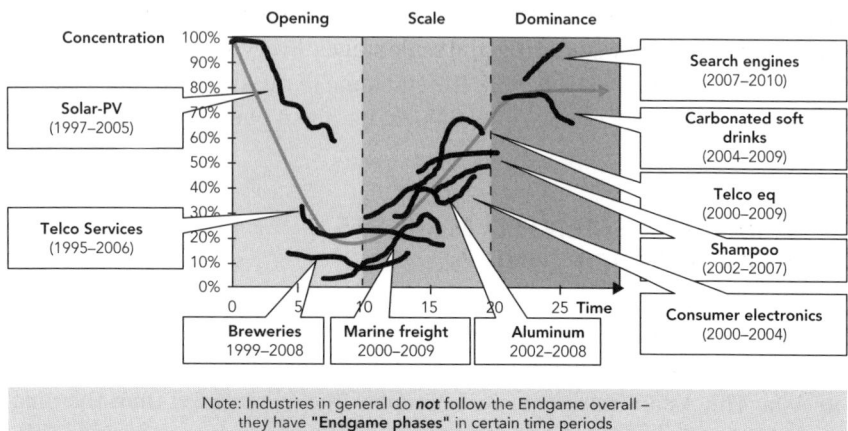

FIGURE 2.1 Endgame Phases Can Be Found in Many Industries
Source: A.T. Kearney analysis.

As one industry completes a round of consolidation, another wave will be touched off in a different industry, which triggers another industry into restructuring mode to increase shareholder value. These waves are transcending borders, pushing the merger and consolidation endgame into the global arena.

The three cycles, or phases, in this endgame scenario create a U curve when mapped out on a graph that compares industry concentration against time (see Figure 2.1).

Though the three-stage merger endgame scenario provides a compelling conceptual underpinning to what we are witnessing in the real world, we need to caution against using it as a definitive predictor of industry scenarios. Many industries can take an inordinate amount of time to reach the scale or dominance phases. Other industries, once reaching the dominance phase, will commence another industry cycle of opening, particularly if new technology or deregulation lowers the entry barriers for new entrants again.

The important takeaway for executives is this: You can determine where on the U curve your industry sits and project what stage is likely to come next. If your company is in the opening phase of an industry, grow organically and keep an eye out for potential acquisitions. As your industry heads toward the scale phase, get ready to eat or be eaten. Know where you want to sit in the pecking order at the end of the dominance phase before it arrives because, by then, it will be too late. Companies that want to be at the top of the food chain in the merger endgame need to develop a plan of attack and build momentum during their industry's opening and scale stages. Every strategic move a company makes should be made with the endgame in mind even if that stage is 5 or 15 years away. Success isn't about luck. It's about planning ahead.

ASIA'S FRAGMENTED MARKETS CREATE OPPORTUNITY

European companies can typically sell a product or brand to a wide target market across the European Union (EU) using one strategy. This is not true in Asia. The Asian market is more complex and fragmented than the many states within the EU. There's a wider array of cultures, languages, and incomes among Asia's consumers. Asia's developing economies are at radically different stages of development; and within each country, many tiers of consumers exist with different purchasing power levels.

To understand how fragmented Asia is as a market, consider some of the following figures. There are 23 official languages spoke in the EU; it sounds like a lot, but it's about half that of Asia. There are 44 languages spoken in Asia's seven major emerging economies alone, namely China, India, Indonesia, Malaysia, Singapore, Thailand, and the Philippines. This doesn't even include regional dialects or languages from Organisation for Economic Co-operation and Development (OECD) countries such as Korea and Japan.

The income gap yawns wider in developing Asia than in the Western markets. Consider the range of per capita GDP, or purchasing power parity, across emerging Asia: At one end, we have Singapore, where per capita GDP hit $62,100 in 2010, outstripping even the United States; at the other end is India and the Philippines, where per capita GDP was just $3,500.[1]

By comparison, the gap is barely noticeable in the West. The United States had a per capita GDP of $47,200 in 2010; the entire EU has a per capita GDP of $32,700. Even if you look at individual European countries, the variance is low: Consider Sweden at $39,100 and Italy at $30,500. The difference is only a few thousand dollars. Asia's variance is so wide, it strips out an entire decimal point.

What does this add up to? Severe segmentation. More than 54 percent of Indians earn less than one dollar a day, yet luxury brands ranging from Louis Vuitton, Mercedes-Benz, and Montblanc do brisk business by targeting the top niche of India's consumers. Income is one difference. Culture, education, language, and location, be it rural or urban, impact spending decisions. And that's just within one country. So many kinds of consumers are all over the marketing map that one bank, telecom company, or beer brand would have difficulty achieving the broad market dominance in Asia the way they do in Europe or the United States.

ASIAN PLAYERS WILL DRIVE LOCAL OPTIMA

All this adds up to a major marketing challenge and an opportunity. Though our global endgame curve indicates that all industries tend to consolidate toward an optimum number of dominant companies, Asia's diverse and segmented markets means there's room for multiple local optima. Instead of two or three companies dominating an entire sector, several companies will dominate a specific price point, or segment, within the industry. Asian companies are best positioned to win that race. Parsing a market by specific tastes, incomes, and cultures requires deep local knowledge.

This is already starting to happen. Our research shows Asian champions are dominating sectors and segments that are in the scale and dominance phases that we described earlier.

We put together a Herfindahl-Hirschman Index (HHI), which measures market concentration, for several key Asian industries including banking, telecoms, retail, automotive, alcohol, soft drinks, and packaged food. A high index figure indicates the industry is concentrated, with a few key players, and a low figure indicates less concentration with many small firms.

The data highlight which industries are concentrated and which are fragmented and, therefore, ripe for future consolidation. The data show Asian companies are emerging as winners in industries that have consolidated. The success of these companies underscores our analysis and provides impetus to other Asian companies in different industries to get their M&A plans in order before their industry moves to the next endgame stage.

Let's zero in on several key industries and examine what stage they're in, what's coming next, and who is in the driver's seat.

CONSOLIDATION LOOMS FOR ASIA'S NASCENT RETAIL SECTOR

Asia's retail sector is one of the most highly fragmented industries in the region. The retail sector in large, developing countries like India, China, and Indonesia is so fragmented that it barely registers on the HHI (see Figure 2.2). To put

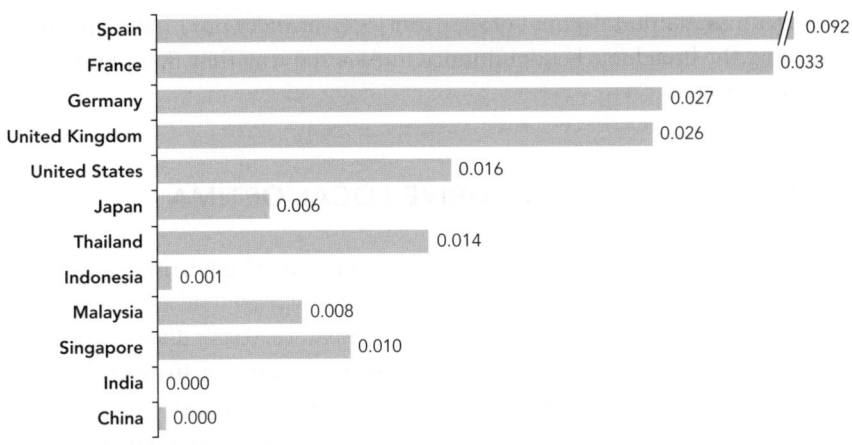

FIGURE 2.2 HHI for Retail Industry
Source: Euromonitor; A.T. Kearney analysis.

Asia in context, we ran the numbers on the retail sector of several developed, Western markets, including Spain, France, Germany, the United Kingdom, and the United States. Those countries have a high index ranking, indicating consolidation has produced a mature, concentrated retail industry dominated by a few large players.

Modern retail formats and chain stores are making inroads in urban areas of most Asian countries, but independent shops and mom-and-pop stores still dominate much of the region. Many countries have imposed ownership limits on foreign retailers: India still doesn't grant licenses to foreign retail companies like U.S.-based Walmart. Malaysia, meanwhile, requires foreign hypermarkets to sell a 30 percent stake to an ethnic Malay partner to secure an operating license. Still, foreign investors are making inroads. France's Carrefour and Walmart have expanded aggressively in China, and UK retailer Tesco has moved into most big Asian markets. Local players have achieved scale, regionally and at home. Hong Kong-based Dairy Farm, which owns the Wellcome, Cold Storage, and Shop 'n Save grocery chains, the Giant hypermarket chain, and the Mannings and Guardian drug store chains, has a strong presence across greater China and Southeast Asia.

If we were to put Asia's emerging retail markets on our consolidation endgame graph, they would populate different parts of the U curve. India's nascent industry is still in the early part of the opening phase. The real estate needed to bolster modern retail—namely shopping malls—is taking off. Protectionist laws keep foreign retailers out. The unorganized sector, meanwhile, reigns supreme. Modern grocery retailers, for example, commanded just 2 percent of India's grocery market share in 2010, according to Euromonitor. That figure rose from 1 percent in 2005, an important signal that modern retail is growing. Still, the country has a long way to go in this opening phase before consolidation begins. This could spell opportunity for savvy players who can map out a strategy that will put them on top during these early, go-go growth days.

At the other end of the spectrum is Singapore, which is home to one of emerging Asia's most concentrated, least fragmented retail sectors. The Singapore story offers a glimpse of what's to come for countries like India and lends credence to our theory that Asian champions will emerge. The four biggest retailers, in terms of value, are Asian companies: NTUC FairPrice Co-operative Limited, a Singaporean grocery chain; Hong Kong's Dairy Farm International, whose Cold Storage grocery chain and Mannings and Guardian pharmacy chain dot the city-state; Sheng Siong Supermarket, a Singaporean low-cost grocery store; and Takashimaya, a Japanese department store. Western brands and chains do figure but way down on the list.

China and the rest of Southeast Asia fall in between India and Singapore on our endgame curve. These countries are moving into a critical stage where size starts to matter, and M&A will drive consolidation.

China's retail sector is growing fast but is consolidating and becoming an increasingly important theme. Carrefour and Walmart helped build the organized retail sector during the mid-1990s with big box hypermarket retail outlets that attracted local shoppers in droves. Local retailers followed suit and have built on their momentum. To achieve the kind of price advantages that heavyweights like Walmart and Carrefour command, leading Chinese retailers are scrambling to expand their distribution networks by opening new outlets, accepting franchising agreements for third-party operated outlets and engaging in M&A activities.[2]

The market is hitting the bottom of our U curve in China: The combined market share of the top 10 retailers in China rose from 4 percent in 2004 to 7 percent in 2010, according to Euromonitor. That's a long way off the situation in the United States, where the top 10 retailers accounted for 30 percent of sales. Still, the sharp rise in the combined share of the biggest players indicates that China is heading into the scale stage of the consolidation cycle. The biggest companies are gaining competitive advantage and will snap up smaller companies who fall behind.

Consider China Resources Enterprise Limited: Its flagship Vanguard supermarket chain purchased around 2,000 stores from regional players between

2004 and 2010.[3] The Hong Kong-listed company, which is majority-owned by state-owned enterprise China Resources Group, has interests in retailing, beverage, food processing and distribution, and real estate. It's still much on the acquisition trail: In July 2011, it bought Hongkelong Department Store, which runs 21 hypermarkets in Jiangxi province, for RMB3.69 billion ($573 million).

China Resources Enterprise Limited had more than 3,300 stores in China as of March 2011—including supermarkets, drug stores, and Pacific Coffee outlets—and plans to double that figure. "We aim to have 6,592 retail outlets by 2015 and make it to the top three retailers in China; one effective way of accomplishing that task would be mergers and acquisitions," China Resources Group chief executive officer Hong Jie told Business China in March.[4] Gome Electrical Appliances Holdings Limited, one of the largest electronics and appliance specialist retailers in China, plans to have 2,000 outlets bringing in RMB180 billion ($28 billion) in sales by the end of 2014. These kinds of aggressive targets signal that retailing in China will continue to consolidate and centralize over the next few years.

Chinese retailers have outperformed their international competitors, lending credence to our theory that local champions will emerge in Asia's merger endgame. The top three retailers in China, by market share, are all local companies: Suning Appliance Company Limited, China Resources Enterprise Co. Ltd., and GOME Electrical Appliances Holdings Ltd. (see Table 2.1).

To be sure, the foreigners are big contenders: France's Auchan, Carrefour, and Walmart come in third, fifth, and sixth respectively. But the local players dominate. Chinese companies account for seven of the top 10 retailers.

One of the biggest stories in Southeast Asia's retail sector in 2010 was Carrefour's decision to pull out of the region, where it helped build the hypermarket sector, and to concentrate on markets such as China, where it held a more dominant position. In November 2010, the company sold its Thai holdings to French competitor Casino Guichard-Perrachon, which owns the Big C hypermarket brand in Thailand but immediately backtracked on the rest. Shortly after the sale of its Thai assets, Carrefour announced it had canceled plans to sell its stores in Singapore and Malaysia. A number of analysts believe the rush of bidders, combined with strong economic data, made Carrefour realize it was exiting the region at the wrong time.

Southeast Asia's retail sector looks ripe for further consolidation, and the next few years will likely produce a smaller slate of dominant players as modern retailers draw more of the local consumers and the larger players eat the smaller players.

Retailers have expanded aggressively in Malaysia, and the sector is moving toward saturation, according to Euromonitor. Sales growth will come from

TABLE 2.1 Local Companies Dominate China's Retail Scene

Retailing Company's Shares: % Value 2006 to 2010 (% retail value excluding sales tax)

Company	2006	2007	2008	2009	2010
Suning Appliance Co. Ltd.	0.8	0.7	0.8	0.9	1.0
China Resources Enterprises Co. Ltd.	0.7	0.8	0.9	0.9	0.9
GOME Electrical Appliances Holding Ltd.	0.6	0.9	0.9	0.8	0.9
Auchan China	0.4	0.5	0.5	0.6	0.6
Lianhua Supermarket Holdings Co. Ltd.	0.5	0.5	0.5	0.6	0.6
Carrefour (China) Hypermarket Co. Ltd.	0.4	0.5	0.5	0.5	0.5
Wal-Mart (China) Investment Co. Ltd.	0.3	0.3	0.4	0.4	0.5
Dashang Group	0.4	0.4	0.4	0.4	0.4
Taobao.com	—	—	—	—	0.4
Shanghai Nong Gon Shang Supermarket Co. Ltd.	0.4	0.4	0.4	0.4	0.4
Amway (China) Co. Ltd.	0.2	0.3	0.3	0.3	0.3
Belle International Holdings Ltd.	0.1	0.2	0.3	0.3	0.3
Shenzhen A-Best Supermarket Co. Ltd.	0.3	0.3	0.3	0.3	0.2
Hisap High Technology Corp.	0.2	0.3	0.3	0.2	0.2
Parkson Retail Group Ltd.	0.1	0.2	0.2	0.2	0.2
Trust-Mart Co. Ltd.	0.2	0.2	0.2	0.2	0.2
Wuhan Zhongbai Group Co. Ltd.	0.1	0.1	0.2	0.2	0.2
Beijing Wangfujing Department Store Co. Ltd.	0.1	0.2	0.2	0.2	0.2
Shanghai Lotus Supermarket Chain Co. Ltd.	0.3	0.3	0.2	0.2	0.2
Wumart Stores Inc.	0.1	0.1	0.1	0.2	0.2
Hualian Supermarket Co. Ltd.	0.3	0.2	0.1	—	—
Others	93.4	92.8	9.2	92.3	91.6
Total	100	100	100	100	100

Source: Euromonitor's January 2011 "Retail China" report.

higher-priced products, not from organic growth. A saturated market populated with many players gripped by slowing margins means consolidation is around the corner. Small retailers will start to lose market share, and the larger players will grow because they have the resources to plow into new stores and acquisitions.

A quick look at the top retail companies, by market share, shows that Asian champions are ahead of the game. Six of the top 10 players in Malaysia are Asian, including Malaysia-based The Store Corporation, which operates grocery, department, and hyperstore outlets; Econsave Cash & Carry, another local hypermarket company; Dairy Farm International and Hutchison Whampoa, both from Hong Kong; and AEON Group and Seven &i Holdings, which are both from Japan. Seven &i Holdings, which operates 7-Eleven stores, was bought from its U.S. founders in 2005 by Seven-Eleven Japan Company Limited. The three foreign retailers in the top 10 are Tesco PLC, Carrefour SA, and Amway.

The picture in Thailand mirrors Malaysia to a certain degree: Five of the top 10 retail companies, by market share, are Asian, including Thai-owned retailers Central Group, Home Product Center PCL, The Mall Group Co., and Fresh Mart International, which operates a local chain of convenience stores, and Japan's Seven &i Holdings.

Foreign retailers do have a big presence in the hypermarket space. Tesco had the second-largest retail market share in Thailand in 2010, and French hypermarket owner Casino Guichard-Perrachon, which operates the ubiquitous Big C Hypermarket brand in Thailand, was number four. In 2010, Casino bought out Carrefour's Thai hyperstores, which held the number five spot, further expanding its reach.

The retail sector in Thailand sits somewhere between the opening and scale phases on our endgame graph. There is still plenty of room for multiple players to achieve organic growth, but the larger companies are keen to acquire competitive advantage through M&A, as evidenced by the rush to snap up Carrefour's assets. As Malaysia's retail sector moves into consolidation mode, it could trigger a wave in neighboring Thailand as these dominant companies move to cement their position and match shareholder returns.

THE TALE OF TWO SOFT DRINK MARKETS: WHY LOCAL OPTIMA WILL EMERGE

The soft drink sector offers up informative lessons for any company striving to tap Asia's consumer boom. Consider how China's soft drink market is evolving: The urban market is starting to look saturated, and growth will come in the rural areas and from new products. Manufacturers have moved quickly to segment soft drinks to target different price points and different tastes to spur drink sales and fight saturation.

Global and local companies are investing heavily in product development to cater to consumer's specific needs. China Huiyuan Juice Group Limited, for example, has recently launched a drink called Huiyuan Juizee Pop, which contains more than 10 percent real juice to meet a demand from increasingly health-conscious consumers. The company intends to invest RM5 billion to develop the sales and marketing reach of this new product, which analysts think could alter the competitive landscape of the carbonated drinks category, according to Euromonitor.

Multinational soft drink companies such as Coca-Cola and PepsiCo hold the leadership position on a national scale, but a strong demand exists from lower-tier cities and rural areas for more affordable, economy brands, according to Euromonitor. Asian companies, particularly from China and Taiwan, know that and are working to produce products to tap that demand. Although Pepsi and Coke might lead nationally, local companies dominate a number of regional markets. For example, Ting Hsin International has a leading position in the Northwest China region. The company, which is owned by a Taiwanese family but headquartered in Tianjin, China, is spending heavily to keep a lock on that position. In 2010, Ting Hsin International announced plans to invest $440 million in a new factory and operations center in Shaanxi.

In East China, Coca-Cola and Ting Hsin dominate sales, but Guangdong Jiaduobao Beverage & Food Company Limited saw the largest increase in sales, by value, in Southern China in 2010. Its best-selling Wong Lo Kat brand of canned herbal tea helped buoy its position, illustrating that consumers prefer tastes that are familiar to them. Indeed, ready-to-drink tea and Asian specialty drinks saw the fastest growth in the key South China market in 2010. These segments are dominated by Chinese and Taiwanese brands, underscoring how local insights on taste and preferences give Asian companies the advantage.

A similar scene is playing out in India. Coke and Pepsi dominate national sales, but local companies such as Parle Agro and Dabur are leading the charge in customization. Like their Chinese counterparts, they are investing heavily to develop new products with new tastes and price points to cater to different segments among the diverse Indian demographic, according to Euromonitor. Strong demand for value-for-money products has led to a proliferation of powder concentrate versions of existing drink products. Price is one issue; taste is another. Indian consumers like what they know and veer toward products that suit their palate. One of the most competitive subsegments is lemon/lime drinks that taste similar to a traditional lemon drink called nimbu pani. Local companies have understood that for a while, but the global companies aren't standing still. Coca-Cola launched a new lemon-flavored juice drink in 2010 in a bid to squeeze into this particular niche.

Local flavor is fast becoming an important theme in India. Soft drink companies that operate in every segment—energy drinks, fruit juice, carbonates, and concentrates—introduced new products in 2010 that have favored flavors. Some companies ran ad campaigns that year that highlighted the tradition and "Indianness" of their products to establish brand equity, according to Euromonitor. Pepsi and Coke may dominate overall sales, but it'll be tough to "out-India" the Indians as this competition heats up.

India's consumers, like those in China, are becoming increasingly health conscious, and Euromonitor predicts the carbonated drink segment, in particular, will see a steady shift away from dominant colas toward lemon/lime drinks, non-colas, and lower calorie options. That may open up another avenue that favors local champions.

Companies have plenty of time to plan their endgame strategy. India's soft drink industry is in the growth phase and remains broad and diverse. Parts of the country's soft drink sector are so localized and fragmented that the national brands don't hold much sway. Consider, for example, India's Northeast. Low incomes and political unrest have kept national brands at bay, and numerous regional companies have sprouted instead, offering low-cost, locally made drinks. India's per capita consumption of soft drinks was around eight liters in 2010; that figure is forecast to double as national soft drink companies begin to pay more attention to the less developed parts of India.

HENAN BROUHAHA HERALDS BEER CONSOLIDATION DRIVE

China is home to the world's largest beer market, and everyone wants a piece of the pie. Every world-class beer company operates in China through their own facility or a joint venture. Though a few big brands dominate, the rest of the market is fragmented with many small local players. The industry is hitting saturation, and the consolidation race is well under way.

Consider the activity that took place in Henan over the past two years. Henan, China's second most populous province, was home to about 40 small and mid-sized beer companies. National and global breweries have flocked to the province to snap up stakes in the province's fragmented beer industry. Beijing Yanjing Brewery Group Corporation, for example, paid RM227 million ($35 million) for a 90 percent stake in Henan Yueshan Brewery, the province's third-biggest brewer, in August 2010. The acquisition gave Beijing Yanjing, the fourth-largest beer producer in China, a beachhead in Henan to compete with market leaders China Resources Enterprise Ltd., Tsingtao, and Anheuser-Busch InBev in the key mid-China region, according to Euromonitor.

The floodgates opened the following year. Anheuser-Busch InBev paid RM 520 million ($69 million) to buy three breweries and two brands from Weixue Beer Group, Henan's second-largest brewer, in March. China Resources Snow Breweries, China's largest brewer and a joint venture between China Resources Enterprise Ltd. and SABMiller, acquired Henan-based Lanpai Brewery in July, after snapping up three Henan-based plants from Henan Aoke Beer Industry Company in January and Yuequan Beer in November the year before. China Resources Enterprise Ltd. announced the deal less than one week after it bought 49 percent in another Chinese brewer, Jiangsu DaFuHao Breweries Company, and 100 percent of Shanghai Asia Pacific Brewery Company from Heineken N.V. Belgium's Anheuser-Busch InBev spent RM2.7 billion ($419 million) on a new manufacturing facility in Xinxiang, Henan, the same year. China Resources' Snow Breweries' general manager told local reporters the brewer was just getting going in Henan, indicating that more buyouts lie ahead.[5]

Henan's large market, low costs, and connectivity make it a pivotal battleground in China's beer wars. "Whoever can control Central Plains (Henan) will be able to dominate the whole market in China," Song Yugang, deputy secretary general of the marketing committee of Henan's association of distillers and wine makers, said.[6]

The flurry of activity in Henan illustrates how China's booming beer market is zooming toward consolidation. The top three spots in China's beer market are held by China Resources Enterprise Co. Ltd., which brews Snow, China's top-selling beer, in a joint venture with SABMiller; Tsingtao, which is 27 percent owned by Anheuser-Busch; and Anheuser-Busch's own brands. Those three companies held 46 percent of the beer market in 2010, according to Euromonitor. The next four contenders are local, including Beijing Yanjing Brewery Group and Henan Jinxing Beer Group. Beijing Yanjing's ambitions to take on the big boys in Henan illustrates that local players with more affordable brands intend to work hard to win key segments in the consolidation game.

BANKING AND TELECOM SECTORS DOMINATED BY ASIAN CHAMPIONS

The HHI shows that much of Asia's banking sector has achieved a level of concentration that meets or beats key Western markets, including the United States, the United Kingdom, Germany, France, and Spain. Thailand is on par with the United Kingdom and Spain, Malaysia outstrips France, Indonesia just surpasses the United States, and Singapore, Asia's most concentrated market, beats them all. The telecom sector is as concentrated, if not more, than key Western markets. The exception is India, which is the most fragmented in Asia.

What's more, Asian companies dominate these concentrated markets. Some of this can be attributed to trade barriers. The telecom and financial sectors were historically viewed as industries of national importance and remained sheltered from foreign competition until recently. Asian governments worked hard to encourage consolidation ahead of liberalization to ensure the optimum number of local incumbents remained in control of the market before foreign competitors came in.

The most interesting story, however, is the transformation of key Asian banks and telcos into dominant regional players. Companies like Singapore Telecommunications (SingTel), CIMB Bank, and Axiata Group have been able to capitalize on their understanding of the region—and its consumers—to carve out a strong position as a regional champion.

Singapore Telecommunications, for example, has become Southeast Asia's biggest telecommunications company by acquiring strategic stakes in mobile operators across Asia, including India, Thailand, and the Philippines. SingTel owns Optus, Australia's second-largest telecommunications company. (See "The Quest for New Markets" section in Chapter 3.) Likewise, Axiata Group, formerly Telekom Malaysia International, is moving quickly to establish itself as a regional competitor. Axiata owns controlling stakes in mobile companies in Malaysia, Indonesia, Sri Lanka, Bangladesh, and Cambodia and owns significant minority stakes in companies in India and Singapore.

Both of these companies have built a regional strength that beats Telenor and Vodafone, the most active global players in Asia. Telenor, which controls mobile companies in Pakistan, India, Bangladesh, Malaysia, and Thailand, claimed 100 million subscribers in Asia as of February 2011. That figure remains firmly in the shadow of regional powerhouse SingTel, which hit 416 million subscribers at the second quarter of 2011. Axiata weighed in with

168 million, as of March 2011. Both Asian telecommunications firms continue to hunt for more acquisition targets to further expand their regional market share.

Malaysian CIMB Bank has leveraged its strong domestic position to expand across Southeast Asia, bolstering organic growth with strategic acquisitions. (See "Regional Ambitions" sidebar in Chapter 3.) CIMB Bank, which aims to capitalize on the demand for regional banking services that will come when the Association of Southeast Asian Nations (ASEAN) becomes a free trade zone in 2015, continues to make acquisitions to cement its position as one of Southeast Asia's dominant banks.

Asian banks are building competitiveness in other areas, such as investment banking, that have traditionally been the stronghold of their Western peers. Western investment banks that have ruled Wall Street, Frankfurt, and London for generations have dominated Asia as well. Asian companies that want to raise capital need access to global investors and have veered to global investment banks with connections and a track record. The experience foreign banks have at helping companies raise capital on global markets has put them in a better position to reap the rewards of Asia's economic boom until now.

Local banks are fast building the expertise required to compete on equal footing on international exchanges. The investment banking subsidiaries of Chinese banks are proving they can raise the kind of capital needed to compete with the big boys. Ping An Securities and Guosen Securities earned the fifth and sixth largest amount of investment banking fees in Asia, excluding Japan, between January 1 and May 1, 2011, according to Dealogic.[7] They beat out Bank of America Merrill Lynch, Credit Suisse, Citigroup, and J.P. Morgan. As Asia's economies continue to lead global growth and the region's consumers look for new ways to invest their money, local banks with access to local investors will continue to build muscle and clout.

THE EXCEPTIONS: SOME INDUSTRIES LIKELY TO BE DOMINATED BY GLOBAL PLAYERS WHILE OTHERS RESIST CONSOLIDATION

Our Asian endgame theory has some important exceptions. Global companies will dominate in a couple of key industries because these are high-capital expenditure industries or they face limited access to raw materials. Some will not consolidate because governments, for nationalistic reasons, will never cede control.

Consider the steel industry. The iron ore industry is consolidated, and three big companies produce around 80 percent of the world's iron ore. That necessitates consolidation on a global level, and these global players will dominate Asia, too. Steel companies must become large to negotiate with suppliers in this powerful position. When you look at the value chain of any industry, you can make a call about where the profit will lie: When companies on one part of the value chain have an asymmetrical advantage because of a lock over customers or patent rights or control over raw materials, that group of companies drives the price. In the steel industry, the value lies in the hand of the iron ore companies. The steel companies that can survive and make a profit in a situation like this are the large ones or integrated steel companies that have downstream capabilities and can supply their own iron ore.

The concentration of the iron ore sector has driven global consolidation in the steel industry. China, which prohibits foreign companies from taking controlling stakes in its steel industry, remains the exception. Even there, the Chinese government is attempting to drive consolidation of its domestic industry to better negotiate with the big iron ore majors. China's steel industry acts as a collective in negotiating iron ore prices to achieve the same effect. There are thousands of steel companies in China, and the government has indicated it wants 10 of them to produce 50 percent of the country's volumes. In 2010, the government of Hebei, China's top steel-producing province, announced it planned to whittle the number of steel mills from 88 to 10 within five years and would cut electricity and deny credit to companies that refused to participate in consolidation.[8]

Asia's auto sector is another that global companies will dominate. The world's auto industry is gripped by over-capacity, over-supply, and high-capital expenditure costs as continual research and development is needed to keep up with consumer tastes: Consolidation will continue as carmakers look to spread their high development and production cost over a larger customer base, and it will be led by the few that can afford it. When it comes to cars, consumers across the world do have common tastes, usages, and preferences, unlike other products, such as beer and soft drinks.

Though these industries do prove an exception to our local optima theory, it doesn't mean Asian companies won't emerge as global champions of these sectors. Many existing global champions are local. Indian-born Lakshmi Mittal's ArcelorMittal is the world's largest steel company. During some periods in the recent past, Japanese automaker Toyota produced more cars than any other; and China's Geely, which bought Volvo from Ford in 2010 and plans to increase China sales fivefold by 2015, is a fast-moving contender for an Asian champion role.

Other industries that are deemed to be of national interest will remain local because governments will make sure of it. The oil and gas industry is one example, and airlines are another.

The upstream oil sector can be divided into three categories: international oil companies (IOCs), which includes the six oil majors that dominate the business; national oil companies (NOCs), such as Malaysia's Petronas and Indonesia's state-owned equivalent, Pertamina; and oil support service companies that do everything from exploring and drilling to providing support services to the NOCs and IOCs. At the start of the century, IOCs controlled the industry. They came to less developed countries, extracted the oil, and left. Local governments got wise to this and decided to get in the game and keep some of that wealth at home. During the 1960s, a wave of nationalization created NOCs that became competent players in their own right. IOCs are able to collaborate with NOCs, but typically regulations exist to ensure NOCs can displace the local incumbent. That picture is going to stay static. We do foresee that NOCs may buy up support service companies, but this industry will not see a fundamental shift.

The story is similar with airlines. The airline industry is a high-capital expenditure industry, and the more flights and higher connectivity (i.e., the number of routes globally) an airline has, the more a network effect kicks in, leading to lower unit operating costs. This means that the natural evolution for this industry is toward a few large airlines dominating the skies. In reality, we have plenty of national flag carriers typically owned by the government, which won't let them go broke no matter how much trouble they're in, as they are viewed as a source of national pride or are needed to serve low-population centers. As a result, airline capacity is an oversupply in the market. In addition, low-cost airlines, typically run by private shareholders, such as AirAsia, are becoming cost competitive, making life even more difficult for national carriers. No national full-service carriers in Asia are making money, except Singapore Airlines. AirAsia, which is profitable, was recently allowed to take a stake in state-owned Malaysia Airlines (MAS) as a way to rationalize the sector. Hong Kong-based Cathay Pacific, the region's other profitable full-service airline, is not state-owned and serves as proof that governments could step away from this industry and let it fly its own course.

THE CONSOLIDATION TREND IN ASIA: SAME DRIVERS, DIFFERENT OUTCOMES

1. Industries tend to go through a series of phases: opening, scale, and dominance.
2. Asia's fragmented markets will create opportunities for several clusters of local optima to dominate specific sub-segments of an industry. The scenario where two or three global companies dominate an entire industry, which is common in Western markets, is unlikely to emerge in this region.
3. Local companies, which leverage strong local understanding to win in the market and gain increasingly better access to capital and resources to acquire competitors, will have an edge.
4. Companies that figure out early on where their industries lie on the consolidation curve can make moves to ensure they come out on top during the scale and dominance phases.
5. Asian players that plan are positioned to emerge as national or regional champions in the merger endgame.

 ACKNOWLEDGMENTS

The following A.T. Kearney document was used as background material for this chapter: "Merger Endgame Phases" by Jürgen Rothenbücher, a partner and head of the firm's strategy practice in Europe, and Joerg Schrottke, a partner in our Munich office and member of the firm's strategy practice. The authors provided the original framework that was modified for this book.

CHAPTER THREE

The Rise and Rise of Cross-Border M&A

Over the past decade, several attention-grabbing Asian cross-border M&A deals have occurred. What has been surprising is that they have been done before these firms consolidated their local markets. We will explore the drivers behind cross-border deals and suggest this trend will increase. We will explore the added complexity that cross-border mergers and acquisitions (M&A) bring to deals and how firms will have to work harder to extract full value.

ASIAN COMPANIES HAVE TAKEN the standard M&A metrics that have long governed who buys what and when, and thrown them out the door. We have witnessed a sharp rise in cross-border merger activity in many Asian industries before domestic consolidation has begun. Young, aggressive Asian corporations are moving forward more quickly than you'd expect given the state of development of Asia's economies, and these corporations are snapping up companies in other parts of the world. China's fledgling automotive sector, for example, has more than 100 players and has many rounds of consolidation ahead. Geely, for one, decided not to wait. In 2010, the Hangzhou-based company, which makes its own brand of mid-sized, mid-tier cars, paid $1.8 billion for Volvo, one of the world's best-known auto brands.

The kinds of Asian companies that are driving cross-border M&A are surprising. They're not the type of world-beating champions that led global mergers during the 1980s and 1990s but instead are often mid-sized companies with smaller balance sheets and little experience of M&A in their own domestic markets. These acquisitive companies are proving that size and experience don't always matter. Companies such as Tata and Geely are breaking the mold as they move swiftly to snap up the assets they need to leapfrog competitors, access new markets, and move up the technology and branding curve.

TATA TEA LEADS GLOBAL ACQUISITION CHARGE

Tata Tea's takeover of the hallmark British Tetley Tea brand in 2000 was dubbed "the acquisition of a global shark by an Indian minnow" by India's media. That minnow has quickly moved to the top of the food chain.

Tata Tea was a small, $114 million company that sold commodity tea. Its target, Tetley, was the world's second-largest producer of tea bags and an iconic tea brand that was three times its size in terms of revenue. The move transformed Tata Tea from a farming operation that ran tea plantations to a high-margin global distributor of teas and other beverages.[1] After the acquisition, Tata Tea exited the commodity tea business and sold its vast plantations—the majority to its own former employees—to concentrate on its new, higher-value added, consumer-focused business model.

Tiny Tata Tea outbid global heavyweights, including Nestlé and Sara Lee, for Tetley. The tea brand had suffered from rapidly shrinking demand in its core U.K. market, which is steadily switching to coffee, and stiff competition from rivals like Brooke Bond.[2] Tetley's pretax profit fell to £4.98 million in the year ended March 1999 from £35.7 million the year before.

The headline-grabbing merger was the largest cross-border takeover of an international brand by an Indian company. "It is a bold move and I hope that other Indian corporates will follow," Tata Group chairman Ratan Tata said.[3]

They certainly did. In the past decade, Indian companies, including Tata, Bharti Telecom, and Mukesh Ambani's Reliance Industries have snapped up stakes in companies in nearly every industry, from steel and textiles to telecommunications and auto manufacturing. The Tata Group, which operates in a range of businesses, has led the charge.

In 2004, the Tata Group hired Alan Rosling, chairman of Hong Kong's Jardine Matheson Group and a former director of a Jardine-Tata automotive joint venture, to come on board as an executive director in charge of acquisitions. Rosling designed an M&A strategy that transformed Tata into a global name.

That year, Tata Motors bought Korea's Daewoo Commercial Vehicle Co. for $100 million. In 2007, Tata Steel acquired the Anglo-Dutch steel giant Corus Ltd. for $12.1 billion; Tata's Indian Hotels Ltd. paid $134 million for the Ritz-Carlton hotel in Boston the same year and renamed it the Taj Boston. In 2008, Tata Motors spent $2.3 billion to buy Jaguar Land Rover from Ford Motor Company.

The acquisition spree prompted some criticism from stock market analysts, many of whom felt the company paid too much for Jaguar Land Rover and worried it had leveraged itself too high, too fast. The timing of some of its overseas purchases, particularly the Corus and Jaguar Land Rover deals, was far from ideal: The 2008–2009 global financial crisis hit both industries hard. Global steel prices fell nearly 40 percent during the peak of the crisis, and auto sales in Europe practically stalled.

The economic recovery, however, has brought vindication. By mid-2010, both Corus and Jaguar Land Rover had turned around. Jaguar Land Rover accounted for nearly 70 percent of Tata Motors' net profit and 60 percent of its revenues in the quarter ended June 2010. Tata Steel, meanwhile, reported a major improvement in profitability in the second half of 2010; the company said in a statement that results were enhanced "by the dramatic turnaround" of Tata Steel Europe, which reported a positive earnings before interest, tax, depreciation, and amortization (EBITDA) of $513 million compared to an $813 million loss during the first half of 2010.

The outlook for the tea business has also improved. Tata Tea, which renamed itself Tata Global Beverages in 2010, has seen sales grow by about 20 percent each year for the past three years.

The total revenue of all the Tata companies, taken together, was $67.4 billion in 2009–2010, with 57 percent of this coming from business outside India, according to the company's website. This represents a 548 percent increase in revenue since 2001–2002, the start of the company's global push.

At the time of the Tetley takeover, Tata's Krishna Kumar, now chairman of Tetley Tea, said: "If you want to be a strong player, you can't not be a global player."[4] That seems to have turned into something of a corporate motto at the Tata Group. ▪

We are seeing this trend play out in our own practice at A.T. Kearney. Most of our Asian clients have grown rapidly in the past five years, and they're concerned about the ability of organic growth to continue to deliver the same kind of returns. The companies we deal with are putting more thought and effort into building an M&A strategy: They're talking to more bankers, considering more deals, and setting up their own internal departments to find and flesh out potential M&A.

Asia's fast rebound from the 2008–2009 global financial crisis added fresh momentum to the region's cross-border acquisition trend. Asia wasn't as hard hit as the West, and the region's economies and stock markets recovered far more quickly. Asia is driving global growth, and Asian companies have more cash, more confidence, and stronger balance sheets than many of their global peers. They're in a position to buy, and they want a big bang for their buck.

THE NUMBERS POINT EAST

The sharp rise in Asian outbound M&A underscores how active Asian companies have become on the global stage.

Asia's share of the world's total number of cross-border M&A has more than quintupled in the last decade (see Figure 3.1). Asian acquirers did $169 billion worth of cross-border deals in 2010, which accounted for 22 percent of global outbound M&A, up sharply from Asia's 4 percent share in 2001, according to data from Dealogic.

We excluded Japan and Australia from our analysis to get a clearer picture of the cross-border trend in emerging Asia. For cultural or geographic reasons, these developed countries traditionally have had lower cross-border transactions.

Asian companies did 1,887 cross-border deals to hit that $169 billion mark in 2010, up sharply from 490 deals worth $26 billion in 2001, according to data

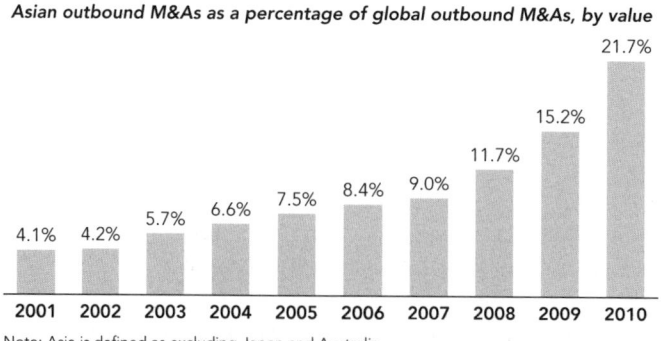

Asian outbound M&As as a percentage of global outbound M&As, by value

Note: Asia is defined as excluding Japan and Australia

FIGURE 3.1   Rise and Rise of Asian Cross-Border M&A
Source: Dealogic; A.T. Kearney analysis.

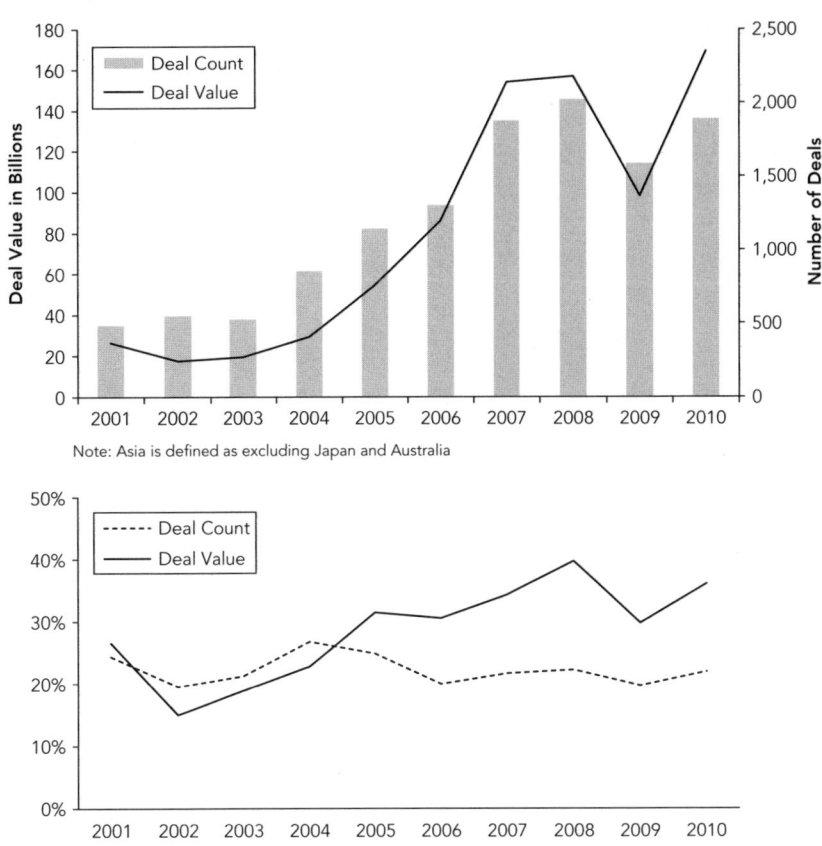

FIGURE 3.2 (a) Asian Cross-Border M&A and (b) Asian Cross-Border M&A as a Percentage of Total Asian M&A
Source: Dealogic; A.T. Kearney analysis.

from Dealogic (see Figure 3.2). Cross-border mergers and acquisitions represented 36 percent of all Asian M&A value in 2010.

Asian companies are not just acquiring companies in other parts of the region; they are increasingly eyeing up assets in developed countries. The value of deals that involved an Asian company making an acquisition in a developed country grew from $2.4 billion in 2001 to $44 billion in 2010, as shown in Figure 3.3.

Though the value of acquisitions of Asian corporations by companies from developed nations has grown over the past decade, the reverse—Asian companies

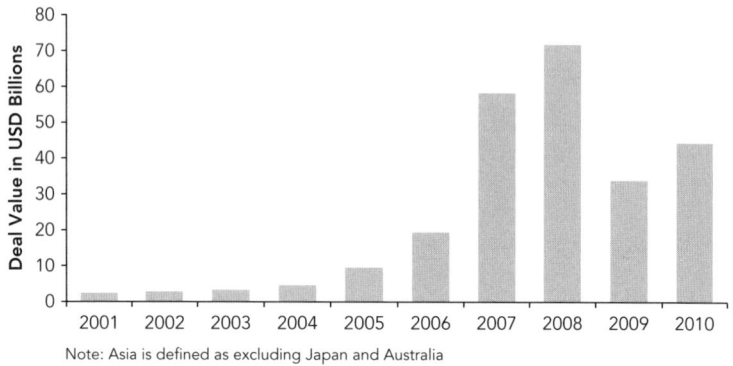

Note: Asia is defined as excluding Japan and Australia

FIGURE 3.3 Acquisitions by Asian Companies in Developed Countries
Source: Dealogic; A.T. Kearney analysis.

Note: Asia is defined as excluding Japan and Australia

FIGURE 3.4 Changing Directional Flow
Source: Dealogic; A.T. Kearney analysis.

buying in developed countries—has grown the fastest (see Figure 3.4). This reflects the fact that Asian companies emerged relatively unscathed by the recent financial crises and well-positioned to take advantage of undervalued assets in developed countries.

China and India are spearheading these acquisitions. The two giants accounted for 60 percent and 19 percent, respectively, of the value of the deals done by companies from developing Asian countries in developed markets in 2010, according to data from Dealogic.

What is interesting, however, is that Malaysia came in at a surprising third at 13 percent. (In 2009, Malaysia even inched out India, ranking second place that year.) A key factor here is that oil-producing nations such as Malaysia and the Gulf countries, and high-growth economies such as China and India, have gained large current account surpluses and are looking to diversify into global assets to reduce currency volatility and stabilize their economies. Given that China has $2.13 trillion in currency reserves that can be deployed, developing countries are going to have a dramatic effect on corporate configurations.

THE DRIVERS BEHIND ASIA'S CROSS-BORDER M&A BOOM

Companies in developed markets typically pursue M&A as a way to cut costs, to strengthen their competitive positions, or to broaden their presence in high-growth markets. They are constantly on the lookout for acquisitions with growth prospects, and they're interested in manufacturing and sourcing targets in low-cost environments to strengthen their competitive position.

Emerging-economy acquiring companies, on the other hand, often see M&A as more of a leapfrogging exercise. For young Asian companies seeking to become global players, M&A offers a shortcut to the markets, distribution networks, brand names, and new technologies they need (see Figure 3.5). These firms are entering established markets to maximize the advantages of their low-cost structure against traditional competitors. The expansion strategy of these

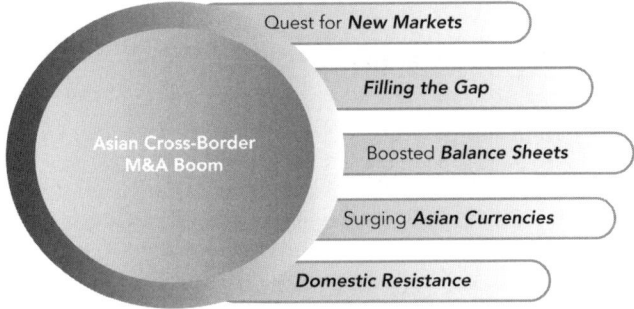

FIGURE 3.5 Why Are Asian Cross-Border M&A Booming?
Source: A.T. Kearney analysis.

companies is more focused on broadening the customer base and increasing market share. Other important drivers of cross-border M&A are Asia's increasing access to government support, global capital to finance its purchases, and its strengthening currency.

The Quest for New Markets

Singapore Telecommunications (SingTel) and Indian outsourcing firm Infosys Technologies are from two different countries and industries. The same driver, however, underpins the M&A strategies of these two companies: access to new markets.

Tiny Singapore offers few growth prospects for national telecommunications company SingTel. Competition from other players is stiff. SingTel, like other Singaporean companies, had no choice but to expand beyond its own shores.

The company started buying stakes in mobile phone companies around Asia in the 1990s, including Globe Telecom in the Philippines and Advanced Info Service in Thailand. In 2000, it paid $400 million for a 20 percent stake in India's Bharti Telecom and a 15 percent stake in Bharti Televentures; at the time, the deal represented the largest foreign investment in India's telco sector. The year 2001 was a particularly busy one for SingTel: It paid $7.3 billion for Optus, the second-largest phone company in Australia, and went on to buy a 22.3 percent stake in Indonesia's Telkomsel.[5] The Optus deal helped turn SingTel into one of the region's biggest telecommunications companies and the largest in Southeast Asia. After that acquisition, SingTel began generating more than half its revenues outside of Singapore.[6]

REGIONAL AMBITIONS

Strengthened by the success of its first round of regional acquisitions, CIMB Group, Malaysia's second-largest lender, has mapped out a plan to turn itself into one of Southeast Asia's top three regional banks.

The group, currently the fifth-largest lender in Southeast Asia, hopes to hit a top-three position by 2015. The company plans to continue along the acquisition trail to achieve that goal. "I do foresee over this period to 2015, we'll do more M&As to grow," CIMB's Group Chief Executive, Dato' Sri Nazir Razak, told reporters in April 2011.[7]

CIMB is particularly interested in acquiring a bank in the Philippines, where it has yet to build a presence, Razak indicated. The company would consider a second acquisition in Thailand, one of the bank's fastest-growing markets.[8]

CIMB was a relatively minor bank until 2005, when it acquired Bumiputra-Commerce Group, a large Malaysian lender. In 2008, CIMB merged its Indonesian unit, PT Bank CIMB Niaga, with PT Bank Lippo, and the unit became Indonesia's sixth-largest bank. CIMB acquired BankThai PCL that same year, expanding its presence in another core Southeast Asian market.[9] In 2009, it took a 19.99 percent stake in Bank of Yingkou Co. Ltd, becoming the largest shareholder of the bank, itself the largest bank in the city of Yingkou, China.

The Association of Southeast Asian Nations (ASEAN) plans to drop trade barriers and become a single market by 2015. CIMB is betting its Southeast Asian push will position the bank to capitalize on that enlarged, free trade economy. When the free trade plan goes ahead, a growing number of companies will want banking services that span the 10-nation region. ASEAN nations have a combined population of 600 million and a combined economic output of $1.2 trillion.[10]

CIMB has operations in Malaysia, Indonesia, Thailand, Singapore, and Brunei, with more than 1,100 branches throughout the region. The company has applied for banking licenses in Cambodia and Vietnam.

The Malaysian bank's regional foray has paid off so far. About 30 percent of CIMB's earnings come from non-Malaysian operations, according to Citigroup. The bank has posted record profits in several of the past five years, and its market capitalization surged to $14 billion from $3.3 billion between 2005 and 2010, making it one of the fastest-growing banks in the region.[11] CIMB Group Holdings' revenue has soared to 11.8 billion ringgit ($3.88 billion) in 2010 from 601 million ringgit in 2004, before its regional push.

The company's investment and Islamic banking units have become strong brands in their own segments. CIMB Islamic Bank, a major player in shariah banking, has been the world's biggest underwriter of sukuk, or Islamic bonds, since 2006. The company's investment bank, CIMB Investment Bank Bhd., has offices in Malaysia, Singapore, Indonesia, Hong Kong, Thailand, Brunei, the United Kingdom, and the United States. CIMB, which bought Singapore broker G.K. Goh in 2005, struck a deal in 2010 to take a 10 percent stake in VFC Securities, a Vietnam-based brokerage, with an option to increase its shareholding to 40 percent. ■

When the company announced its quarterly earnings in February 2003, then-CEO Lee Hsien Yang reported that SingTel's acquisition spree had decoupled its growth trajectory from the Singapore market. "I am happy to report that our results today demonstrate the success of our regional expansion strategy," he said in a press statement. "Our results in Australia and the strong performance of our other overseas investments mean that we have significantly reduced our dependency on our Singapore operations to maintain earnings growth."[12]

SingTel has since upped the stakes it owns in many of these overseas companies, including Bharti Telecom, Globe Telecom, Indosat, and AIS. It has bought stakes in Pacific Bangladesh Telecom and Warid Telecom, in Pakistan. All told, SingTel has invested around S$7.5 billion in overseas investments.[13]

It has not always been smooth sailing. SingTel's foray into Indonesia, through Telkomsel, was complicated by the presence of Temasek, the investment arm of the Singapore government, in the same sector. Temasek is SingTel's largest shareholder and owns ST Telemedia, which took a 41 percent stake in Indosat, another Indonesian telco. In 2007, Indonesia's antitrust watchdog said it found Temasek guilty of engaging in monopolistic and anticompetitive behavior in Indonesia's cellular market through Telkomsel and Indosat. The case dragged on in court for years, and in 2010, Temasek lost its appeal. Indonesia's Supreme Court ruled that Temasek and nine parties, including SingTel, each had to pay a S$2.3 million fine.[14]

Still, SingTel plans to stay the course. The company's current CEO, Chua Sock Koong, said in 2010 that SingTel is looking for acquisitions in Asia, Africa, and the Middle East, to boost growth.

Infosys doesn't have the constraints of SingTel's tiny home market. The world is the market for a company like Infosys that provides global outsourcing services, and Infosys, India's second-largest outsourcing firm, earns more than 60 percent of its revenue from the United States. Still, the company is looking at new ways to expand its reach into the United States and other markets. In 2009, Infosys BPO bought Atlanta-based McCamish Systems, a company that provides back-office business process solutions for insurance and retirement companies. The company's CFO said in February 2011 that Infosys plans to spend up to $200 million to acquire companies in the United States so it can bid on government contracts.[15]

The company is hunting for acquisitions in Europe and Japan in areas including healthcare and public services. "We are doing acquisitions for strategic fit and adding capability at this point in time," Infosys CEO S. Gopalakrishnan told Reuters in May 2011.[16]

Still other Asian companies see M&A as a quick way to access new emerging markets like Africa. India's Bharti Airtel paid $10.7 billion to acquire the African assets of Kuwait's Zain Group in 2010. The deal, one of the biggest acquisitions of the year, turned Bharti into the world's fifth-largest telecom firm, with operations in 18 countries.[17] Bharti's chairman and founder Sunil

Mittal described the acquisition of Zain Africa as "a game changer" for the company.

"With this acquisition, Bharti Airtel will be transformed into a truly global company," said Mittal in a press statement.

Taking the M&A route gave Bharti a big-bang entry into Africa's fledgling telecoms market since expanding organically into each country and obtaining coveted licenses would have taken years. Zain Africa has 42 million subscribers in 15 African countries and annual revenues of $3.6 billion, providing Bharti with a strong start. Bharti aims to grow to 100 million subscribers and $5 billion in revenue by 2013.[18]

Mittal had been working hard to get into Africa: The Zain deal was his third attempt to crack the continent. Two earlier bids to pull off a merger with MTN, a South African telecom company, fell apart after months of negotiations.[19]

The company plans to transplant the successful low-cost model it developed in India to Africa, which Mittal described in a press statement as "the continent of hope and opportunity."

Many Asian companies, like Bharti, have built their business model on serving the middle- to low-end consumer sector in their own emerging market at home, a skill many Western conglomerates are scrambling to acquire. Decades before companies like Nokia began making low-cost, durable phones with an extra-long battery life to tap India's rural markets, India's CavinKare was selling tiny, affordable sachets of soap and shampoo in the country's most remote nooks. Companies like CavinKare wrote the book on rural and "bottom of the pyramid" marketing well before Western companies started looking beyond the city limits. Multinationals that came to Asia during the 1990s typically stuck to the middle to high ground, and have only shifted their focus to the large, untapped lower end of the sector in the last few years. A range of Asian companies, cutting across almost every industry, has figured out how to design, distribute, and market products for the region's large numbers of mid- to low-income consumers.

Bharti, for one, built its large market share by providing affordable mobile phone products and services to India's vast rural hinterland, and consumer companies from China, India, and other Asian countries will likely follow its push into Africa.

Bharti had something to sell to Africa that worked in its own emerging market back home, but important push factors existed, too. About 15 million new subscribers are signing up each month for mobile phone services in India, making this the fastest-growing wireless market in the world. That's attracted new foreign competitors like Sistema and Telenor. Intense competition, from local and foreign players, has driven down call charges in India, squeezing margins and earnings growth.[20]

The fact that Bharti, the leading telecommunications company in the world's fastest-growing market, feels compelled to seek other new, emerging markets to ensure growth underscores the upward trajectory of Asia's cross-border M&A trend. More companies are going to contemplate similar strategies as pressure mounts to maintain profit margins.

Filling the Gap: Acquiring Access to Distribution, Brands, New Technologies, and Resources

M&A has proven a powerful tool for Asian companies seeking to build a global brand. Consider Lenovo's acquisition of IBM's personal computer (PC) business. Until 2005, Lenovo was unknown outside China. It had tried to branch out into new products and markets only to beat a hasty retreat after losing market share in its core markets. With the acquisition of IBM's PC business, however, it found access to more than 100 foreign markets and became a major global player overnight instead of struggling for years in the intensely competitive industry. As part of the deal, Lenovo gained the rights to the "ThinkPad" brand, which continues to dominate the PC market.

By marrying IBM's efficient supply chain and distribution network with a low-cost manufacturing base, the deal was underpinned by sound industrial logic. The merger integration had its share of challenges, but after two years of perseverance, the combined entity showed blazing results in 2007.

China's rise as a manufacturing power was driven by low production costs and low product prices, but if Chinese companies want to persevere in the face of growing foreign competition, they need to close the technology and brand gap. Chinese companies aren't alone in this respect: Many Asian manufacturing companies failed to invest in innovation or branding, choosing instead to rely on low prices to drive volume sales. As margins continue to fall, more Asian companies are thinking about how to move up the value chain.

Lenovo's executives acknowledged that the play for IBM was motivated by the realization that their grip on their home market is vulnerable.[21] The company's products were being squeezed at the high end by the likes of Dell and at the low end by cheaper local competitors. "We are losing our brand advantage in China's domestic market," Liu Chuanzhi, then Lenovo's chairman, said in a 2004 interview in the Beijing-based *Xinjing* newspaper. "We seek to build an internationally recognized brand, which will require plenty of courage and capital."[22]

Some Asian companies that have managed to build a strong brand at home are using M&A as a tool to get better access to technology and distribution and to boost the profile of their homegrown brand on the global stage.

Tata, one of India's more acquisitive conglomerates, achieved all three goals when its automotive unit bought the Jaguar and Land Rover brands. In March 2008, Mumbai-listed Tata Motors paid $2 billion for Jaguar Land Rover from Ford Motor Company, which needed to restructure its own business to return to profitability. The deal initially raised eyebrows: Tata had built its business making small, inexpensive cars for the Indian market. It had no experience making or managing a luxury brand like Jaguar.

Not everyone took that view. When the deal was announced, Tom Purves, who was then CEO of BMW North America, described Tata as "probably the best possible owner for Jaguar and Land Rover."[23] Tata was an experienced and profitable automaker, he noted. North America's own stable of carmakers, meanwhile, have struggled in recent years in the face of competition from Japanese and Korean automakers. "Actually, they are probably the only company that could come in and do this," Purves added.

For Tata, the deal brought two big-name brands into its stable, giving the Indian automaker an opportunity to move its portfolio up the value curve. It gained access to a top-end automotive design and engineering operation. Tata, meanwhile, infused cash and emerging-market know-how into the business.

In May 2010, the company announced plans to build Jaguar and Land Rover cars in China to cut costs and expand sales of both brands in emerging markets. In the meantime, the company opened more showrooms in India and set up a sales company in China.[24] That effort quickly paid off. In February 2011, Tata Motors reported a nearly fourfold rise in its third quarter consolidated net profit, led by higher sales at its U.K.-based Jaguar Land Rover business and at home. Jaguar Land Rover's sales, which had taken a dip during the global financial crisis when consumers in Europe and the United States reined in spending, began to recover in 2010, partly as a result of expanded sales in China, the company reported.[25]

M&A offers Asian companies a quick way to build up their distribution reach. Japanese beverage company Kirin Holdings spent about 1 trillion yen between 2006 and 2010 on M&A to expand its reach into Asia. The company, which owns Australian dairy firm National Foods and Australian brewery Lion Nathan, and a 48 percent stake in Philippine beer company San Miguel, took a 14.7 percent stake in Singaporean beverage company Fraser & Neave (F&N) in 2010 for $953 million, making it F&N's second-largest shareholder. F&N is the largest beverage company in Malaysia and Singapore. It bottles and distributes

Tiger, Anchor, and Heineken beer through Asia Pacific Breweries, a joint venture between F&N and Heineken N.V., and is the regional anchor bottler for Coke, through F&N Coca-Cola. F&N, which makes its own brands of fruit and soft drinks, has operations in Thailand, Vietnam, and China.

Kirin's executives said the company planned to use F&N's extensive sales network in Southeast Asia to expand its distribution, citing dairy products from its National Food subsidiary as an example of its distribution-expansion goal.[26] "This deal will give us a base in Southeast Asia, an area where we have been weak," said Hirotake Kobayashi, Kirin's managing director. "The stake is small, at 14.7 percent, but it is strategically important."[27]

In August 2011, Kirin struck further afield, spending $2.57 billion to acquire slightly more than 50 percent of Schincariol, Brazil's second-biggest beer brewer. The acquisition was the third largest ever done by a Japanese company, after Takeda Pharmaceutical's $14 billion purchase of Nycomed. Kirin later stepped in and bought the remaining 50 percent, making it the full owner of the Brazilian brewer. That deal further underscored the push factor for many Japanese companies, who face a dwindling market at home. Industrywide beer shipments in Japan fell 3.5 percent in the first half of 2011, according to an August 3, 2011, report by the *Wall Street Journal*. In 2001, Japanese brewers were among world's most acquisitive companies, snapping up $4 billion in deals in the first eight months of the year, the report said.

Tata gained production and distribution reach, and a technology boost, when it bought Corus Steel, Europe's second-largest steel producer, in 2007, for $12 billion. Through that deal, Tata acquired production sites in the United Kingdom, the Netherlands, Germany, France, Norway, and Belgium, giving it a strong European presence to balance its Asian operations. Tata Steel has operations in Thailand and India, and a stake in Singapore's NatSteel. The acquisition of Corus helped Tata Steel up its technology game: Corus has particularly strong research and development (R&D) and product development capabilities for value-added products in the global construction, packaging, and automotive markets.[28]

Other Asian companies are acquiring global assets to supply raw materials and energy to their own home market. Chinese companies, hungry for resources like coal and oil to fuel economic growth back home, are leading this charge, snapping up stakes in resource companies from Australia and Africa to South America.

In 2010, China Petrochemical Corporation (also known as Sinopec Group) paid $7.1 billion for a 40 percent equity stake in oil and gas company Repsol YPF Brasil SA, China's largest single outbound deal of the year. Yanzhou Coal made China's largest-ever investment in Australian resources when it paid $3 billion to take over Felix Resources in 2009.

Indeed, China accounted for nearly two-thirds of Australia's US$10.6 billion mining M&A deals in 2009, up from 13 percent in 2008, according to Ernst & Young. The global financial crisis, which choked off access to debt and capital for mining and metal companies in Australia and other parts of the world, paved the way for China's push into Australia's mining sector.[29]

Asian resource companies have focused on Africa. State-owned Jinchuan Group Ltd., China's largest platinum producer, penned a deal to take over Johannesburg-based Wesizwe Platinum Ltd. in December 2010. The deal includes a debt commitment, giving Wesizwe $877 million to build its first mine in South Africa, the world's largest supplier of platinum. China Guangdong Nuclear Power Group of Shenzhen, the nation's second-largest reactor builder, made a $1.2 billion bid for London-based Kalahari Minerals Plc. in March 2011. That deal, if it goes ahead, will give the state-owned company access to Perth-based Extract Resources Ltd.'s Husab uranium project in Namibia. Kalahari owns about 43 percent of Extract.[30]

The value of M&A transactions in Africa surged to a record high of US$44 billion in 2010, more than double the US$17.5 billion worth of deals done in 2009, and China and India accounted for 36 percent of the value of all transactions, according to a report by Deloitte.[31]

Boosted Balance Sheets: Asia's Stock Markets and Governments Underwrite the M&A Boom

Asia's booming stock markets have provided companies with the means to go on global shopping sprees. The region's governments, meanwhile, are doing everything in their power to encourage the trend—including giving out low-interest loans.

Since the late 1990s, Asia's stock markets have outperformed their peers, churning out billionaire businessmen like Ratan Tata, who have the confidence to fulfill their increasingly global ambitions (see Figure 3.6). Many companies across Asia have a higher price-earnings multiple than their global peers. Globalization, meanwhile, has given more Asian companies access to global capital. Bankers are beating a path to Asia's corporate offices, hoping to profit from the region's economic boom. Investors in the most rural parts of the United States are putting money into the most remote parts of Asia. The world is focused on Asia's growth story. Share prices are up, and appetite is strong for Asian equity and debt. Indeed, Asia's share of global stock issuance has doubled

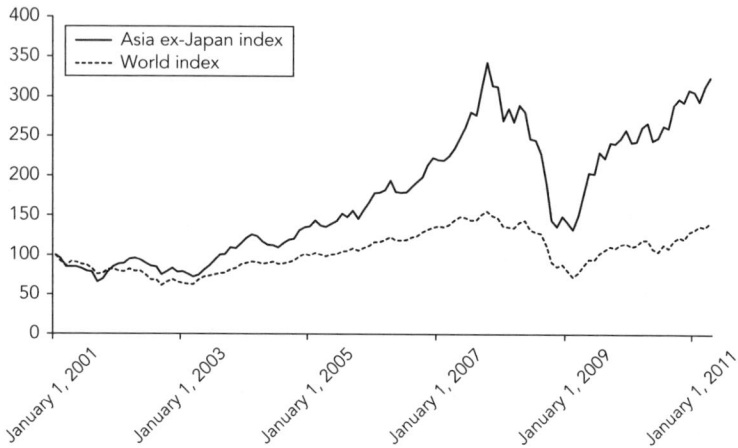

FIGURE 3.6   Morgan Stanley Capital International (MSCI) Index Performance
Source: www.msci.com.

in the last decade. Asia's equity offerings comprised 41 percent of the world's equity offerings in 2010, up sharply from 18 percent in 2001, according to data from Bloomberg. It's easier than ever for Asian companies to raise the money they need to go global.

Consider how quickly and easily Tata Motor was able to restructure and repay the loans it took to buy Jaguar and Land Rover. In October 2009, Tata raised $750 million in a combined shared placement and convertible bond issue that allowed the company to repay the remainder of the bridge loans it had taken out to buy Jaguar and Land Rover the year before. Demand for the issue was so high that Tata, which had initially planned to raise $300 million from each issue, increased the size of each tranche to $375 million. The strong response to the issue, which took place in the depths of the global financial crisis, highlighted the strength of demand from international investors for Indian assets.[32]

Asian governments, meanwhile, are encouraging cross-border M&A to diversify their own markets and economies. Some governments are putting state money where their mouth is. China, for one, is sitting on more than $2.5 trillion in foreign reserves and is actively spending some of that cash for global acquisitions.

China's $300 billion sovereign wealth fund, China Investment Corp. (CIC), which was set up in 2007, has stakes in a range of companies, including Morgan Stanley, U.S. private equity firm Blackstone Group, Singapore-listed commodities supply chain manager Noble Group and Canadian oil and gas company Penn West Energy. The fund holds sizeable stakes in a number of China's major state-owned banks. In April 2011, the *Financial Times* reported that the Chinese government may provide CIC with another $100 billion to $200 billion to reduce its exposure to U.S. government debt.

China's premier, Wen Jiabao, said in 2009 that Beijing intends to use those foreign exchange reserves—the largest in the world—to support and accelerate overseas acquisitions by Chinese companies. "We should hasten the implementation of our 'going out' strategy and combine the utilization of foreign exchange reserves with the going out of our enterprises," he said.[33] That comment was the first official articulation of Beijing's intention to support Chinese corporations' bids to buy offshore assets. One way to do that is for CIC to take stakes in Chinese companies listed offshore or to beef up stakes in companies that are investing overseas.

Private and state-owned Chinese companies have become active global acquirers. Outbound M&A grew 49 percent, by value, to $44 billion in 2010 over the year before, according to Dealogic. Public capital, meanwhile, is increasingly being used to fund those cross-border acquisitions. The China National Petroleum Corp. (CNPC), for example, announced in 2009 that it had received a low-interest $30 billion loan to fund its overseas acquisition spree. "The credit agreement is of great importance for CNPC to speed up its overseas expansion strategy and secure the nation's energy supplies," the company's chairman, Jiang Jiemin, said in a statement.[34]

Sweet deals like this underscore China's commitment to spend what it takes to ensure its enterprises can acquire the resources the country needs.

Surging Asian Currencies Support Spending Spree

Stronger Asian currencies have given Asian companies much bigger purchasing power. Consider the yen, which, in August 2010, hit a 15-year high against the dollar. Faced with a shrinking domestic market and bolstered by the stronger yen, a wide range of Japanese companies began looking for M&A opportunities that year to help them tap into new growth markets abroad.[35]

One such company was Nippon Telegraph and Telephone Corp. (NTT), which agreed in July 2010 to pay $3.2 billion for South African technology service provider Dimension Data. The two companies actually began talks in 2009 but parted company because they were too far apart on price. They returned to the table a year later, after the yen had surged against the dollar. The same deal, at the same price proposed by Dimension, had become 10 percent cheaper for NTT.

In 2011, the bargain hunting continued at breakneck speed. According to Dealogic, outbound M&A by Japanese companies hit $34.7 billion in the first five months of the year, outstripping the $34.2 billion achieved in the whole of 2010. Headline deals included Takeda Pharmaceutical Co.'s $13.7 billion purchase of Swiss drug maker Nycomed. That deal, announced in May, was the second-biggest overseas acquisition ever by a Japanese company.[36] The same month, Toshiba Corp. announced it had agreed to spend $2.3 billion to buy Swiss meter maker Landis+Gyr.

Stronger domestic currencies were one of the key drivers behind Asia's 2010 M&A boom. Currencies like the Thai baht, the Indonesian rupiah, and the yen strengthened sharply against the dollar, sparking a wave of cross-border M&A.

In July 2010, ThaiUnion Frozen became one of the world's largest canned tuna firms, by sales, when it bought French canned seafood business MWBrands (MWB) for €680 million ($884 million). MWB owns brands like John West, Petit Navire, and Mareblu. ThaiUnion owns Chicken of the Sea. Backed by a strong baht, ThaiUnion beat out well-known private equity firms like the Blackstone Group to secure the deal.[37]

Stronger Asian currencies also provide a cushion for Asian companies. Mergers often fail because companies pay too much of a premium, notes Wharton management professor Lawrence G. Hrebiniak in a recent report. The rise in value of the region's currencies defrays some of that risk by providing relative bargains (see Figure 3.7).

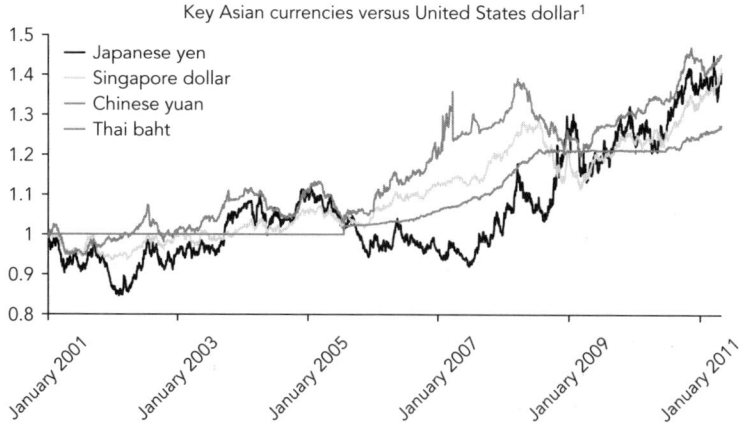

Key Asian currencies versus United States dollar[1]

— Japanese yen
   Singapore dollar
— Chinese yuan
— Thai baht

[1]Rebased with January 1, 2001's exchange rates

FIGURE 3.7   Rising Asian Currencies Allowing Asian Acquirers to Buy on the Cheap
Source: Factiva; A.T. Kearney analysis.

Asia's strong reserves will likely continue to buoy local currencies. That means companies on the lookout for global acquisitions will get a bigger bang for their non-U.S. buck, adding yet more momentum to the M&A trend.

Domestic Resistance to Merger Pushes Companies beyond Their Borders

Some Asian companies look for acquisitions outside their own borders because it's just too difficult to land a deal at home. Many Asian companies are linked to governments or family owned, and often majority shareholders don't want to sell out, even to a good offer. Some even opt for deals that may not deliver the best price.

Asian countries don't always have the strict governance codes that apply in much of the West, which require a board to put any valid offer to the company's shareholders, especially minority shareholders in family majority-owned firms. This leaves family-owned companies free to dodge offers that could dilute their holdings or to favor deals that offer other bells and whistles that mean little to shareholders. Deals based on something other than price-driven logic leave acquiring companies in an uncertain place, prompting many Asian companies that operate in industries that have not yet consolidated to start looking overseas even though deals should be available—or so it would seem—at home.

Asia's financial sector offers up several examples. In 2005, SinoPac Holdings, one of Taiwan's smallest banks, rejected a takeover offer from Taishin Holdings, one of the country's most profitable banks, because some of the shareholders preferred a merger with International Bank of Taipei (IBT) even though Taishin had offered a higher price. Paul Lo, SinoPac's founder and president, was believed to have preferred IBT because it had agreed to retain his post and to keep the bank's brand alive. Two previous merger talks fell apart because SinoPac's management insisted the prospective buyers maintain their posts and the company brand. Like many Asian countries, including Thailand, Malaysia, and Singapore, Taiwan's government had set a consolidation target to reduce the number of players in the finance industry to a few, stronger banking operations. The failure of Taishin's merger bid illustrated the obstacles that founders and family shareholders in many Taiwanese financial institutions could create to M&A.[38] SinoPac ultimately approved the sale to IBT.

Still many more family-owned or founder-owned operations resist mergers altogether. For Asian companies looking to buy, it's often easier to look elsewhere.

 ## THE RISKS INHERENT IN M&A ARE MORE PRONOUNCED IN ASIA

The rise of cross-border M&A looks set to continue its momentum. Yet M&A is a risky business: The failure rate is high. Past A.T. Kearney studies indicate that only 29 percent of companies worldwide see an increase in aggregate profitability, and 57 percent see a decline. That figure drops lower in Asia. Our study showed that just 24 percent of Southeast Asian mergers delivered the expected benefits.

The risk level steepens when companies venture beyond their own backyard. Cross-border synergies are hard to pull off. Culture clashes, poor communication, and lack of local market know-how derail many newly merged cross-border ventures. These risks, which apply to the most seasoned global giant, may be more acute in Asia. The companies fueling Asia's M&A boom are relatively young and immature and lack experience in M&A. These companies may be doing deals for multiple reasons, which can cause executives to lose focus when they consider potential acquisition targets (see Figure 3.8).

The thirst for M&A by Asia's government-linked companies carries its own set of risks. Political leaders worldwide are sensitive about the sale of critical resource or logistics assets to companies owned by foreign governments, particularly where China's concerned. In 2009, the British-Australian mining giant Rio Tinto walked away from a $19.5 billion offer from Chinalco, which would have doubled the Chinese state-owned company's stake to 18.5 percent, after the deal became a political issue. Several Australian politicians proclaimed the deal would effectively give the Chinese government control of national resources. "Chinalco is an arm of the Chinese government, so you've got a customer, competitor, and sovereign government embedded in the structure, and we feel troubled by that," Ross Barker, managing director of the Australian Foundation Investment Company, told the newspaper *The Australian*.[39] Rio Tinto's shareholders eventually panned the deal.

China is not the only bogeyman. Australia killed a proposed merger between the Australian and Singapore stock exchanges in 2011 after a huge

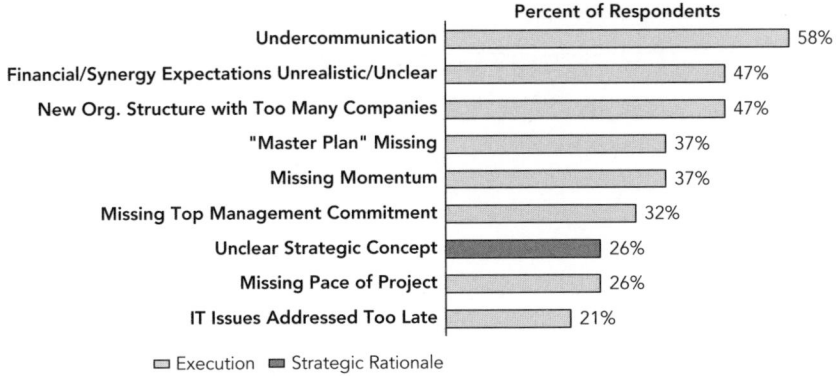

FIGURE 3.8 Problems Identified in Post-Merger Integration
Source: Global Merger Integration Survey; A.T. Kearney analysis.

political outcry. In April, Australian Treasurer Wayne Swan forbade the merger, saying it was not in the country's national interest.[40]

Another hurdle in Asia's cross-border M&A race is rising valuations. The post-crisis gold rush for undervalued assets has pushed up prices, particularly within Asia. Many of our clients at A.T. Kearney are focused on buying companies that will help expand their regional reach. Asia is getting pricey, and Asian deals are getting harder to find. Most Asian companies have the same ambitions, and increasingly, not enough deals exist. Many of the companies that are on the block have serious issues. They tend not to have perfect governance structures, for example, and they have poor financial reporting. Those issues, which typically come up during the due diligence process, are surmountable but do tend to slow down deals.

Another risk we see is that executives are sometimes too anxious to do a deal; they'll grab at any deal rather than the right deal. Investment bankers in Asia, keen to capitalize on the boom, are continually throwing up possible targets to companies that are in buy mode. We advise our clients to focus a little more on how these deals will fit into their overall strategy before they go too far down the road.

The gamut of risks and hurdles doesn't mean that Asian corporations should walk away from cross-border mergers. Instead, executives need to think about how to do it better.

FIVE KEY POINTS BEHIND ASIA'S CROSS-BORDER BOOM

1. Cross-border M&A are on the rise in Asia and the trend has plenty of steam left. Cross-border deals accounted for 36 percent of Asia's total M&A value in 2010, up from 15 percent eight years before.
2. Asian companies undertaking mergers are breaking the Western mold: They're going abroad faster and younger and with less reserve, driven by markedly different reasons than their Western peers.
3. Asian companies see M&A as a tool to fast-track up the technology and branding curve, expand distribution, and access new markets.
4. Asia's booming stock markets and the region's cash-infused governments are underwriting the cross-border merger boom.
5. Plenty of risks exist, particularly for young Asian companies with no merger experience. Executives, however, still need to consider M&A if they want to seize new markets and secure growth.

 ## ACKNOWLEDGMENTS

The following A.T. Kearney documents were used as background material in writing this chapter: "Deal Making—Now Is as Good a Time as Any," a white paper by Vikram Chakravarty, Karambir Anand, and Rizal Paramarta; "Drivers of Successful M&A Integration," a PowerPoint presentation for the Mergers and Acquisitions Conference, October 20, 2005.

CHAPTER FOUR

Transforming Government-Linked Companies through Mergers and Acquisitions

The drivers for mergers and acquisitions (M&A) do not typically include a desire for culture change. However, we suggest that for some government-linked firms, with a heavy hold of the bureaucracy, this could be a real and transformative benefit. The post-acquisition period shakes established habits and could allow for a new regime. We have identified several mechanisms for engineering a mindset shift and suggest this might be a better way to kick-start a transformative program.

G OVERNMENT-OWNED OR GOVERNMENT-LINKED companies dominate a large part of the domestic economy in most Asian countries. These incumbent government players tend to be somewhat lethargic, ponderous, and bureaucratic. They are typically slow to adapt, slow to change, and slow to make decisions. They can't, however, afford to continue to operate that way.

Consider the onslaught of private sector competition that has emerged in the past decade in high-cost industries that have traditionally been dominated by government companies, including airlines, energy, and telecoms. In most cases, when faced with newfound competitive pressures, government incumbents have looked inward and opted to take on moderate improvement initiatives.

A viable, aggressive, and more proactive strategy to address their competitive shortcomings is the pursuit of M&A. M&A provides access to new products, technology, strategies, and ideas, and this kind of event offers a unique chance to shake up the corporate culture. M&A can be transformative. During a merger or acquisition, legal day one offers companies a chance to reinvent themselves: It can be a new day for a new company that plans to approach the market in a new way. This fresh-start approach gives executives a chance to reassess whether their processes make sense, whether the culture makes sense, and whether their internal promotion cycle makes sense. As the merger team maps out the strategy of the enlarged entity—ranging from products to markets to processes—it has a unique opportunity to chart a new course and shake up an otherwise large, moribund institution.

This may be critical to Asia's economies, which remain dominated by government-linked corporations (GLCs) and state-owned enterprises (SOEs). Governments that want to continue to use GLCs to nurture and grow their economies must use the most powerful tool on hand to get those enterprises into fighting form. M&A is the tool.

THE ROLE OF THE PUBLIC SECTOR IN KEY ASIAN ECONOMIES

Asia's public sector typically plays a large role in its local domestic economy through myriad state-owned companies or GLCs. GLCs may be publicly listed, but the government remains the largest—usually the majority—shareholder.

We compiled a list of GLCs in key Asian countries and calculated their 2010 revenue as a percentage of the country's gross domestic product (GDP) as a proxy for how big the GLCs are relative to the size of their respective domestic economies. This allows us to make some comparison across countries although it doesn't precisely map out the exact contribution of GLCs, private players, and multinational corporations in each country, as revenue of GLCs will include contribution from overseas. The revenues of China's state-owned companies and GLCs constitute 14.5 percent of GDP, which is on par with Thailand; India's revenue of GDP makes up 6.5 percent and Malaysia's is 17.4 percent. Singapore stands out at 48 percent. The revenue earned by Australia's GLCs equates to 3 percent of GDP; the ratio in the United States is 1.68 percent. We included GLCs in which the respective government had a stake of 50 percent or more. The actual list is much higher; some government investment agencies control GLCs through a minority stake that leaves them as the largest, controlling shareholder.

Even though Asia's GLCs command a sizeable portion of the economy, they're not doing a standout job. Singapore's GLCs are competitive, but they are probably the exception: Most of these companies are nowhere near as nimble or well run as their private sector peers. As an example, consider the gap between Asia's state-owned banks and their private sector peers. We compared the average return on assets (ROA) of Asian government-linked banks in 2010 against the average ROA of private sector banks. We included all banks in our GLC list in which the government has a controlling stake even if that stake was less than 50 percent. There is a consistent lag in returns.

The average return on assets of India's government-owned banks was just 0.88 percent, but their private sector peers returned 1.4 percent, as shown in Table 4.1. In Japan, GLC banks underperformed as well, with a 0.18 percent ROA, compared to 0.26 percent from the private sector. The picture is worse in parts of Southeast Asia. Indonesia's government-owned banks returned an average of 2.3 percent, compared to the 3.5 percent average of the private sector banks. Thai government-linked banks underperformed by the widest margin of all, with an ROA that was less than half of that of their private sector peers.

If government-run companies continue to claim such a large slice of the economic pie, surely they owe it to the country's taxpayers, and shareholders, to operate in the most efficient and competitive manner. By merging with competing state-linked companies to gain better synergies and reduced costs, by acquiring private players who can galvanize their operations, or by selling a majority stake to a market leader who can provide the cutting edge technology, services, and competitive returns required, these companies can better

TABLE 4.1 Private Sector Banks Outshine GLC Peers: 2010 ROA of Publicly Listed Banks versus Government-Linked Banks in Selected Countries

Asian Countries	GLCs ROA (Weighted over Assets)	Non-GLCs ROA (Weighted over Assets)
China-People's Rep.	1.089	1.068
India	0.887	1.397
Indonesia	2.255	3.489
Japan	0.182	0.257
Malaysia	1.214	1.350
Singapore	0.692	1.307
Thailand	0.665	1.354

Source: Bankscope; A.T. Kearney analysis.

justify their outsized presence in the country's economy by delivering more to shareholders and voters. Privatization may not be the best answer for state-linked companies that offer critical services in thinly populated markets, but in thriving industries crowded with nimble competitors, the option should be on the table.

M&A: A TOOL THAT MAKES BOTH COMPANIES AND ECONOMIES MORE COMPETITIVE

Many Asian governments have traditionally used state-owned companies and state-linked companies to execute broader economic policy. Singapore's GLCs, for example, were a core part of the government's strategy to develop its external economy. Singapore, with few natural resources, had to look outward for growth momentum since the earliest days of nationhood. Outbound M&A have been a key part of that strategy. Singapore's GLCs have led the city-state's corporate push into the region, and indeed the world, by snapping up stakes in everything from telecoms to ports to financial institutions. China's SOEs are doing the same, pushed by the need to secure natural resources to fuel economic growth back home.

Still, there are few examples of GLCs undertaking domestic mergers to consolidate fragmented industries at home, to gain better synergies, or to use M&A to shake up the organization. Across Asia, a lot of resistance exists to M&A within the public corporate sector even though they are active in cross-border acquisitions.

Many of these organizations could do with some transformative changes. China's SOEs, for example, remain largely opaque, and the listed companies lack transparency. These enterprises are acquiring companies all over the world, but they're not transferring the business know-how or the commercially driven corporate culture of those targets back to their own operation.

In May 2011, China's National Audit Office published a report that revealed irregularities and disciplinary violations in the financial statements of 17 high-profile SOEs in the 2009 fiscal year. The state agency that supervises the country's SOEs said it would work to make the SOEs' management more transparent in the wake of the report. In a statement posted to its website, the supervising agency said the SOEs have made progress in management, risk controls, and social responsibilities in the past years but noted they still lag far behind top-level international enterprises and should take advantage of the disclosures to enact further changes, according to a report by *The China Daily*. Acquiring or merging with private sector competitors and harnessing their best practices and top talent would help propel the typical state-owned entity up the ladder.

Even Singapore's GLCs, which are run on a commercial basis and held up as the gold standard in Asia, could do more to leverage M&A. The city-state's GLCs have been criticized as being less nimble than their private sector peers partly because GLC managers are often appointed from the ranks of senior civil service and not from private industry.[1]

Sovereign Wealth Funds, which typically hold the government's stakes in the GLCs, have taken a few steps to drive change at GLCs through M&A. Malaysia's state investment fund Permodalan Nasional Berhad (PNB), for example, drove the three-way merger of Malaysia's government-linked plantation companies. Khazanah Nasional Berhad, the investment-holding arm of the Malaysian government, has been active in driving change in Malaysia's public sector.

In 2005, Khazanah, which owned a 22.7 percent stake in Commerce Asset-Holdings Berhad, then the country's second-largest financial group, encouraged the merger of two of Commerce Asset's majority-owned units: Bumiputra-Commerce Bank (BCB), a large bank that was widely viewed as badly run, and CIMB, a much smaller but more nimble investment bank.[2] The move, which transformed CIMB into a dominant player, came at a time when Malaysia was promoting consolidation within its banking sector ahead of plans to open the market to foreign competition in 2008.

The outcome of that forced marriage has been stellar. Since it swallowed BCB, CIMB has gone on to become Malaysia's second-largest financial services provider and Southeast Asia's fifth-largest lender (see "Regional Ambitions" sidebar in Chapter 3).

Asia's governments should use M&A to prepare the domestic sector for foreign competition. Trade barriers are coming down all over Asian groups, including the Association of Southeast Asian Nations (ASEAN), the Asia-Pacific Economic Cooperation (APEC) forum, and the World Trade Organization (WTO), as the Trans-Pacific Strategic Economic Partnership Agreement (TPP) phases in agreements to liberalize trade. Many Asian nations are busily signing bilateral trade agreements with each other and Western countries to bolster economic activity, adding to the momentum of deregulation. State-owned companies across Asia are going to have to become more competitive to survive in this new era.

Many state-owned companies were set up to help build nascent industries, from telecoms to automotive manufacturing, to help diversify Asian economies; protectionist laws were put in place to keep foreign competitors out to ensure they could achieve those goals. That era is drawing to a close.

Asian governments are working on a host of regional and bilateral trade agreements designed to bolster economic activity by cutting import duties, lifting ownership limits, and improving two-way access for investors and companies. The members of ASEAN, a combined population of 550 million, have committed to remove obstacles by 2015 to the cross-border flow of goods, services, and investment. The six most developed economies of ASEAN—Thailand, Malaysia, the Philippines, Indonesia, Singapore, and Brunei—have removed import taxes for ASEAN companies. The four least developed—Vietnam, Cambodia, Laos, and Burma—are scheduled to follow suit by the 2015 deadline. In 2010, China got on board and signed the ASEAN-China Free Trade Agreement, which, with a combined population of 1.9 billion, will create the world's largest free trade zone.

The 21 members of APEC plan to create a pan-Asian free trade zone by 2020. Many Asian countries have pushed ahead of that goal; there are more than 120 bilateral free trade agreements with the Asia-Pacific region. Others are also signing up for the TPP, another multilateral free trade agreement that aims to liberalize the economies of the Asia-Pacific region. The TPP requires members to eliminate trade barriers in a range of sectors, including manufacturing, agriculture, and services, within a period of 10 years from entry. Singapore, New Zealand, Brunei, and Chile are members of the TPP, and five other nations—the United States, Australia, Peru, Vietnam, and Malaysia—are negotiating to join the agreement.

One way to prepare a sector for the tidal wave of liberalization is to trim the number of state-run companies, encourage consolidation, and create larger, more competitive enterprises. There are a few examples of this: Singapore's DBS Bank, for one, merged with POSBank, another government-linked bank, in 1998, to gain dominant market share. The deal came one year ahead of a five-year plan, announced by the Monetary Authority in 1999, to liberalize access and participation by foreign banks in the domestic finance sector.

The move by Malaysia's state-run investment fund to push for the merger of three state-linked palm oil companies is another example. That deal created the world's largest palm oil producer and created economies of scale that enhanced the company's competitiveness in the international arena.

There's plenty of scope and many drivers for more of these kinds of deals. Many state-linked companies, from India to China, need improvement. Meanwhile, GLCs or state-owned companies could make much better use of M&A to pave the way for the inevitable liberalization of industries that remain largely sheltered from international competition and from China's finance sector to Malaysia's automotive industry.

THE EMERGING THREAT FROM THE PRIVATE SECTOR

The encroachment of private companies into industries traditionally dominated by government companies is not a new phenomenon. In most countries, prior government dominance of the financial sector, agricultural commodity trading, broadcasting, and transportation has long been eroded. However, several industries remained strongholds for government incumbents until recently. The lack of private players was brought about by factors inherent in these industries: high asset or investment requirements, prohibitively high economies of scale that caused a natural monopoly, a lack of private actors with financial or technical capabilities (particularly in developing countries), significant first-mover advantages enjoyed by the incumbent, and regulatory restrictions, such as state ownership over strategic industries.

However, the wave of private competition that we see emerging in recent decades is unique. Whereas past private sector incursions occurred in industries where initial capital investment is not exceedingly large and businesses are highly scalable, the private sector is increasingly targeting industries with high initial investment and technical requirements, such as air travel. Even though previous erosions of government companies' dominance occur sporadically at a national scale, the recent waves of private sector encroachment occurred simultaneously on an international scale. The explosion of competition in wireless telecommunications in emerging countries is an excellent example. Lastly, where previous private sector challengers limited their focus to their respective domestic markets, private competition is appearing in industries such as metals and mining, which have a high degree of international linkages or may not serve the domestic market at all.

Industries that strongly exhibit this trend are airlines, telecom, energy upstream/exploration and production (E&P), refining and downstream oil and gas, mining, metals, and complex manufacturing. This phenomenon is facilitated by several developments. Wireless technology, for example, invalidates the natural monopoly that was inherent in telecommunications; more than one operator can compete in a single area. Increasing sophistication and specialization of businesses allow the outsourcing of highly complex tasks and delivery of end-to-end solutions and turnkey projects, all of which reduce the technical barriers for new entrants. The largest enabler has been the trend toward liberalization and deregulation that dismantles artificial barriers to entry into areas previously designated as "government-exclusive." Whatever the causes, one thing is certain: These changes are here to stay.

In some cases, the erosion of the incumbent's dominance can progress more quickly than anticipated. The cautionary tale of the Indonesian aviation industry, where government-owned flag carrier Garuda Indonesia held a dominant share of the domestic and international passenger market a little more than a decade ago, is a prime example. Garuda, which was hard hit by the 1997–1998 Asian financial crisis, was simply not ready for the onslaught of nimble, private-sector low-cost carriers that sprang up across Southeast Asia after the post-crisis period. Garuda's share of Indonesia's international market plummeted from 65 percent in 2001 to just 18 percent in 2011. The airline's share of the domestic market shrunk from an estimated 55 percent to 23 percent over the same period.

 ## MEETING THE CHALLENGES

Despite these challenges, government incumbents, lulled into complacency by decades of low competition, look inward and undertake moderate improvement initiatives (often half heartedly) as the sole way to address these competitive pressures. Few top-line initiatives are undertaken other than attempts to mimic innovations or strategies developed by the new entrants. Efforts to match the cost efficiency of industry leaders are pursued in a lukewarm manner and/or to a limited scope. Underlying these is the factor of complacency: Rarely is there an urgency to change until it is too late, often until the point of financial distress and/or privatization by the government under unpleasant circumstances.

Government incumbents must consider an alternative approach to regain supremacy. Rather than undertaking improvement initiatives internally and moderately, the transformation toward competitive leadership—in technology, business innovation, or operational efficiency and productivity—can be jump-started through the right M&A deal. Several M&A and inorganic growth options are available, of which four relevant ones are outlined next.

Acquisition of a Competitor

Though this strategy provides the incumbent with control over the acquired target, effectiveness may be enhanced if the target is in possession of a significant competency in its innovations, technologies, markets, brands, distribution channels, business know-how, or talent. Additionally, this strategy bears the advantage of eliminating a degree of competition in the market, provided approval by market regulators is forthcoming.

Acquirers often fail to leverage significant value from the target as initially envisioned. Extracting value from a target company is not always easy. State-owned companies with little merger experience, in particular, face a high risk of failure. Even when a state-linked company uses M&A to move up the value curve, lack of planning and poor strategy can derail the entire exercise.

Consider the short-lived attempt of Shanghai Automotive Industry Corporation (SAIC) to run South Korean automaker SsangYong. SAIC bought a 49 percent stake in SsangYong for $500 million in 2004, outbidding global giants, including General Motors (GM).[3] SsangYong had a 10 percent share of Korea's car market and was the country's fourth-largest automaker. The company was struggling with a large debt burden but was starting to grow exports of its sport utility vehicles (SUVs); SAIC hoped the acquisition would help boost its own development capabilities and gain entry to new global markets, including the United States.

The new joint-management team decided to swiftly expand manufacturing capabilities and launched five new models worldwide. In 2006, gas prices shot up, and Europe and the United States came out with tough, new emissions standards. Both factors hit SUV sales hard, straining relations between SAIC and SsangYong's powerful trade unions, which went out on a seven-week strike. Chinese and Korean executives disagreed, partly because of cultural differences, on how to improve the company's performance. The global financial crisis dealt the struggling company another blow. SsangYong's sales fell 53 percent in December 2008 over the same month the year before.

SAIC supported its subsidiary by buying $4.5 million worth of vehicles to sell in China. Eventually, SAIC put a restructuring plan in place that cut the workforce by 36 percent and included a number of measures to improve productivity. The Korean unions refused to sign off on the plan and initiated legal action against SAIC, accusing the company of transferring designs and technology developed with Korean government funds to China, a charge SAIC denied. SsangYong eventually filed for bankruptcy protection in January 2009, prompting another round of strikes and protests. SAIC wrote off most of its investment and reduced its stake to 3.7 percent in July 2010. In the five years that SAIC controlled SsangYong, the company pumped more than $618 million into the venture and walked away with nothing.[4]

SAIC had the right idea but failed to extract the synergies it hoped to gain from the deal. The key in such acquisitions is to proactively develop early on a clear strategy of what value is to be captured from where and how to optimally extract that value. A good risk management plan might have helped troubleshoot some of the problems that ran the company aground. Perhaps more could have been done to incentivize workers to meet the productivity goals needed to extract value from the merger. Private or public companies that want to unlock value from a merger must create an integration strategy that covers all these bases and more. Companies should only execute acquisitions after developing a strategy instead of pursuing an opportunistic approach to acquisitions. Concrete and immediately realizable synergistic assets such as patents and distribution networks are advantages.

Partnership and Joint Venturing

Perhaps the biggest advantage of a joint venture (JV) is the benefit of maintaining ownership of its organization while gaining access to a competitor's know-how at substantially lower costs than an acquisition. The training ground it offers allows the incumbent to develop leaner, more efficient business models, and talent can later be leveraged into the parent organization.

The difficulty in striking such deals, however, is the lack of incentive for the counterparty and the government incumbent to form the partnership. The government incumbent is typically only able to offer greater access to markets in which it dominates, and this directly risks eroding its market share, thus leading to the halfhearted pursuit of partnerships by incumbents over minuscule and meaningless projects and preventing the creation of a viable platform with sufficient critical mass to turn around its parent organization. Incumbents should seek to build open and dynamic relationships with their partners, expanding or modifying scope and partners and seizing advantages wherever possible.

Consider the petrochemical joint ventures formed by Malaysia's state-owned oil company, Petronas. Facing depleting oil reserves in the 1980s, Petronas needed to diversify into other sources of income. It chose to build petrochemical capability by engaging with established players who were looking to build a base in the region. Petronas, which largely focused on refining crudes for domestic consumption before the 1990s, is the largest and most diversified petrochemical producer in the region. In 2009, Petronas took over the independent operation of its three most advanced petrochemical JVs after it paid around $700 million for the shares of its JV partners, including Dow Chemical Company's Union Carbide Corporation. That move was a testament to Petronas' success at building capability.

Malaysia's state-owned investment agency, Khazanah, took a particularly bold step in August 2011, when it engineered a share swap between the ailing, state-controlled flag carrier, Malaysia Airlines (MAS), and upstart rival AirAsia,

Asia's first and most successful low-cost carrier. The $364 million deal created an alliance between the two adversaries and put AirAsia's outspoken, entrepreneurial founder in a position to make real changes at Malaysia Airlines.

This is a fine example of a state-linked company creating an alliance with the clear intention of bringing private sector expertise on board to breathe new life into its operation. Under the agreement, AirAsia founder Tony Fernandes and his partner Kamarudin Meranun, who hold about 30 percent of AirAsia through their holding company, Tune Air, will sell a 10 percent stake in AirAsia to Khazanah, which owns 69 percent of MAS. In return, Tune Air will get a 20.5 percent stake in MAS. As part of the planned collaboration, the airlines aim to realize savings and increase revenues in key areas, including aircraft purchasing, engineering, ground support services, cargo services, catering, and training. The two airlines compete head-on on numerous domestic routes, and analysts widely expect the deal could lead to a more profitable route rationalization.

MAS has plenty to learn from AirAsia, which has grown routes, services, and profits at a time when MAS has struggled, paring routes and firing staff to avoid bankruptcy.[5] In the quarter ended March 31, 2011, MAS had an operating loss of RM267.4 million ($86 million) on revenue of RM3.14 billion ($1 billion). AirAsia had an operating profit of RM241.72 million ($77.4 million) on RM1.05 billion ($336 million) revenue.

The deal will end a bitter rivalry between the two airlines and put one of Southeast Asia's most colorful, market-oriented entrepreneurs in the cockpit of one of the region's stodgier, more troubled state-owned companies. In 2001, Mr. Fernandes, the former head of Warner Music's Southeast Asian operations, bought AirAsia—then a small, two-plane operation owned by an automotive conglomerate—for 27 cents, plus an agreement to assume the $10 million debt the airline carried. He revamped the airline into a low-cost carrier and, within three years, turned AirAsia into a regional budget carrier. A slew of budget carriers and Asian government-linked airlines scrambled to copy his formula, giving birth to a new segment of Asia's airline industry.[6]

AirAsia had to fight MAS and Malaysia's regulators tooth and nail during the early years. The Malaysian government balked at giving AirAsia the domestic routes it requested for fear of hurting the incumbent state carrier. The country's chief airline regulator, who approved routes, was a member of MAS's board. Mr. Fernandes had to lobby senior government officials hard to win new routes. He even crashed a tony cocktail party to get a moment with the transport minister. When customers rushed to snap up AirAsia's low fares, MAS responded with a price war, slashing many domestic fares by half.

AirAsia accused MAS of using government money to push it out of business. Mr. Fernandes wrote then–Prime Minister Mahathir Mohamad a blistering letter, accusing MAS of "state-sponsored economic terrorism." MAS denied it had started a fare war and told the *Wall Street Journal* that it had extended "promotional fares" to a host of groups, including senior citizens, students, police, armed forces personnel, families, and people who fly at night.

Malaysia's move to put the man whom local aviation officials once eyed warily onto the board of its troubled flag carrier indicates how serious the government is about revitalizing MAS. Shortly after the share swap, Khazanah announced a management revamp, replacing MAS's chairman and managing director and appointing two new businessmen to the board, besides AirAsia's duo.[7] Equity research analysts, who welcomed the deal, are watching to see how much room the airline gives Mr. Fernandes to maneuver.

Mergers with Peer Government Companies

This avenue offers the typical revenue and cost synergies that accrue from a merger. More importantly for the government incumbents, a large-scale merger provides management with a platform for reform and transformation. It allows management an opportunity to intensify the pace of change and precipitate a "step-change" through actions it would otherwise find difficult to take, such as capacity reduction, workforce rationalization, and divestment of non-productive assets. In other words, it presents management with an opportunity to address legacy issues, start with a clean slate, and go forward with a performance-oriented culture more suited to the increasingly competitive industry.

This strategy comes with the typical merger challenges. A well-publicized A.T. Kearney study found that fewer than 50 percent of mergers create value. The top attributing factors in merger failure were identified as lack of stakeholder buy-in, loss of momentum, and an organization structure that is too compromised. These factors would be magnified in the merger of government companies, where cultural, legacy, and political complications are undoubtedly more intense than in private sector mergers. To navigate through a merger, the company must rigorously commit to synergy realization. It needs to integrate synergy realization into top management key performance indicators (KPIs), create an empowered project management office to run the integration, put in place measures to motivate employees, and have continuous change management interventions.

The worst move a government can make is to order two state-owned companies to merge without having a highly detailed road map and change management team in place, as with the disastrous merger of Air India and

Indian Airlines. This is a classic example of a merger of GLCs that was deeply resisted and poorly implemented. In 1986, India's government began talking about merging Indian Airlines, the main domestic carrier, with Air India, the country's flagship international airline. Rajiv Gandhi, then prime minister, appointed a committee to draw up a merger plan with an eye to improving service; making more efficient use of staff, fleet, and maintenance operations; and increasing the odds that the state-backed airlines would achieve long-term self-sufficiency.[8] The airlines and their internal unions resisted the merger, concerned about job cuts and rollbacks. Over the next two decades, the government proposed variations of the deal, from creating a holding company that would oversee the two airlines, which would be left intact, to creating closer cooperation between common units, such as engineering and ground handling. They met resistance at every step.

Finally, in 2007, India's government pushed ahead and merged the two airlines. The results have been nothing short of dismal. Air India, the merged entity, has not turned a profit since 2007 and was expected to report a pretax loss of 70 billion rupees in 2011. The airline failed to synergize operations, trim unprofitable flights, pare high debt costs, and tackle an inflated wage bill that plagued both operations.

Air India, saddled with a cumbersome and bureaucratic structure, unyielding unions, and a host of operational efficiencies, has struggled in the face of growing competition from the more nimble private sector. Air India has the largest fleet in India, yet it holds a 15 percent market share, well behind private competitors such as Jet, Kingfishers, and IndiGo.[9] Competing airlines have their aircraft in the air for up to 14 hours a day; Air India's fleet is airborne for fewer than 10 hours. The state-owned carrier has about 250 employees per aircraft, over one-third more than the industry norm. IndiGo, in contrast, has 102 employees per aircraft. Powerful unions and local laws that make it tough to fire workers are part of the problem, but a poorly planned integration is also to blame. The government had two decades' worth of warning that resistance would run deep, and more could have been done to map out synergies, create incentives to motivate staff, and mitigate the highly visible risks that have cramped the merger.

The government response has continued to lack speed and decisiveness. In 2009, India's Prime Minister Manmohan Singh promised to create a turnaround plan for the airline, which is only now being finalized. Critics say this particular plan focuses only on restructuring debt, not on fixing the problems in operations. "Hardware is not an issue. Air India has the best fleet," Jitender Bhargava, a former executive director of the airline, told Singapore's *The Straits Times*. "But it is the software that needs to be fixed."[10]

In August 2011, the government appointed Civil Aviation Secretary Nasim Zaidi as chairman and Rohit Nandan, a joint secretary at the Ministry of Civil Aviation, as managing director, as part of a management shakeup. "Government will not allow Air India to fail because the political repercussions would be too severe," said Madhavan Nambiar, a former aviation secretary. "But my worry is that too little is being done too late."[11]

Done properly, a merger of GLCs can unlock massive value. A prime example of such success is the three-way merger of Sime Darby, Golden Hope, and Kumpulan Guthrie to create the world's largest palm plantation company and Malaysia's largest market capitalization firm. State-owned fund manager PNB, which controlled the three groups, initiated the deal: The goal was to use the merger as a transformation platform to achieve competitive leadership in the palm oil industry. However, they were aware that mergers often fail to create value, let alone be a platform for change. To avoid such an outcome, they set forth numerous top-line and bottom-line improvement initiatives, committed to the projected synergy numbers, and appointed a program management office (PMO) with a direct reporting line to manage the initiatives. The plantation operations reported a 139 percent increase in operating profit the year after. Notwithstanding the increase in global palm oil prices, significant productivity and cost improvements contributed to this increase. Since the merger, the company has always exceeded its annual revenue and profit targets. Although, in recent years, some have called for the company to spin off its palm oil group from other non-palm oil related ventures such as engineering, utilities, and automotive, the rationale for consolidation of the three palm oil companies has never been questioned.

Self-Initiated Sale to a Nonhostile Party

This strategy provides management with a platform for transformation to a greater degree than a merger because reduction or elimination of government ownership will reduce legacy and public service constraints. Although this avenue is typically controversial politically, it is a better option than a privatization out of the incumbent's control. For the management, it provides a more suitable platform for transformation than if the company is privatized through a public offering. New owners can provide financial and know-how support. During the turnaround phase, management is often afforded greater flexibility in taking unpopular or short-term loss-making decisions for the eventual turnaround if a sympathetic owner backs them.

Even though the key challenges of fit issues and finding a non-hostile buyer might seem to make this an improbable option, consider the case of Skoda. After the Velvet Revolution, the Czech government sought to divest the business, seeking to turn it into a viable contemporary car producer rather than dismantling the business. Skoda was a healthy business at this point. Despite its dated image, Skoda has remained a common sight in Western Europe. Volkswagen (VW) was selected to be the eventual purchaser, primarily because it committed to technology transfer and producing high-value models in Czech factories. Since its acquisition, Skoda sales volume has quadrupled. More impressively, its revenue has increased over 20 times, a fivefold increase in the value of its cars and a testament to its successful modernization.

 ## A BETTER WAY TO ACHIEVE TRANSFORMATION

As government incumbents embark on these journeys of regaining supremacy through M&A, a successful deal involves the right partner and terms and the execution of the integration process. Transformation involves envisioning a clear, consistent view of the end state, generating and maintaining momentum for change, and maintaining agility to adapt to new information and shifting circumstances. These can be difficult for government incumbents as they are the weaknesses that bred in them in the first place. But what better time to start the process of turning over a new leaf than with the coming together of two companies?

FIVE THINGS GLCS OUGHT TO CONSIDER

1. **Liberalization is unstoppable:** Liberalization is sweeping Asia, and governments need to prepare the domestic sector for completion. Merging GLCs that operate in the same sector can help winnow the industry and create a few strong players.
2. **Competition is inevitable:** Government incumbents in every sector are facing more competition from local and global players. More pressure is yet to come. GLCs can use M&A to help innovate their operations.
3. **Sitting still is unthinkable:** Air India, once the country's dominant carrier, today holds a 15 percent market share. Nimble, private competitors are eating them for lunch. This is a cautionary tale for every Asian GLC.

(continued)

(continued)

4. **Underperformance is unacceptable:** GLCs command a large share of Asia's economies. These companies owe it to taxpayers and shareholders to meet or beat the returns achieved by their private sector peers. That's not happening in most Asian countries today.
5. **Change is undeniable:** GLCs need to up their game and quickly change from within. Though many GLCs are making international acquisitions to secure resources or expand markets, few are using M&A to transform their own operations. Transformation must be moved to the top of the corporate agenda.

ACKNOWLEDGMENTS

The following A.T. Kearney white paper was used as background material in writing this chapter: "Turning Over a New Leaf: Transforming Government-Linked Companies through M&A," by Vikram Chakravarty, Karambir Anand, Navin Nathani, and Rizal Paramarta.

5

Getting It Right Before You Begin

Many companies stumble into mergers and acquisitions (M&A) before they are ready, resulting in botched deals or expensive and chaotic acquisitions. Companies can do several things to prepare themselves before they go down the M&A path. The first thing to do is to use our debt-equity framework to figure out whether the company should be considering M&A. A system should be put in place to methodically track and screen potential M&A targets. Building an acquisition factory focused on smaller deals can increase the chances of success. Understanding whether the company can shape industry dynamics using M&A will be an important consideration. Finally, a company should not be shy about surrounding itself with expertise to support the deal.

THE SEEDS OF A successful merger or acquisition are planted early, long before executives zero in on a target company or make an offer.

The failure rate of mergers is high. Our research indicates that 29 percent of mergers result in an increase in aggregate profitability. According to one A.T. Kearney study that measured long-term market capitalization trends of companies involved in mergers, slightly less than half of all M&A deals create value.

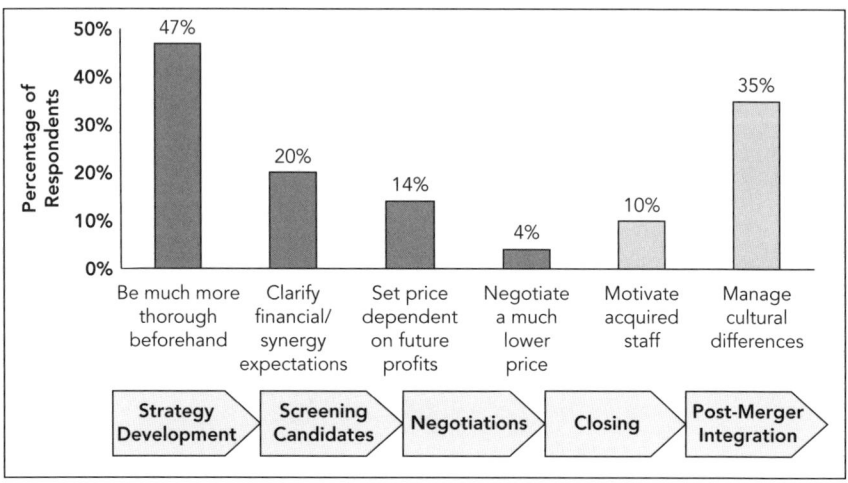

FIGURE 5.1 Factors Attributed to Successful M&A
Source: A.T. Kearney global survey.

The companies that do succeed usually have a framework in place that signals when they should consider mergers, helps identify and track targets early on, and guides executives through the deal itself once it materializes. We believe M&A should be planned and considered. They should never be opportunistic.

One of the biggest drivers of M&A success is an up-front strategy. We conducted a survey of M&A deals that worked and asked what factors contributed to their success: 47 percent of respondents said success hinged on being "much more thorough beforehand." By comparison, 4 percent rated "negotiating a much lower price" as a factor behind success (see Figure 5.1). Getting it right early on is one of the two most important parts of the game; the other is the ability to integrate the M&A successfully.

Our analysis shows that many Asian companies are well-placed to achieve steady inorganic growth through M&A. Many opportunities are available in the wake of the global financial crisis and as economic activities shift from the developed Western economies to the emerging Asian countries. Asian companies are in a strong position to capitalize on this situation. Few Asian companies, however, have the processes in place to map out and execute planned M&A. Asian executives should take several key pre-merger steps to ensure the best deals get done (see Figure 5.2).

Leaders need to put a framework in place to determine whether M&A is right for their company, create a mechanism to track and screen candidates

| Plan for M&As | Screening and Tracking | Building Expertise and Partnership | Due Diligence |

FIGURE 5.2 Four Key Pre-Merger Steps
Source: A.T. Kearney analysis.

methodically, and determine which of several merger strategies will best achieve their goals and build expertise in that area. Finally, they need to conduct a deeper-than-normal due diligence, which we'll cover in the following chapter.

 ## STEP 1: A FRAMEWORK HELPS FORWARD PLANNING

When the leaders of most Asian companies sit down each year to come up with their forecasts and budgets, they typically focus on organic growth. Executives think about new sales points, new products, and new target markets. Inorganic growth is rarely part of the agenda during their annual planning cycle. Our research shows that M&A can play a key role in maintaining a company's growth momentum. Companies that fail to put M&A on their agenda risk missing out on this important opportunity. If you want to grow ahead of the industry, M&A have to be part of the plan.

Consider the example in Figure 5.3, from a utility industry manufacturing company. The growth targets laid out for this particular company indicate that inorganic growth could meet or beat the company's projected organic growth plans.

In Asia, corporate leaders typically think about M&A only after an investment banker has thrown an opportunistic deal their way. Too often, executives wake up in the morning, see a good deal, and think, "We should grab it." We think that's a mistake.

We advocate a more methodical approach. A.T. Kearney has developed a framework for clients that allows them to pinpoint where their company sits on the M&A spectrum at any time and signals what they should do: whether they should buy, whether they should sell out, or whether they need to stabilize before making any more moves.

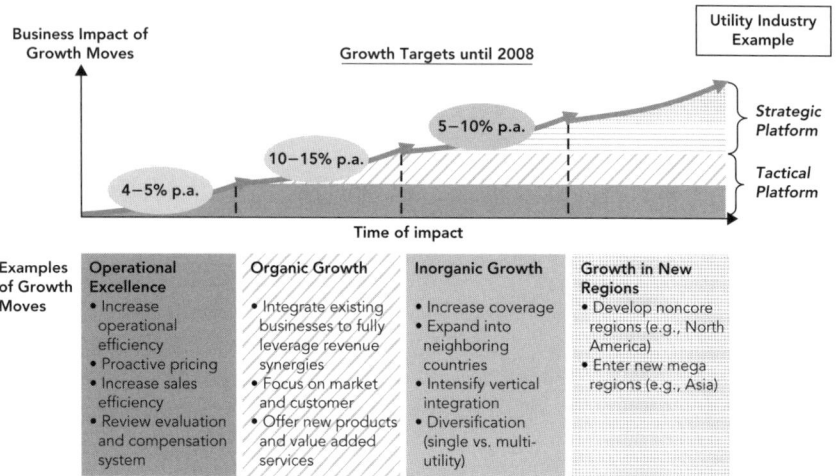

FIGURE 5.3   M&A Play a Critical Role in Ensuring Growth Momentum
Source: A.T. Kearney analysis.

Our framework compares the ratio of a company's net debt to EBITDA (earnings before interest, taxes, depreciation, and amortization) to the ratio of its price-earnings multiple to the rest of its industry. In other words, we analyze how leveraged a company is and whether the company can use its stock as currency to fund its acquisition drive. Using these data, we generate a matrix that indicates whether a company should attack, rebuild, or defend.

The attack stance is reserved for companies with access to liquidity and limited debt. These companies are in a position to leverage their strong balance sheet and a rising market cap to pursue M&A. Rebuilding the organization is for safe-haven companies with limited ability to exploit market opportunities. Their focus is on strengthening their operational performance and cost position. Companies that get defensive do so because they are the most vulnerable to hostile takeovers. The best strategy for these companies is to pursue "friendly" buyers to divest equity stakes to guard against hostile takeovers.

We ran the top Asian companies through our framework and mapped out where they should be (see Figure 5.4). Our analysis highlighted several Asian companies that seemed well-placed to make some aggressive moves: Reliance, Petronas, SingTel, Tata Consultancy Services, and NTT Docomo fall firmly into the "attack" position on our matrix.

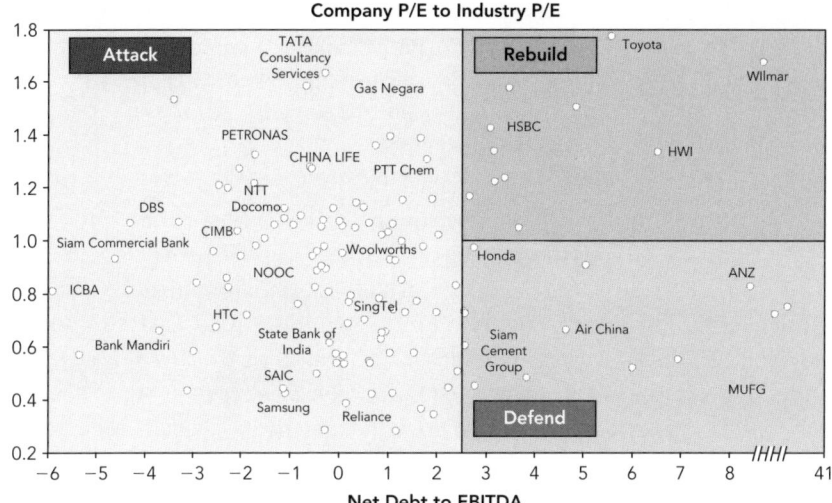

FIGURE 5.4 Attack, Rebuild, Defend Matrix
Source: Bloomberg data; A.T. Kearney analysis.

SingTel has implemented a series of M&A deals as market entry strategies in countries such as Thailand, the Philippines, Indonesia, India, and Pakistan. It pushed for entry into the African telecom market via its interests in Bharti Airtel. SingTel had announced in 2010 that it was on the lookout for more acquisitions, but given the limited opportunities relative to what it was willing to pay for, subsequently decided to return part of its cash hoard to shareholders as a special dividend.

Reliance Industries is also on the move. The Indian company has a sizeable presence in the refining and petrochemical businesses, including the world's largest refinery complex at Jamnagar. A few years ago, Reliance made inroads into the upstream oil and gas segment and identified it as an area of growth. The company went on to buy the U.S. shale assets of Pioneer Natural Resources, Atlas Energy, and Carrizo Oil & Gas for $3 billion in 2010.

Reliance could take advantage of the current situation to enhance its presence in the upstream business outside India and add to its recent acquisitions. The company could also acquire downstream assets outside India to provide a channel for its refinery products. This strategy could help secure future entry into the more profitable upstream segment of the respective countries. Reliance could also make acquisitions in relevant parts of the chemical business that would allow it to become a price setter in a commodity environment. It attempted to do this with its bid on the petrochemical company LyondellBasell (which would have created the world's largest petrochemical company ahead of BASF and Dow Chemical Company), but the bid was rejected.

Industry experts predict China's airline industry is set for another round of consolidation, and could move toward the emergence of a mega-carrier that could compete with global giants such as British Airways or United.[1] This could put Air China in "defend" mode. After a previous wave of consolidation in 2010, when China Eastern Airlines took control of Shanghai Airlines Co., and Air China acquired Shenzhen Airlines, China Airlines, China Eastern Airlines, and China Southern Airlines emerged as the country's top three carriers. Air China, the country's flagship, was left vulnerable as a result of high oil prices, rising interest rates, and its acquisition, which pushed its gearing high and its share price low. The company had raised its stake in Shenzhen Airlines to 51 percent from 25 percent in 2010, a move that boosted net income that year, but by 2011, its outlook had dimmed, and in May it announced that first-quarter profits were down 23 percent from a year before. It forecast that full-year profits would fall below that of 2010.

Air China should take care to recognize its defensive position if competitors, such as China Eastern Airlines, do aspire to giant status.

HSBC fell into the "rebuild" section of our matrix. Recent news reflects our analysis: In May 2011, the bank announced it plans to sell businesses and exit retail banking in markets where it doesn't have scale. The bank shares reported lackluster first-quarter results that showed rising costs and flat revenue.[2]

A framework such as this is an important tool in today's competitive market. Companies that are aware of where they sit on a matrix such as this one can plan ahead better. Armed with this kind of knowledge, executives can embed the M&A option into their annual planning cycle.

We believe that companies should run a regular health check to determine whether they should be in attack or defend mode to augment or protect their growth. It's not enough to map out new products and marketing strategies each year. It's important to clarify strategy for inorganic growth, too. The realization that you should be looking to buy—or are likely to be bought—should never come out of the blue.

We used this matrix as part of strategic work we did for an Asian downstream gas utility. We looked at where the company was and decided it needed to go upstream. The first thing we did was clear up its debt position. The company replaced its debt with low-cost funding and did a rights issue to build some cash. We used our matrix to map its position against global and regional industry players. This exercise signaled that our client should be on the attack and highlighted a number of acquisition targets that fell into the defend quadrant.

We are looking aggressively at gas assets upstream to target for acquisition. In many cases, these are small companies that do exploration work, or large companies such as Shell or British Petroleum (BP) that are offloading assets in parts of the world where our client can do well. We didn't come across these prospective deals by chance. Instead, we discovered them because we'd created a matrix of key competitors and industry players and tracked them for nearly a year.

STEP 2: METHODICAL TRACKING AND SCREENING UNDERPIN SUCCESSFUL M&A

Every CEO or CFO in Asia is being pestered by investment bankers with deal books that lack imagination. Bankers and lawyers are constantly bringing ideas—good, bad, and ugly—to senior management. It's hard to separate the so-so ideas from the great ones unless you have a clear strategy.

Once a company has figured out where it sits on the M&A spectrum, the next step is to develop a sound target assessment framework to track and screen candidates. M&A should be about planned acquisitions. This is the fundamental difference between companies that succeed at M&A and those that fail. Top acquirers set M&A objectives, constantly monitor the market for potential M&A opportunities, and execute the plan quickly when such opportunities arise.

A target assessment framework should be based on three core criteria: strategic, organizational, and financial fits. Companies need to look for candidates that fulfill strategic and synergy requirements, including products, technologies, and markets that complement or augment their own. Financial fit is crucial. Acquirers need to assess the target company's price, debt structure, and profit picture, and see how it impacts their own balance sheet. Companies shouldn't take on something they can't handle. With organizational fit, a company must gauge how easily a candidate can be integrated. Nationality, leadership style, and the degree of centralization of the target operation can impact a merger.

Armed with these criteria, companies on "M&A watch" should generate a list of a group of companies they'd like to acquire and list the reasons and rationale for each. This framework should be able to filter candidates by quantitative metrics, such as price, and should detail the risks associated with each potential acquisition. Risks could include concern over whether the target company can achieve its growth targets, for example, or improve profit margins. If a company is tracking these potential targets systematically over time, executives should be able to reduce the risk, gauge the best price, and zero in on companies with the best strategic fit.

Consider the work we did for an Asian investment fund that wanted to enter the region's banking sector. We helped that client create a short list of 10 banks that we tracked for four years. Over that period, the fund took a stake in five of those banks when it gauged the price, timing, and risk levels were right.

Companies that have built M&A into their annual planning cycle and have the discipline and process in place to track their candidates are in a strong position: When the target becomes available, they know how much they'd like to pay for it and have offset much of the risk that can undermine a typical acquisition.

The Asian fund, for example, mitigated the risk inherent in two deals thanks to our tracking system. The fund was considering a stake in a global bank, but the asking price seemed steep. The bank's cost/income ratio was high, and though the bank's executives insisted they could lower it, it wasn't clear if they could achieve their goals. We advised our client to track the bank for six quarters, to see if they could deliver. They did. The client felt assured the stake was worth the price, and the deal went ahead.

In another instance, the fund was eying an Indonesian bank that wanted to diversify its corporate-focused business by expanding into consumer banking. After tracking the company for several years, we felt it had managed the transition badly. The consumer banking heads weren't up to par and branch performance was poor. The acquiring fund put together a team of bankers with global experience to deploy to the Indonesian bank's consumer business, and it moved ahead with the deal.

For each element of risk, companies who take a methodical approach to M&A can work out a mitigation plan. Patience and discipline help ensure the target is right, the price is right, and the level of risk is low.

 ## STEP 3: CHOOSE YOUR MODEL: CLASSIC M&A VERSUS THE ACQUISITION FACTORY

Companies use two major M&A strategies to boost inorganic growth: classic M&A, which entail a large, one-off transformative deal; and the buy-and-build approach, where companies set up an in-house "acquisition factory," generating growth through a higher number of smaller deals. Here, the buyer focuses on improving the bottom-line performance of a growing pool of acquired companies.

Classic M&A are about getting a big bang for a big buck. This is historically how deals were done. The Daimler-Chrysler merger, the Royal Dutch-Shell deal, and AOL's acquisition of Time Warner are all textbook examples of transformative, classic M&A.

Today, however, more companies are taking the buy-and-build approach. These kinds of deals are less dramatic but less risky, too. Big, weighty mergers have proven hard to pull off. Creating value by merging two behemoths is difficult. Prominent failures of classic M&A, including Daimler and Chrysler, Time Warner and AOL, Adidas and Salomon Sports, and Siemens and Nixdorf underscore the pitfalls. Typically, the larger the deal, the tougher the challenges; the larger the parties, the higher the organizational complexity and the stronger the corporate culture of each party. Money and executive attention are focused toward managing a big deal, integrating a complex organization, and capturing synergies, and are diverted away from markets and customers, thus hampering profitable growth. Besides, regulators don't take a kind view when one Goliath suddenly rules the market.

Many companies shy away from M&A because they believe it's going to be an all-consuming, transformative undertaking. It doesn't have to be. We believe that the buy-and-build approach offers a more sustainable route to growth and market leadership. It's easier to accelerate growth by using a serial, standardized acquisition factory strategy to generate a series of frequent, smaller deals that don't strain the entire operation.

A services company that A.T. Kearney worked with (see Figure 5.5) did an astonishing 397 small deals, worth an average of $14 million each, over 10 years. The company's revenue grew on a compounded annual growth rate of 19 percent over the 10-year period, while maintaining solid profitability. To be sure, this was a large corporation with a big budget. In some sectors and some countries, serial deals are often small, ranging from $1.5 million to $5.8 million.

The acquisition factory angle is still below the radar screen of many Asian executives, but this strategy provides many benefits: profitable growth, superior value creation, and market leadership in a far shorter time and at reduced risk, especially in industries in the opening and scale phases of the consolidation race.

As first movers, companies operating an acquisition factory can shape the consolidation of their industry and realize organic growth at the same time. Successful operators identify favorable market conditions, such as the availability of small acquisition targets in a fragmented industry, and confirm the target fits with their own strategy and business model.

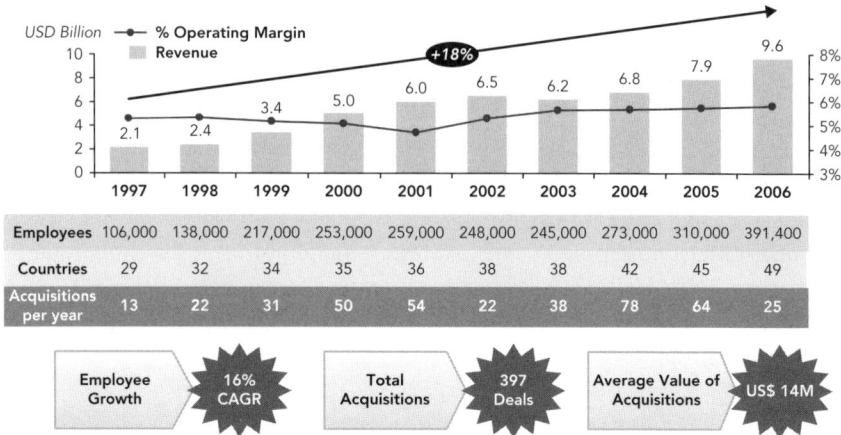

	1997	1998	1999	2000	2001	2002	2003	2004	2005	2006
Employees	106,000	138,000	217,000	253,000	259,000	248,000	245,000	273,000	310,000	391,400
Countries	29	32	34	35	36	38	38	42	45	49
Acquisitions per year	13	22	31	50	54	22	38	78	64	25

Employee Growth	16% CAGR	Total Acquisitions	397 Deals	Average Value of Acquisitions	US$ 14M

FIGURE 5.5 Overview of a Services Company
Source: Company reports; A.T. Kearney analysis.

Companies that run acquisition factories follow three simple principles:

▪ Leverage the relatively lower enterprise value (lower multiples) of smaller companies.
▪ Focus on shaping the acquired business to the core business model even if it leads to a limited loss of revenue.
▪ Improve performance throughout the acquired company in all functions, particularly by leveraging scale and centralizing most overhead functions as well as by leveraging best practices in the other functions.

Acquisition factories create value by applying an efficient serial acquisition process while improving mainly the bottom-line performance of the acquired business. The result is a significantly higher valuation multiple with the integrated businesses compared to their stand-alone valuation. Consider the following case study: A company with sales of $1.4 million and an earnings before interest and tax (EBIT) margin of 24 percent is acquired for $2 million, which reflects an EBIT multiple "as acquired" of around six. Post-acquisition, the company focuses on its more profitable core competencies and sales drop to $1.2 million, yet the EBIT margin rises to 43 percent. Combined with active performance improvement, this transaction created value in the range of

50 to 150 percent, which yielded an "integrated-company" multiple of about 10 and an enterprise value of $5.2 million.

Successful acquisition factories keep busy. Over a period of 5 to 10 years, they may do tens or hundreds of deals. Accordingly, they need a dedicated organizational entity and ongoing resources and capabilities for target search, acquisition, and integration. The factory organization and the company as a whole benefit from the focus on small, hidden champions as opposed to large-scale blockbusters or mega-deals. The benefits of focusing on smaller companies occur throughout and after the acquisition process.

The pre-acquisition and transaction phases, for example, are typically quicker and require fewer resources when dealing with smaller companies. Target selection and evaluation criteria are clear. Bidder competition is reduced and the target company is usually in the weaker bargaining position.

Smaller companies with few or simple products are less complex. That means due diligence teams have less to examine and integration can take place more rapidly. Acquisition and integration risks are typically lower and spread more broadly.

Value generation, meanwhile, often exceeds industry performance. Over the past 10 years, the 25 most active acquirers in the A.T. Kearney merger endgames database consistently outperformed the Morgan Stanley Capital International (MSCI) Index by double the growth rates. Our merger endgames database includes more than 13,000 M&A that have taken place over the past decade.

First movers who make several acquisitions each year and integrate them rapidly can instantly enhance their market presence. Leaders who shape a consolidating industry can quickly gain market leadership and overwhelm competitors.

Acquisition Factory Winners Offer Insight into Strategy

Oracle's CEO Larry Ellison was once quoted in the *New York Times* as stating, "It's crazy to say you will only grow through innovation." It is no secret that Oracle is consolidating the information technology (IT) industry by buying software rather than developing programs internally. Since 2005, Oracle has acquired more than 50 companies; although some deals are high profile, including the acquisitions of Sun, PeopleSoft, and Hyperion, most are under $1 billion. In 2009, despite the recession, Oracle spent $1.2 billion on three acquisitions, aside from the Sun deal. Oracle's revenues doubled to $23 billion between 2005 and 2009, and maintained operating profits at around 50 percent.

Success stories of companies operating an acquisition factory can be found across industries and countries. Copenhagen-based Integrated Service Solutions, Inc. (ISS) is another interesting example.

ISS is one of the world's largest facility management service providers, with market presence in Europe, Asia, Latin America, and Australia. The Danish company employs more than 400,000 people and serves more than 100,000 business-to-business (B2B) and public sector customers in 50 countries. ISS's services include shop floor and office cleaning, maintenance, catering, and security. In many markets, ISS faces strong competition due to low entry barriers in cleaning and related services. Since personnel expenses are the primary cost driver, competitors undercutting minimum wages and pursuing questionable labor practices are key challenges for ISS.

Foreseeing the global trend of outsourcing facility services to external providers, ISS started its acquisition factory in 1997. It initially targeted companies that were in or close to its core business of facilities cleaning, and later turned to more diversified areas such as catering and security.

ISS's strategy aimed to build a full-service network and increase customer value by offering a one-stop, integrated offering for all relevant facility services. Its centralized customer relationship management enabled increased service quality and streamlined processes. The strategy enabled ISS to expand regionally, gaining access to overseas markets. The company acquired more than 450 small firms, increasing sales to more than $11 billion. Most acquisitions had revenues of fewer than $19 million when they were taken over. ISS made two large-scale acquisitions: Abilis in France in 1999, and Tempo in Australia in 2006.

With its acquisition factory, ISS consolidated the market substantially and continues to focus on small acquisitions to minimize transaction and integration risks and leverage local market knowledge.

The Key Elements of a Successful Acquisition Factory

Out of the many cases of successful acquisition factories A.T. Kearney has tracked, we have extracted three key factors for success (see Figure 5.6):

1. The first is a good fit between the company's market and corporate strategy and the acquisition factory approach. The more suitable the market and business model, the greater the opportunities and impact of an acquisition factory. A suitable market is one where industry consolidation is ideally low to medium, with only a few competitors following a similar strategy. That gives the lead acquirers a first-mover advantage. With respect to the

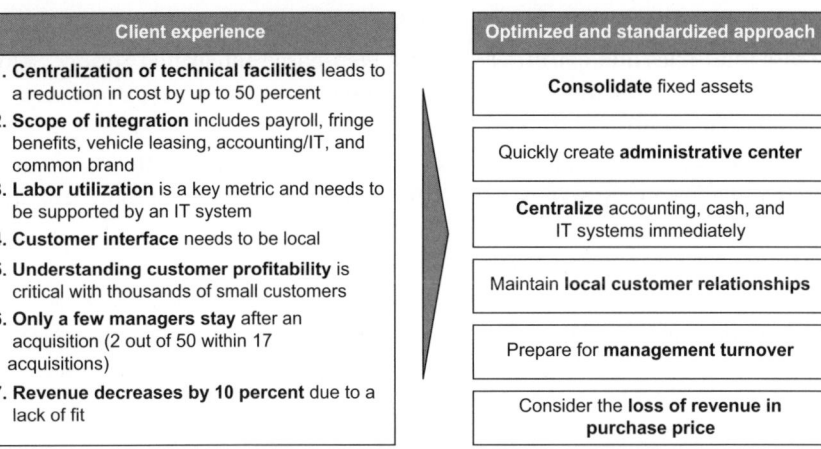

FIGURE 5.6 A Consistent Consolidation Approach Is Vital for Business Success
Source: A.T. Kearney analysis.

corporate or divisional business model, the acquirer should be able to centralize and apply its model to various acquisitions.

2. The second key to success is having a systematic target selection process. Systematic and continuous market scan, screening, and selection processes supported by modern decision tools can deliver high-quality targets. Such processes should result in more successful takeovers executed faster and with less risk than when targets are chosen opportunistically or reactively. The process includes a clear evaluation scheme and catalogue of criteria for long-list and short-list smaller or equal-sized companies in similar or complementary market segments. The targets should enhance and possibly complete the buyer's offering and service portfolio and increase market share.

3. The third factor for success is to develop a standardized integration framework for implementation. The target should be integrated rapidly based on best practices from acquisition experience and lessons learned.

Companies can capture synergies and upgrade performance by centralizing, consolidating, and instituting initiatives such as better labor utilization. Another execution element may be to outsource noncore activities, accepting a loss in revenues. However, integration teams should focus on cost synergies and bottom-line activities to create value and on actions that enable profitable growth, by setting clear priorities for short-term growth and by strengthening the sales and marketing function. These measures include maintaining local customer interfaces and preparing for management turnover, through non-competition clauses.

Companies across all industries can learn from the systematic and efficient approach underlying an acquisition factory. At the right time and with careful strategic alignment, this industrial process approach to M&A produces profitable growth and value generation faster and with less risk than other strategies, resulting in industry leadership. However, we recommend keeping large M&A opportunities and organic growth moves in mind as well. Companies can combine these strategies to maintain their growth momentum under changing market and economic conditions.

Asian Industries Where Acquisition Factories Would Work Well

An acquisition factory is most useful to companies in fragmented industries where plenty of small competitors exist and buying opportunities abound. That's what makes this strategy so compelling for Asia, where many companies operate in markets that have yet to go through consolidation.

Asia's IT, retail, and telecommunications industries, for example, offer up many opportunities. Though early waves of M&A by the likes of SingTel have sewn up the obvious, major deals in the region, many telecommunications providers are snapping up smaller service providers and applications and content companies. Large, organized retailers around Asia are mopping up smaller players in a bid to boost growth in a low-margin industry. India's IT services and IT hardware industries are fragmented, and deal opportunities abound. We are seeing a huge amount of M&A in this sector and expect more to come.

The commodity, agriculture, and food industries in Asia are ripe for serial deals. Little consolidation has occurred here and these industries are fragmented across the entire region. Indeed, many of our Asian commodity clients are working fast to snap up controlling stakes in downstream operations and competitors.

It's an active industry. Hong Kong–headquartered, Singapore-listed Noble Group has been aggressively using M&A to transform itself from a supplier of raw materials and commodities into a diversified commodities company with stakes in a range of upstream energy and agricultural operations. Since 2007, the company has made six acquisitions and bought stakes in another six companies.

In 2009 and 2010, Noble bought stakes in Gloucester Coal, Blackwood Corp, and East Energy Resources, all Australian coal mining companies. Noble spent $950 million in 2010 to buy two Brazilian sugar cane and ethanol plants.

The consolidation trend in Asia's commodities industry is expected to gain momentum. Noble, with its strong balance sheet, will continue to be an active player. Singapore-listed Olam International is also in M&A mode. Olam, like competitor Noble, a supply chain manager, announced several deals in 2010 in sugar, timber, fertilizer, and palm oil.

Another competitor, Wilmar International, has slipped into rebuild mode, according to our M&A framework. Wilmar International, the world's largest palm oil trader, has been expanding quickly through M&A into ventures in sugar, palm oil, and other edible oils over the past few years. However, when we put Wilmar through our M&A matrix, the company appears in the rebuild position. The company's financials deteriorated as it took on more debt to fund its M&A push, and its gearing ratio, which measures net debt to EBITDA, jumped from 1.7 times in 2009 to 5.5 times a year later. Stock analysts still like the company despite its increased leverage because its earnings prospects and credit facilities remain in good stead. But Wilmar's slide down our matrix illustrates how important it is for companies in M&A mode to put a framework such as this in place, especially when other competitors are in attack mode.

 ## STEP 4: SURROUND YOURSELF WITH EXPERTS

Ensuring that an acquisition is a good fit, not just on paper but as an integrated business, demands more than traditional financial due diligence; it requires a detailed value assessment. We call this a pre-assessment or improved due diligence. It takes place before a memo of understanding is signed and includes an examination of operational and management issues and risks. The insights gained are used to value the target, communicate to the board of directors, create a bidding strategy, plan negotiations, and accelerate the integration of the target company.

This early analysis provides a comprehensive perspective of the acquisition's potential to create lasting shareholder value, and should influence how the market reacts to the acquisition announcement.

To get beyond the numbers and to challenge traditional assumptions about risk and value, winners pull together expert internal and externalresources that understand base business value and growth and can evaluate cost and revenue synergies.

For example, as a spreadsheet exercise, valuing a target's base business can be straightforward. What acquirers often miss in their number-crunching process, however, is spotting problems in the target's base business. These are usually not apparent from routine inspections of publicly available documents and will not be readily disclosed by the target company.

Another common mistake is failing to assess the target's future growth rate and profitability and then neglecting to "sanity check" the findings against changing conditions in the macroeconomic, foreign exchange, and competitive environments. Forecasting an unrealistic growth rate for the target can have dire consequences for its valuation. If the base business is overvalued by 20 percent, an accurate evaluation of potential synergies will be of little comfort.

One way to manage these issues is to reach out to experts who have experience in working through this type of maze. Interviews with third-party industry or trade experts, customers, or suppliers will help if they can be done discreetly and out of public view. These people should be able to offer objective information about the quality of the target's business, its executive talent and workforce, and its processes and products. For example, if a target company has a poor history of bringing successful products to market, the acquirer has the right to be skeptical of its positive claims about an upcoming product launch. If the company has a history of investing less in research and development (R&D), physical capital, or maintenance, the acquisition business case should anticipate and plan for increased investment in these areas. This will ensure reliable product supply and head off sudden unexpected increases in operating costs.

In evaluating cost and revenue synergies, many companies struggle with striking the right balance between the two. They place too much emphasis on cost synergies and ignore those that will point to future growth, or they overestimate growth potential and miss the short-term value that comes from improving efficiency. Analyzing synergies beyond financial statements is complex: Opportunities can cross functions, product families, and processes, but sorting through the complexity is worth the effort. An acquisition that gives appropriate weight to cost and growth synergies is more likely to succeed.

Again, for this effort, the top acquirers call on experts who have experience in helping companies identify and realize cost and revenue synergies, and navigate the legal and regulatory requirements needed to get the deal done.

A company considering M&A should build a team of experts that includes bankers, consultants, lawyers, accountants, and tax and regulatory experts. Investment bankers have a large role to play. Investment banks can provide specialized industry knowledge and contacts, and they can help sellers shop the company and assist buyers with valuation and negotiation strategy. They can help companies raise the capital they need to fund the purchase, by underwriting a debt or share issue or by arranging a private placement.

Accountants and tax experts play a critical role in performing financial due diligence, preparing fund flow statements, and working capital analysis, and advising on the tax structure and tax planning for the merged entity. They play a key role in the post-merger integration of the acquired business. Lawyers perform legal due diligence (LDD), create the legal documents that underpin the transaction, and assist negotiations of the terms of the deal.

Investment bankers, lawyers, and tax specialists are often called transaction advisors; they lend technical assistance leading up to the deal. Sometimes, these experts may overlook or underestimate the problems of post-merger integration; their job is to get the deal done. Most transaction advisors are paid on a contingency fee basis tied to the value of the deal. Though they remain as professional and objective as possible, they are often decidedly optimistic about the synergies of the two companies.[3]

Merger consultants are typically hired to provide unbiased analysis, benchmark organizational processes against a range of best practices, and provide big-picture perspective. Consultants track, screen, and select candidates, conduct due diligence, and analyze strategic fit; they can validate future growth rates of acquisition candidates, assess revenue and cost synergies, and help buyers unlock value by identifying areas within operations that could be streamlined or restructured. Consultants stay on to see the entire process through, working with the newly merged company through the entire integration process. After closing a deal, a company such as A.T. Kearney helps with integration, aligning cost synergies and promoting a fast and complete implementation of turnover strategies to ensure value capture. Comprehensive merger management support, from finding the right deal to making it work, is crucial in a world where most M&A fail to deliver the returns expected by executives and shareholders.

Winners make sure they tap their own team of internal experts in identifying and realizing cost and revenue synergies. Sales, marketing, and operations people should always be part of the value assessment because they are typically charged with, and held accountable for, integrating the two companies after the deal is signed.

Sun Microsystems does this well. Sun involves its sales and marketing team at the beginning of every potential acquisition to analyze the target's products. The team explores the possible risks related to the products, including their success rate to date, projected growth in customer demand, "fit" with other products in Sun's portfolio, and the likelihood that the products will enable Sun to expand its presence in desirable geographic, technology, or industrial markets.

By assessing potential synergies beforehand, a buyer can quantify the likely costs (expenses and capital) of implementing the acquisition and estimate the time it might take to realize the benefits. Both will influence how much the acquirer should pay for the target. With today's constant refrain of "know what you are getting into" from investors, this value assessment will help identify the target's viable potential. Essentially, it offers insight on the true net value of the deal, which confers an advantage at the negotiation table.

 ## PLAN EARLY, THINK SMALL: THE RISK-AVERSE ROUTE TO SUCCESS

In short, it's all about getting organized. Corporate leaders who know their own mind and put inorganic growth on their annual planning agenda and mechanisms in place to track potential prey methodically will have the upper hand. Companies that plan to do many small deals will achieve steadier growth with lower risk than those that opt for the classic "big bang for a big buck" M&A. And the more you do, the better you get at it. Companies across Asia should consider doing a few small transactions to understand the landscape, learn how to do deals, and understand the complexities of integration. This will allow them to get bigger and bolder with their inorganic growth plans, without taking on too much risk.

PREPARING FOR A DEAL

Getting it right before you begin goes a long way to ensuring success in any merger or acquisition. Here are five things to think about before embarking on the hunt for a target:

1. **Know your position:** Figure out where you are on the M&A framework, either in attack, rebuild, or defend mode.
2. **Know your targets:** Create a system that methodically tracks and screens potential targets and signals the best time to buy when risks are low and the price is right.
3. **Know your model:** The risks inherent in classic M&A put off many Asian corporations. Build an acquisition factory that can do a series of small deals, which helps reduce risk, build experience, and maintain a steadier rate of growth.

4. **Know your industry:** Many industries and sectors in Asia remain fragmented and ripe for consolidation, offering up many opportunities for serial deals. Figure out where you are in the pecking order and chart out where you'd like to be before a competitor gets there first. Early movers will shape the direction of a consolidating industry.

5. **Know your team:** You don't have to do it alone. Build a team of experts that draws on expertise within and outside your company.

 ACKNOWLEDGMENTS

The following A.T. Kearney white papers and documents were used as background material in writing this chapter: "Impact of Crisis," by Naveen Menon, a partner and head of the firm's Asia Telecom practice; Kiran Karunakaran, a manager in the firm's Australia practice, supplied the original Attack-Rebuild-Defend framework that was modified for this book; "Build Your Own Acquisition Factory," by Jürgen Rothenbücher, a partner and head of the firm's strategy practice in Europe, Martin Handschuh, a partner and member of the firm's utility practice in Europe, Sandra Niewiem, a consultant and member of the firm's strategy practice in Europe, and Michael Maxelon, an alumnus of the firm who acts as the spokesman of the board at SWK Netze, a utility company, in Krefeld; "Deal Making—Now Is as Good a Time as Any," by Vikram Chakravarty, a partner and head of the strategy and corporate finance practice in Asia, Karambir Anand, a consultant in the Singapore office, and Rizal Paramarta, a consultant in the Jakarta office; "Mergers and Acquisitions: Reducing M&A Risk through Improved Due Diligence," *Strategy & Leadership* 32, no. 2 (2004), by Jeffery S. Perry and Thomas Herd, both A.T. Kearney alumni.

6

Due Diligence

Doing a proper due diligence before an acquisition is critical in helping buyers clarify strategy and synergy expectations and uncover hidden issues. Classic due diligence focuses on the company's financial and commercial aspects. Increasingly, operations due diligence is used as a complement to classic due diligence. Operations due diligence (ODD) evaluates the entirety of the target's operations to identify potential improvement opportunities that can drive the target to full operational potential and uncovers hidden land mines that may constrain or even disrupt the growth of the target.

S AD STORIES OF GIGANTIC merger failures have become prime time media fodder over the past few years. The painful sagas of AOL Time Warner, Corus, and Vodafone have become textbook cautionary tales. Veterans of mergers and acquisitions (M&A) trade excruciating war stories among themselves about a multitude of smaller, less notorious debacles.

Historically, half of all M&A activities have fallen short in creating lasting shareholder value. A 10-year A.T. Kearney study on the stock performance of companies following a merger reveals that nearly 50 percent of the biggest mergers and acquisitions failed to produce total shareholder returns greater than those of their industry peers in the first two years after the deal closed. Only 30 percent outperformed their industry peers (by 15 percent or more) and had earned a penny more in profitability. Five years after the merger, 70 percent of the survivors remained chronic underperformers in their industries.

What went wrong with all these deals? In attempting to answer that question, analysts have scrutinized and interpreted vast amounts of information. They concluded that M&A disasters can be attributed to poor synergy, bad timing, incompatible cultures, off-strategy decision making, hubris, and greed. One universal lesson is clear: Making a deal work is one of the hardest tasks in business.

As M&A become increasingly complex, the activities of due diligence become more important. From the outset, the buying company needs to understand what it's getting and what it's getting into. Between recognizing the potential value of a merger or acquisition and achieving a new and fully integrated enterprise is a dangerous middle ground where, without the proper preparation, anything that can go wrong will. The danger is not that companies fail to do due diligence but that they will do it poorly. The good news is that a handful of due diligence best practices can reduce the risk and give the deal a fighting chance.

A proper due diligence exercise can help buyers clarify strategy and synergy expectations at an early stage. An important part of our due diligence work is a 100-day plan, which helps companies think before the deal is done about issues that will matter later on, issues such as breaking down cultural barriers, motivating employees, and moving quickly to integrate the acquired company.

RISK IS ON THE RISE

The M&A deals that companies tend to strike today are far riskier than those of the 1990s. We can trace the increased risk to at least three converging trends. First, companies in maturing industries are rebalancing their portfolios and selling off pieces of the business. An acquiring company has to untangle the target's often-entrenched business processes from its parent company and integrate into its own organization cultures those that are often deeply rooted. Second, cross-border transactions, increasingly common because of the global reach of today's industries, are intrinsically riskier than those within a single country. Third, expectations have changed: In the 1990s, a merger or acquisition was expected to deliver cost reductions, but M&A are often a core growth strategy. Achieving projected growth targets is far less certain than achieving projected cost savings and more difficult to measure.

Despite the waning number of successful M&A, history reminds us that consolidation is inevitable. However, new accounting rules mean the stakeholders will be playing the game differently. Acquirers will need to perform better upstream planning and detail the reasons behind an acquisition. Boards of directors and investors will demand a more thorough assessment of potential targets, and acquisitions will take place only when there are identifiable, quantifiable operational synergies. If a purchasing company fails to gain a full perspective of the potential partner prior to the acquisition, realizing value from the deal will be nearly impossible. CEOs will be motivated to prepare for the acquisition well beforehand even as it is still at the idea stage. The ideal acquisition will begin by pinpointing a target that the acquirer can "fuse" with, and end with a well-handled integration, skillful management of initiatives, projects, and risks, and minimum loss of customers and talent.

FOLLOW THE LEADERS, LEARN FROM THE FAILURES

In recent years, a few companies have demonstrated exceptional proficiency in assessing their target acquisitions, evaluating them first as stand-alone organizations and then factoring in the value of any potential synergies. Cisco Systems' CEO John Chambers avoided large-scale employee turnover and leveraged the acquired firms' products and technologies throughout his acquisition spree of more than 70 companies. Kellogg's rewarded its shareholders with a 25 percent return a year after it acquired Keebler Foods. General Electric (GE) bought 534 companies in six years without much fuss. Granted, few of these deals were complex mergers of equals, but the acquirers achieved speed and success because of thorough integration of the target into the buyer company's business processes and well-defined, time-tested integration practices.

Such stories of skillfully managed mergers rarely make a splash in the media, but their impact on long-term shareholder value is obvious.

Unfortunately, most companies are not as adept. They target and buy without understanding what they have bought. They underestimate integration and deal costs, overestimate savings, and imagine synergies that do not exist. Shortly after the merger of AOL and Time Warner, the new CEO, Richard Parsons, said the synergies ascribed to the deal were oversold. "*Time* has not even been able to get its AOL email to work properly," he told *Newsweek*. Two years after Vivendi's acquisition of Seagram's entertainment business, there was scant evidence of synergies between the company's U.S. and European assets. The merger between British Steel and Hoogovens, in 1999, which formed Corus, was supposed to create one of the largest steel companies in the world with a $6 billion market capitalization. The business was worth a mere $250 million; Tata Steel swooped in and bought the distressed company.

What went wrong for these companies? They did a poor job of planning. They failed to identify the risks in integrating two organizations with different management and operational processes, and the results were predictable: management strife, political interference, employee rebellion, and disastrous financial results. If they had done the right kind of due diligence, these problems could have been identified and dealt with early on.

BRIDGING THE DUE DILIGENCE GAP

Due diligence is a key activity in M&A because it is the point at which the potential for value creation and purchase price are determined. Most acquirers perform commercial due diligence (CDD) or strategic due diligence—a review of financial and commercial data—to assess the state and potential of a target prior to the transaction. Increasingly, companies are going a step further and performing an ODD as part of their standard merger assessment in an effort to capture value sooner and dispel any hint of failure (see Figure 6.1).

Private equity firms were the first to put ODD into practice, and they set the bar higher by forcing today's deals to show value quickly. Historically, private equity funds have been successful in identifying companies with untapped growth potential. By using a mix of financial engineering and some limited operational restructuring, they have been able to increase the value of their targets and generate substantial returns for their investors. However, more competition for good deals has led to higher-priced assets and a simultaneous increase in the required returns hurdle. At the same time, financial engineering has become less of a differentiating factor for value creation. Factor in the global financial crisis, the higher price of debt, and increased level of covenants, and private equity firms have been forced to seek value elsewhere. They settled on ODD as a strategy for discovering short-term value creation potential such as tangible top-line and bottom-line improvements immediately after closing a deal. This strategy has helped mitigate many of the risks that typically undermine M&A.

We firmly believe that operations are an underexploited route to value creation. Among the growing number of successful deals closed by traditional firms following in these first movers' footsteps is the $47 billion merger of Procter & Gamble (P&G) and Gillette in 2005. The prompt integration of

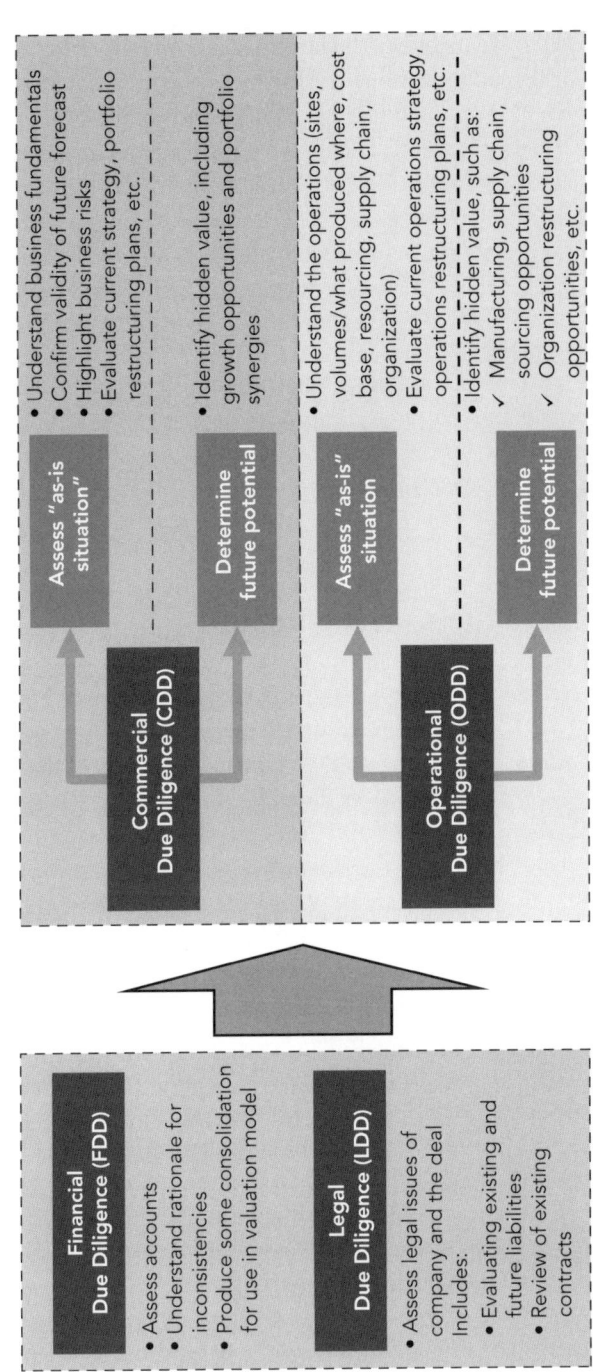

Financial Due Diligence (FDD)
- Assess accounts
- Understand rationale for inconsistencies
- Produce some consolidation for use in valuation model

Legal Due Diligence (LDD)
- Assess legal issues of company and the deal
Includes:
- Evaluating existing and future liabilities
- Review of existing contracts

Commercial Due Diligence (CDD)

Assess "as-is situation"
- Understand business fundamentals
- Confirm validity of future forecast
- Highlight business risks
- Evaluate current strategy, portfolio restructuring plans, etc.

Determine future potential
- Identify hidden value, including growth opportunities and portfolio synergies

Operational Due Diligence (ODD)

Assess "as-is" situation
- Understand the operations (sites, volumes/what produced where, cost base, resourcing, supply chain, organization)
- Evaluate current operations strategy, operations restructuring plans, etc.

Determine future potential
- Identify hidden value, such as:
  ✓ Manufacturing, supply chain, sourcing opportunities
  ✓ Organization restructuring opportunities, etc.

[ ] Performed on most deals   [ ] Rarely undertaken

FIGURE 6.1   An Integrated Approach to Due Diligence Includes Financial, Legal, Commercial, and Operations Due Diligence

Source: A.T. Kearney analysis.

operational processes, particularly in sales and procurement, led to a speedier integration, smoother transition and faster realization of synergies. At P&G and Gillette, and similar companies, ODD and attentive merger planning are quickly boosting the value of the merged company.

Unlocking the value in operations is an art and a science. Doing it well requires the following:

- Understanding the true full operational potential.
- Identifying and quantifying improvement opportunities that can be implemented quickly.
- Determining possible land mines that may constrain or, even worse, disrupt the growth of target companies.
- Developing a resource plan and implementing the initiatives with the cooperation of the operations team (a critical but often neglected element of the due diligence process).

DUE DILIGENCE: THE CLASSIC APPROACH

Due diligence is an overall term that typically refers to three broad areas: CDD or strategic due diligence, which seeks to determine if a market exists, analyze whether it's attractive, and map out the competitive landscape; legal due diligence (LDD), which analyzes contracts and other documents; and financial due diligence (FDD), which looks for inconsistencies in the accounts. We refer to this three-in-one approach as classic due diligence. Though it has served acquirers well in the past when increases in earnings multiples or the ability to increase financial leverage might have been sufficient, the approach fails in evaluating a firm's operations and the ability to execute a business plan.

The FDD and LDD work streams focus on building a historical fact base, particularly in relation to regulatory and compliance issues. They typically provide caveat emptor advice, often with many facts but little prioritization of risks, and are backward-looking by nature. These work streams provide a context within which a target's future performance can be evaluated.

By contrast, the CDD work stream typically provides a forward-looking evaluation of the target's prospects, focusing on the business and industry fundamentals and evaluating the firm's strategy and competitive position. CDD includes analysis of the markets the company is currently in, potential new markets it could address through new products and services, and the degree to which it is suitably positioned to target that growth. It should assess the risks and challenges, such as technology changes, that might impact how the market is likely to evolve, or assess regulatory risk. It could, for example, include an assessment of the likelihood of a mining company obtaining a new license to expand its operations. Often, however, say CDD critics, it places too much emphasis on best-case scenarios.

Investors use CDD analyses and insights to refine their bid-valuation model but this often does not adequately consider the firm's operations. Consequently, performance gaps that could provide short-term value-creation opportunities, when overlooked, lead to two significant challenges for acquiring companies: first, the inability to establish the firm's true full potential and, second, the inability to determine the real business risks. Failure to assess properly a target's internal inefficiencies is often the reason acquisitions that previously appeared attractive ultimately disappoint.

OPERATIONS DUE DILIGENCE

Operations due diligence (ODD) complements the scope of a CDD and, through its focus on the target's operational capabilities, aims to bridge the classic due diligence gap. Operations due diligence is executed in an integrated manner alongside CDD, with the two work streams collaborating to incorporate each other's findings.

Commercial due diligence (see Figure 6.2) focuses on the target's strategy, competitive position, and industry attractiveness, and assesses growth

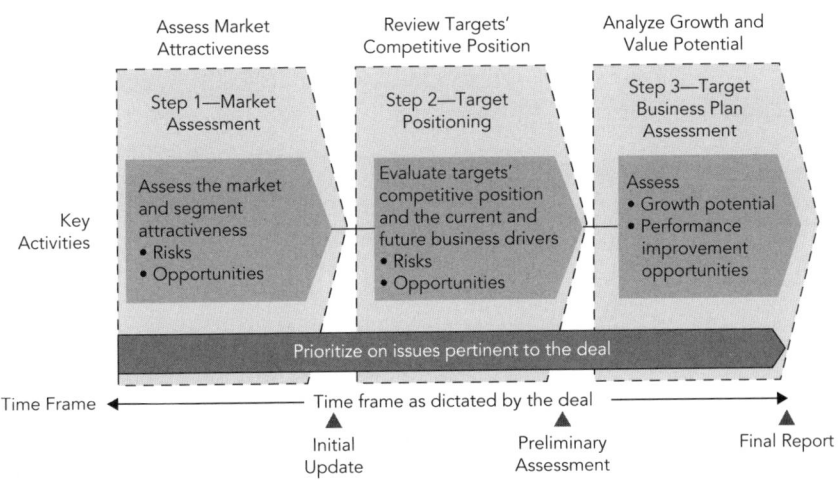

FIGURE 6.2 Typical Commercial Due Diligence Approach
Source: A.T. Kearney analysis.

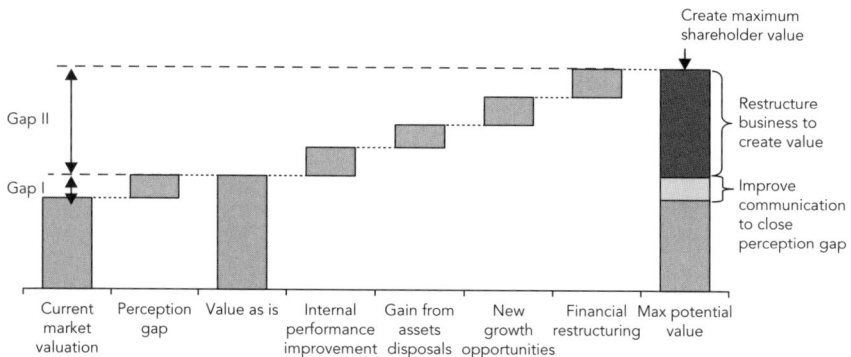

FIGURE 6.3　Operations Due Diligence Evaluates the Target's Entire Operations
Source: A.T. Kearney analysis.

opportunities and portfolio synergies. Operations due diligence (see Figure 6.3) focuses on providing a deeper understanding of the target's business operations, including manufacturing, supply chain, cost base, organizational structure, resourcing, and operations planning, and provides a balanced view of an investment's opportunities and potential pitfalls, nailing down the full potential value. This kind of analysis helps buyers understand what kind of value they can squeeze out of the company from within. Not least, ODD provides the wherewithal for a reality-based conversation with the acquirer about the target business.

Specifically, ODD provides for the following:

- Evaluates target's entire operations, including sites, volume, production content and location, costs, resources, and supply chain efficiency, among others.
- Benchmarks performance and identifies where, how, and when to make improvements, and how to do so as easily as possible.
- Considers the potential capital expenditures and working capital levels required to realize the target's full potential.
- Accounts for the risks and constraints that current operations place upon the target's ability to achieve its business plan.

Acquiring companies obtain significant advantages from this deeper understanding of the target's operations, a chief one of which is the ability to identify opportunities for unlocking incremental value.

For example, as part of the due diligence exercise in a recent project, we assessed the overall operations for a glass manufacturing plant. The objective was to identify opportunities and risk that could potentially impact the overall operations and, in turn, the revenues. Our assessment focused on operational parameters and capital expenditure drivers.

We were able to pinpoint and articulate the potential improvements across key processes of glass manufacturing that would boost the production volumes without compromising on quality. Though the operating teams typically can improve these parameters on a regular basis, our assessment used a combination of three key sources of data to test and stretch the operating parameters further. Our recommendations included the following:

- Tweaking the production scheduling, especially during color and job changes, to minimize losses by up to 3.5 percent.
- Optimizing the recipe to augment output and reduce raw materials cost and energy usage. Our plan cut energy consumption by up to 5 percent and increased output by up to 5 percent.
- Improving furnace operations, operating smarter to increase daily output without causing unreasonable wear.
- Improving machine operation by making adjustments to increase speed without risking excessive defects.

These changes, along with others, improved the overall output of the plant and reduced the costs across several operating areas.

In terms of capital expenditure, we identified an ability to "sweat the existing assets," which meant some of the upgrading plans could be delayed by almost two years.

The result was improved cash flow and, in turn, value. We helped prioritize capital expenditures and developed a business case for the acquisitions, which gave the investor—in this case, a private equity fund—more confidence in the source of earning improvements and allowed it to bid more realistically.

In another example, we were involved in an automotive industry project to conduct an ODD on a power train manufacturing company in Asia. The business was at a crossroads: It was expected to grow, but due to its move from a domestic market to an export market, its complexity was expected to increase and constrain its ability to fulfill overall demand.

Based on the due diligence, we identified three key areas of potential improvement:

1. Manufacturing operations: optimize capacity and improve manufacturing productivity, cost, and quality.
2. Supply chain management: reduce the supply chain cost and improve efficiency through better inventory management and response time.

3. Vendor base management: rationalize vendor base and assess performance on delivery parameters, which were on-time, quality, and quantity.

We used a comprehensive approach to review the current state of the company across the three areas mentioned above. The new owners of the company requested us to help implement the initiatives we identified during the due diligence stage. The benefits delivered across the three areas are listed below:

1. Manufacturing operations: improved overall asset effectiveness of the plant by 10–20 percent.
2. Supply chain management: improved order compliance of 99 percent, with reduction of lead time by up to 10 days and reduction of overall supply chain cost by 25 percent.
3. Vendor base management: a reduced number of vendors, implementation of a new kitting and tiering process, and a roll-out of a new procurement organization.

Because ODD provides an improvement agenda backed by detailed analyses, it can be used to facilitate negotiations with the target's owners and management. The results provide input into the 100-day plan, allowing the acquiring company to link specific short-term improvement initiatives directly to management incentives.

The Approach: Six Areas

The ODD approach focuses on six areas, evaluating a target's internal capabilities and the measure of its effectiveness in interfacing with its external environment (see Figure 6.4).

This balanced assessment, taking into account the target's costs, operations, revenues, and margins, includes an evaluation of support functions, such as finance, human resources, and IT. This ensures that outsourcing and shared services concepts are fully leveraged.

The first operational issue that must be examined lies within the walls of the target company itself: how many production facilities, for example, and their operations efficiency, their employee numbers, the cost per unit, and the bottlenecks and the capital expenditure needed to get rid of them. A lot of this can be accomplished by benchmarking the plants against the industry.

The second operations issue is network effectiveness: If a company has five plants making products for five markets, we need to look at what can be done

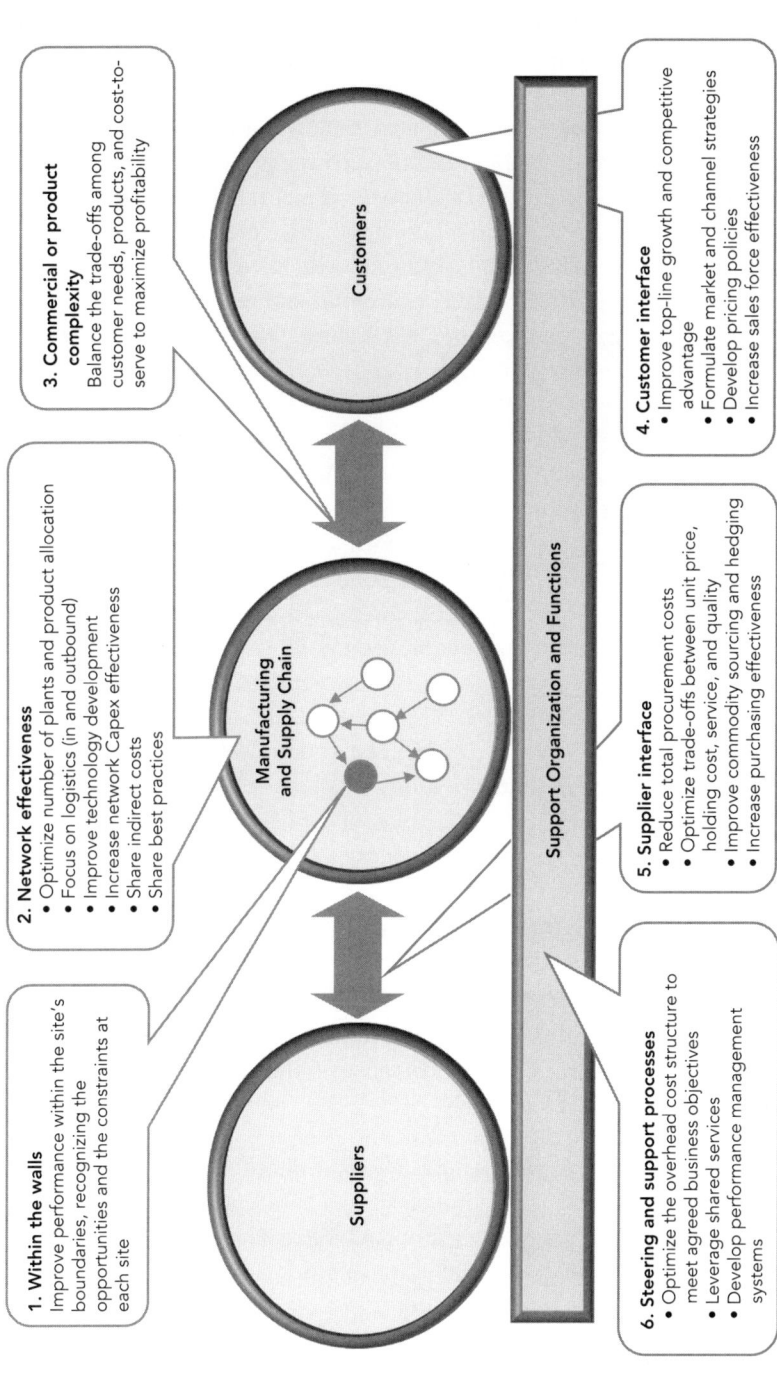

1. Within the walls
Improve performance within the site's boundaries, recognizing the opportunities and the constraints at each site

2. Network effectiveness
- Optimize number of plants and product allocation
- Focus on logistics (in and outbound)
- Improve technology development
- Increase network Capex effectiveness
- Share indirect costs
- Share best practices

3. Commercial or product complexity
Balance the trade-offs among customer needs, products, and cost-to-serve to maximize profitability

4. Customer interface
- Improve top-line growth and competitive advantage
- Formulate market and channel strategies
- Develop pricing policies
- Increase sales force effectiveness

5. Supplier interface
- Reduce total procurement costs
- Optimize trade-offs between unit price, holding cost, service, and quality
- Improve commodity sourcing and hedging
- Increase purchasing effectiveness

6. Steering and support processes
- Optimize the overhead cost structure to meet agreed business objectives
- Leverage shared services
- Develop performance management systems

Customers

Manufacturing and Supply Chain

Suppliers

Support Organization and Functions

FIGURE 6.4 Operational Issues Consist of Six Areas
Source: A.T Kearney analysis.

to improve efficiency by focusing certain plants on certain markets or moving capacity from one to another and potentially shutting down those that aren't needed.

We need to look at the product offering and the customer interface: Is the company offering what the customer wants, or is the product offering too complex? We need to achieve the right balance between product and demand, and link that to the plant network. At the same time, there may be ways to improve pricing, sales force effectiveness, and channel strategies.

Procurement is another big area of potential savings, and this is typically where we find quick, easy-to-tap value. A.T. Kearney has access to information on a range of businesses and can easily assess whether materials prices are too high or priced appropriately.

Capital investments, meanwhile, is one of the most important areas we focus on during operational due diligence. Most companies have a capital expenditure plan designed to push their growth plans. Often, after making a site visit and benchmarking the plant performance, we find that much can be done to boost efficiency at no further cost. Sometimes, the opposite is true, and capital expenditure plans fall short of growth goals. In that case, an acquirer may wind up having to inject more capital later.

The areas of focus for an ODD project are established by assessing the market and the target's unique situation. The objectives, for example, could be conducting a diagnostic to understand current operations, benchmarking current operations, quantifying opportunities for value creation, or a combination of any of these.

Our approach is based on the following:

- Site visits. Crucial information about a target's operational capabilities and a firsthand view of asset health are a couple of the advantages of making a site visit, and they help evaluate the site team's capability.
- Processes and capabilities assessment. Given the ODD time frame, the focus is limited to high-priority, mission-critical processes. The processes for each industry or function are assessed using a comprehensive set of questions and process maps.
- Benchmark operating parameters. The best quantification of operations value comes from benchmarking operating parameters; external consultants and key technical experts in the industry provide a solid database of information that supports the benchmarking.

These three elements feed into the "operations upside model," which is similar to the commercial upside model, and provide information on the following:

the operating expenditures plan, the capital expenditures plan, the potential upside from release of additional capacity, the risks with asset integrity, and the risks and bottlenecks with the current operations setup.

As discussed above, ODD can help potential acquirers unlock a target's full potential value and identify ways to capture this value. In an ODD exercise we conducted on a flexible packaging company in Europe, for example, plant optimization offered the best opportunities for potential value. The company had a fragmented network of more than two dozen small factories, most of which were operating at less than full capacity. We recommended it consolidate its plants and close six, and focus certain plants on certain products, which would allow the company to streamline the technology at each of the remaining plants. The company's supplier base was fragmented in certain categories, and it could achieve considerable savings by consolidating that base. Overall, our team estimated the packaging company could improve earnings before interest and tax by 20.6 million euros and improve cash flow by 22 million euros if it followed the most conservative set of recommendations from our due diligence study.

Several value levers are standard in almost any merger (see Figure 6.5). We've done a wide body of work with manufacturing operations, for example, and have found that plants can typically reduce manpower by around 20 to 30 percent, improve asset utilization by 10 to 20 percent, and reduce working capital by 15 to 20 percent. Most factories we look at can also reduce material losses by 20 to 50 percent. We will find ways to wring a 1 to 2 percent improvement in net profit from pricing improvement alone, and we are typically able to reduce costs by 5 to 10 percent through value engineering.

A solid ODD map can be used to begin a more wide-ranging conversation with the target company's owners. Finally—and perhaps most importantly—ODD helps investors identify the potential risks of an investment before making a financial commitment.

THE 100-DAY PLAN: A ROAD MAP TO SUCCESS

Operational due diligence establishes an opportunity to create the road map that unlocks value during the immediate post-deal phase: the 100-day plan.

About 80 percent of the value of synergies between two companies is typically captured in the first 12 months of a merger. You can't wade in; you have to get off to a flying start from the first moment a merger is legally approved. That's easier said than done. Cultural clashes, low staff morale, and confusion can mire any integration exercise.

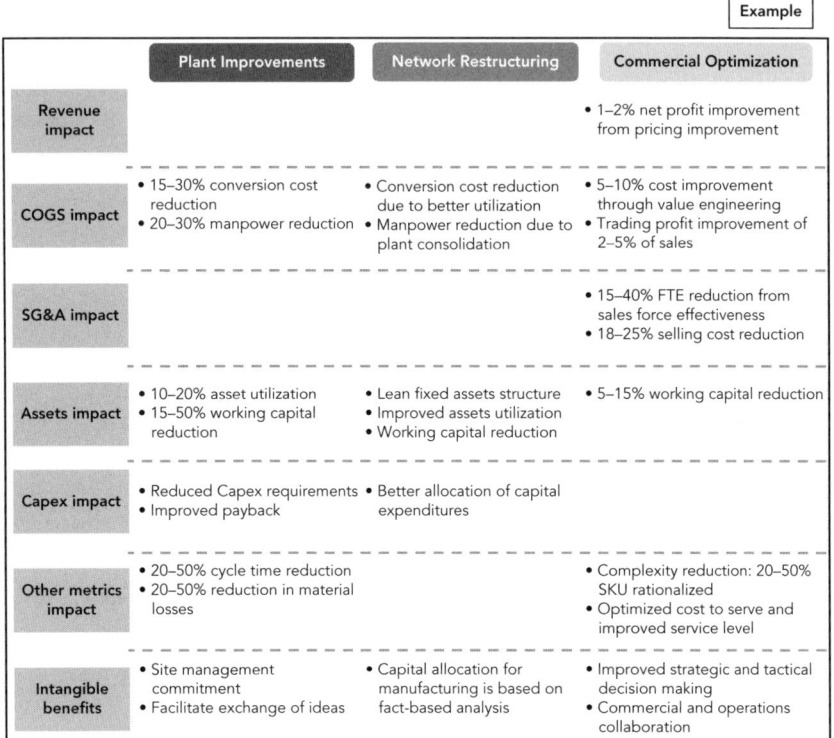

FIGURE 6.5 Implementing Operational Improvements Can Create Substantial Value

Source: A.T. Kearney analysis.

Operational due diligence allows executives to define the value levers, assess the ease of implementation, and analyze the capabilities of the staff. That puts them in a position to prioritize what they want to achieve and lay this out in a 100-day plan. This plan is a precise set of activities to be undertaken during the first 100 days and allows executives to gun for the value creation opportunities identified during the ODD. Figure 6.6 provides an overview of what goes into a detailed 100-day plan.

The plan maps out value creation initiatives—such as rationalizing factories, cross-selling products or consolidating suppliers from the two merged entities, and negotiating better deals—and includes the key enablers

	Week 1–3	Week 4–6	Week 7–9	Week 10–12	Week 13–14
	◆ Announce Merger			◆ Change of Control	
HR—Selection/ Harmonization		Define Company A job scope/grade/ compensation baseline	Convert Company A grade/ compensation to Company B	Announce new scope and positions	Redeploy personnel
HR—Retention	Set up HR integration team and sub-teams	Define retention strategy and identify candidates	Determine retention package (e.g., options, bonus) — Roll-out program		
HR—Separation		Define separation strategy and guidelines	Identify employees for separation, determine separation package and process	Roll out separation program	
HR—Vision/ Mission/Values		Gather feedback on new VMV	Develop and test new VMV — Finalize new VMV	Roll out new corporate vision, mission, and values	
IT	Set up IT integration team	Define IT operating baseline	Determine future IT organization	Develop IT integration blueprint	Roll out IT integration program
Finance	Set up finance integration team	Define finance operating baseline	Determine future finance organization	Develop finance integration blueprint	Roll out finance integration program
Communications	Cascade merger announcement and hold roadshows	Communicate regularly on integration progress and gather stakeholder feedback		Execute change of control communication	
Program Office	Set up program office, guidelines, and tools	Monitor and track integration activities		Prepare for change of control — Prepare for COC and post-merger	Manage and transition integration activities
Sales	Set up sales integration team	Identify synergy possibilities (cross-selling and sales strategy)	Validate synergy targets with baseline, internal/external data — Define organization and process	Develop sales integration blueprint — Transition organization and process	Capture synergy (cross-sell) and go-to-market sales strategy
Customer Service	Set up CS integration team	Identify synergy possibilities (fulfillment, etc.) and CS strategy	Validate synergy targets with baseline, internal/external data (fulfillment and support) — Define organization and process	Develop CS integration blueprint — Transition organization and process	Capture synergy
Branding/ Marcom	Set up branding integration team	Understand current brand positioning — Develop brand options (positioning, logos, identity)	Test and finalize new brand identity	Develop branding implementation plan — Launch new branding and market identity	
Product Line Management	Set up PLM integration team	Identify synergy possibilities (pricing, etc.) and pricing strategy	Define organization and process (pricing)	Develop PLM integration blueprint — Transition organization and process	Capture synergy (pricing alignment)
R&D	Set up R&D integration team and sub-teams (assembly, test, QA)	Identify synergy possibilities (program, etc.)	Validate synergy targets with baseline, internal/external data (R&D—test/assembly/QA) — Define organization and process (R&D—test/assembly/QA)	Develop R&D integration blueprint — Transition organization and process	Capture synergy (rationalize program, start new programs)
Procurement	Set up procurement integration team	Identify synergy possibilities (consolidation, etc.)	Validate synergy targets with baseline, internal/external data — Define organization and process (best practice, limits, etc.)	Develop procurement integration blueprint — Transition organization and process	Capture synergy (supplier sourcing, inventory optimization)
HQ	Set up HQ integration team	Define HQ operating baseline	Define functional and personnel overlap — Determine process to shut down location and transfer	Prepare HQ rationalization plan — Transition organization and process	Capture synergy (terminate lease, reduce personnel cost)
Manufacturing	Set up manufacturing integration team	Define manufacturing strategy (Country X plans, Country Y expansion)	Share best practices and process improvement strategies	Transition organization and process	Implement manufacturing improvements

FIGURE 6.6 Sample 100-Day Plan

Source: A.T. Kearney analysis.

that will support value creation, including human resources, people training, compensation, IT, financial reporting, process changes, and communication with staff and customers.

Putting a 100-day plan down on paper ensures leadership teams from the two merged entities get organized and focused on the goals at hand. It brings people together. Under a typical 100-day plan, executives create joint teams and assign the responsibilities and goals those teams must deliver on. That tends to galvanize staff and have everyone immediately working together, which in turn gives purpose, boosts morale, helps people get comfortable with each other, and dissipates some of the cultural clashes than can slow a merger.

A 100-day plan reduces uncertainty. Talent and customer retention are key issues during a merger. You don't want your best people to walk out the door because they're uncertain about their future or your best customers to jump ship because they're worried about continuity.

 ## JUMP-STARTING THE CLEAN ROOM

The move to capture value can start before a buyer takes legal control of the acquired company. The earlier the work begins, the better. Remember, most synergies are captured within the first year: Every week counts.

The challenge is that a merger is not legally complete until the regulators give approval. That can take weeks or months after a deal is signed. Many restrictions exist on what kind of information two companies can share and what must remain confidential until the legal box is ticked.

Here's where having an independent third party involved can help. Consultants can operate a "clean room" that they can use to analyze confidential data from both companies, work out the synergies, and craft a plan for the first 100 days of the legal, post-merger stage. Companies that undertake an ODD and use a clean room to jump-start their 100-day plan can extract value from a merger almost immediately.

This is not a new idea: When companies are being sold, they typically create a "data room" and release information to the bidder in a systematic way. We take this a few steps further. If the merger is likely to happen, we advise clients to set up a clean room where both parties share the information required to make the value-creation opportunities more specific and tangible.

For example, many synergies can be captured on the cost side in a merger. When two companies come together, they can buy double the raw material, for example, which boosts their negotiating power. Consultants running a clean room can pinpoint cost reductions across the buying cycle, get data from both companies, and map out a strategy to deal with suppliers. On day one, an executive involved in the closing can sit down and start negotiating new contracts with those suppliers. Companies that don't run a clean room can spend six or seven months plodding through the process.

It's all about getting it right early on.

DUE DILIGENCE FAQ

When we first approach companies with our operations due diligence strategy, we typically seek to answer several key questions at the outset:

Q: *Can operations due diligence take place without access to the target?*

A: Unrestricted access to the target company is desirable through the due diligence process but often is limited due to confidentiality and commercial concerns. When such restrictions exist, ODD can be performed by internal industry experts and through the use of intellectual property and global benchmarks.

Q: *Can this be done internally by our company?*

A: Some form of pre-deal assessment of the target's operations should always be undertaken. When an investor has considerable operational expertise in the target's market, an internal review may be sufficient. However, when industry familiarity is lacking or the operations are sufficiently complex, a formal ODD process is preferred.

Q: *How long does the process take?*

A: Operations due diligence is run simultaneously with the CDD work stream and typically spans three to four weeks. The scope of the pre-deal ODD is determined by considering the industry and the target's situation, and initial hypotheses and focus areas are determined in consultation with the client. A two-phase process highlights key "red flags" during the pre-deal evaluation and provides value-creation assistance during the investment-holding period.

ACKNOWLEDGMENTS

The following A.T. Kearney white papers and articles were used as background material in writing this chapter: "Bridging the Due Diligence Gap," by Vikram Chakravarty, Badri Veeraghanta, Francesco Cigala, and Adam Qaiser, 2011; "Due Diligence: Think Operational," by Jürgen Rothenbücher and Sandra Niewiem," 2008; "Mergers and Acquisitions: Reducing M&A Risk through Improved Due Diligence," *Strategy & Leadership* 32, no. 2 (2004), by Jeffery S. Perry and Thomas J. Herd, both A.T. Kearney alumni; "Breakthrough Value Creation in M&A," by Vikram Chakravarty and Navin Nathani, *Financier Worldwide* (e-book), 2009.

7

A Guide to Successful Post-Merger Integration

A large percentage of mergers and acquisitions (M&A) fail because the post-merger integration (PMI) process is mishandled. Successful integrations are about speed, leadership, communication, risk, and cultural management. Establishing a proper PMI team, with three important building blocks—merger management, value capture, and merger enablement—is important. A central program management office with the backing of senior shareholders and management needs to manage and drive the merger. SWAT teams must be formed to identify and deliver the synergies that have been identified as part of the merger proposition, with the full involvement of the eventual business line managers. Finally, key enablers such as information technology (IT) and human resources (HR) need to be aligned to ensure the company has the right technology and capabilities to take it forward.

AFTER THE DEAL HAS been sealed, the hard work begins. Integrating two companies is difficult work. This is the make-or-break juncture, and the odds are stacked against success.

Few mergers create value. Our research shows that in Asia, only one-quarter of M&A deliver the expected benefits. Poor communication, unclear expectations, a muddled post-merger structure, lack of leadership, poor planning, and lack of momentum are often to blame (see Figure 7.1).

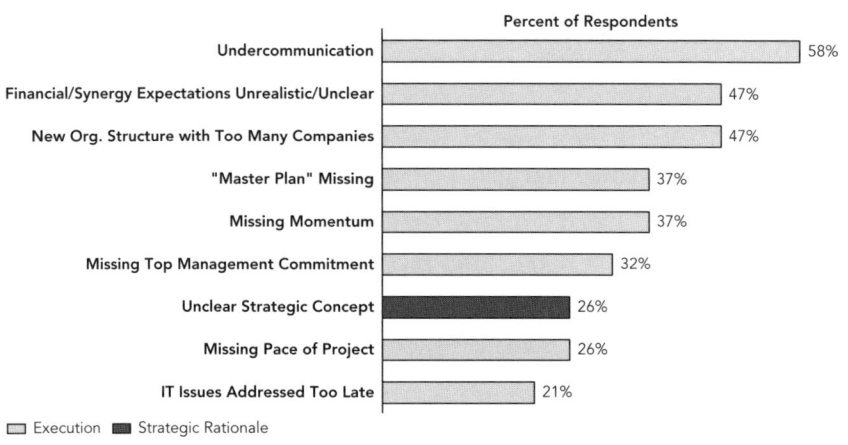

FIGURE 7.1 Problems Identified in Post-Merger Integration
Source: Global Merger Integration Survey; A.T. Kearney analysis.

The success or failure of a merger can be judged in many ways. Some companies look at how well their people work together, whether they integrated the processes smoothly, or whether they managed to acquire or launch a new product or cut some costs out of the operation. We think this is a narrow view of merger activities, and focusing exclusively on these activities can destroy value in the long term. Executives who undertake a merger must take a holistic approach to value creation; value can come out of or be derailed by soft issues, such as culture, and be driven by hard areas, such as direct earnings before interest, tax, and depreciation (EBITD) improvement, revenue upswing, and cost reduction. The success of a merger reflects the sum of all the parts, and each must be given due time and attention during the integration process.

We do not think Asian companies are more likely to face challenges in integration post-merger and acquisition compared to companies from the West. We do think, however, that as Asian companies are newer to the M&A game compared to their Western counterparts, they are probably less familiar with the challenges of PMI and with some of the tools and approaches for integration. In addition, Asian companies are probably less likely to look externally for professional help in these activities, preferring to resolve the issues on their own. Asian executives must develop a good, clear understanding of the PMI process if they want to emerge as winners in Asia's merger endgame.

MERGER INTEGRATION OVERVIEW: THE KEY PILLARS OF A SOLID POST-MERGER PLAN

Integration doesn't happen by itself. You need to plan every step of the process. All too often, companies don't place enough emphasis on proper PMI. These companies buy another company, make some effort to merge production or back-office staff, and then hope for the best. The difference between those who succeed and those who fail comes down to how they manage the process. It always pays to look at what the winners have done. We've worked with a multitude of companies that have pulled off M&A, and we have distilled nine of the core best practices that drove these successful integrations. These are shown in Figure 7.2.

Establish a Sense of Urgency

Time is of the essence in a merger or acquisition. A.T. Kearney studies show that 80 percent of the value of synergies is captured in the first year (see Figure 7.3). Little is achieved beyond that. Miss that 12-month window, and the value equation is largely gone. Creating a sense of urgency is the most vital part of the post-merger plan.

The winners work hard to light this fire well before the legal close of the deal. These companies create teams across multiple functions to plan

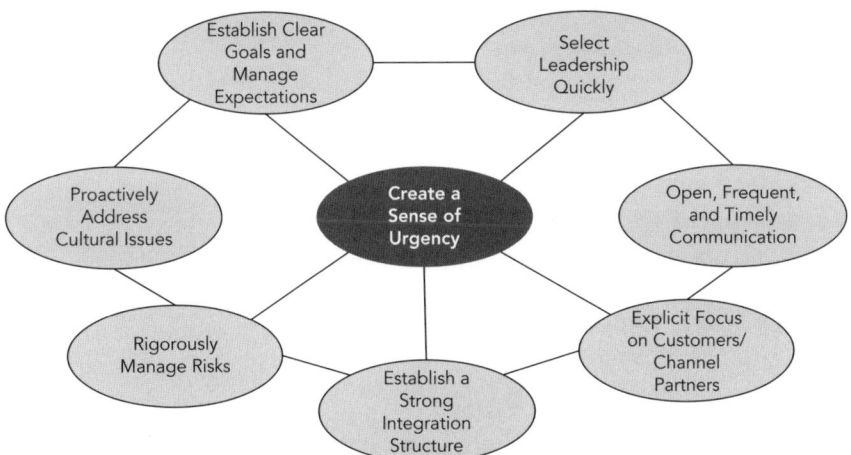

FIGURE 7.2 Successful Mergers and Acquisitions Consistently Exhibit "Best Practices" That Can Be Applied to Guide Value Creation
Source: A.T. Kearney analysis.

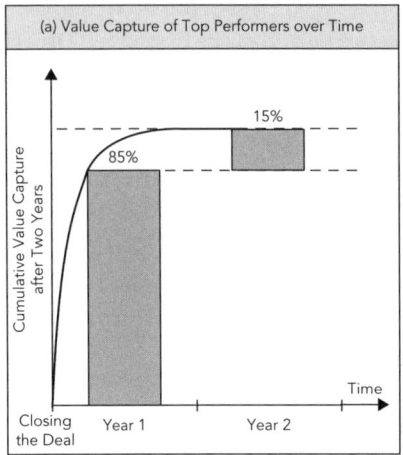
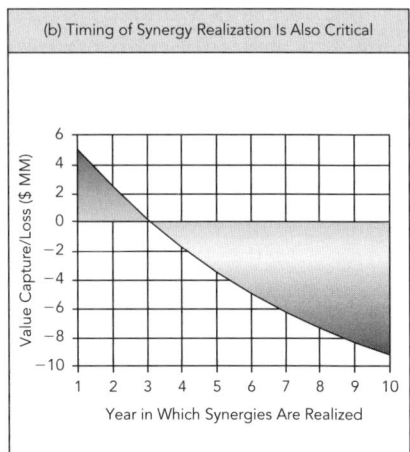

FIGURE 7.3 Key to Achieving Targeted Benefits Is Speed and Sense of Urgency

Source: A.T. Kearney's Global PMI Survey; Mark L. Sirower, *The Synergy Trap* (New York: The Free Press, 1997). Calculated based on a $10 million acquisition premium, representing 50 percent of market value.

for integration before legal day one and work with independent consultants to set up a clean room to analyze data they can't share before the deal is legally closed. Using those data, the consultants help identify and quantify the synergies achievable by the companies and create a plan that the companies can launch on day one after the merger to capture the synergies. The cross-functional teams create a 100-day plan that outlines the key areas of integration, maps out the deliverables, states who is accountable for each item, and creates a system to track the benefits and highlight bottlenecks. These companies know who's going to do what, where, and when to create value before day one dawns for the merged entity.

Select Leadership Quickly

We believe that a large-scale, transformative integration requires a Churchillian leader who knows what the company is shooting for and will go for it at all costs. Any large reorganization and change-management exercise needs a strong leader to champion the process. We encourage companies to decide on the chief executive officer (CEO) before the legal close. Early on, who's in charge must be clear.

The CEO-designate can move quickly to interview candidates from both organizations and settle decisions on the next layer of leadership even before day one. The roles within the first tier of management should be resolved and communicated to the entire organization by the end of the first week. Quickly selecting the leadership team provides clarity, unity, and purpose. The chief financial officer (CFO), chief investment officer (CIO), and head of HR are critical to the success of the merger.

These decisions, however, are tough: Two people are doing the same job at the two entities, and a decision between them must be made. The CEO shouldn't just divvy up these senior roles between the two companies, giving the CFO to one, for example, and HR to another. The new entity will be better served by taking the best person for the role. It helps to bring in a neutral party, such as an HR consultant, to assess the candidates and assist the CEO-designate in making a nonpartisan decision.

Sustain Open, Frequent, and Timely Communication

Communication is critical throughout the integration process. A merger can cause anxiety for multiple stakeholders, including the staff, shareholders, suppliers, consumers, and clients. A steady flow of information eliminates uncertainty, and misinformation that can plague a merger or acquisition. The merger office must take a proactive approach and address issues before they arise. We advise clients to be honest about job losses or let staff know when job decisions will be announced.

Management must also pay attention to the blogosphere. Sources from inside and outside the company will blog about everything from job losses to plant closures, and it's often a mix of accurate information and mere speculation. In our experience, the best way to combat this is to release as much information as you can throughout the process and provide staff with a timeline of decisions on these key issues. If a blog speculates that a certain plant will close, refer to a timeline and say, for example, three plants are under review, but the other 18 are not. Then state when the decision will be made. Letting people know when they will find out what their future holds can help manage anxiety.

Winning companies typically have a day one communication plan that includes a conference call or e-mail conversation with staff on the legal merger's first day, a 1-800 number that allows staff to get answers to critical questions they or their clients may have, and a staff intranet that includes information about how the changes affect jobs, reporting lines, and each business unit's future. A good communication plan should include a schedule of town hall meetings or conference calls with the new entity's leadership and an integration newsletter that goes out by mail and on the staff intranet to keep employees in the loop. Encouraging dialogue bridges differences in corporate or national culture; these can often beset a merger.

Focus Explicitly on Customers and Channel Partners

In a merger, people frequently take their eyes off the ball, and it's easy to become focused on internal issues, such as "Will I have a job?," "Who will my boss be?," or "How do we get this system or that process to work after the merger?" A properly structured PMI plan will keep a company firmly focused on its customers. This is a critical time for customers and suppliers, too. Customers will be worried about disruption to supply, change in sales and supply processes, whether the products they are comfortable with will be eliminated, and whether the sales guy they worked with will be changed. This is a period when competitors know you are the most vulnerable, and they will take advantage of the situation and steal your customers. We frequently see competitors spreading fear, uncertainty and doubt (FUD) in customers' minds, speculating, for example, that products will be phased out or not supported in the future.

Before day one of the merger, winners typically put together a jointly developed customer retention plan that focuses on keeping the lines of communication open. This plan kicks into action before day one, as it will involve the current team of salespeople and executives reassuring their respective customers that their welfare and interest will be covered. Once day one comes around, the plan will typically include visits from the newly merged entity's CEO and top executives to key customers within the first week to reassure them nothing will change or it will change for the better. Without a strong customer focus, the entire merger could become an exercise in futility: Concerned about the future of their business relationship or the ability of the newly merged company to meet their orders or service their account, customers are likely to start exploring back-up options if the phone goes silent during a large transition.

Establish a Strong Integration Structure

A well-organized merger is put into effect by a solid, well-organized team. Key to this is a central program management office (PMO), which coordinates the entire effort, and a series of PMI teams, which execute the many initiatives mapped out by the PMO. Engaging the best people to carry out these roles is critical. Typically, a mix of consultants and in-house staff runs the PMO. The employees selected for this must have strong organizational capabilities and a powerful enough personality and presence to get people on board and motivate them to deliver on time. A PMO should stay in place for a year or more, and the staff selected to do this job must stay focused on integration until the end of the entire process.

To do its job, a PMO must have a strong mandate, clear authority, and the support of top leadership. Underneath the PMO is a set of integration teams that come from every business unit and work stream. An effective PMO has to reach every part of the organization. Companies that have executed successful M&A tend to put this defined, well-resourced integration structure in place for 60 days before the legal merger and keep it on board until the job is done.

Manage Risks Rigorously

Companies need to keep a close eye on a set of indicators aligned to issues that can threaten to derail a merger. We recommend a series of proven reporting tools, which we'll explain later in this chapter, that identify, track, and prioritize risks. The key here is communication: The PMO and the steering committee need to stay on top of where each synergy capture team is and what bottlenecks need to be removed. Risks can be mitigated before they blow up if everyone is aware of what's going on. Figure 7.4 illustrates the levers of change we rely on to ensure a smooth integration. The biggest risks are that high-value staff will walk out, top customers will leave, staff morale and motivation

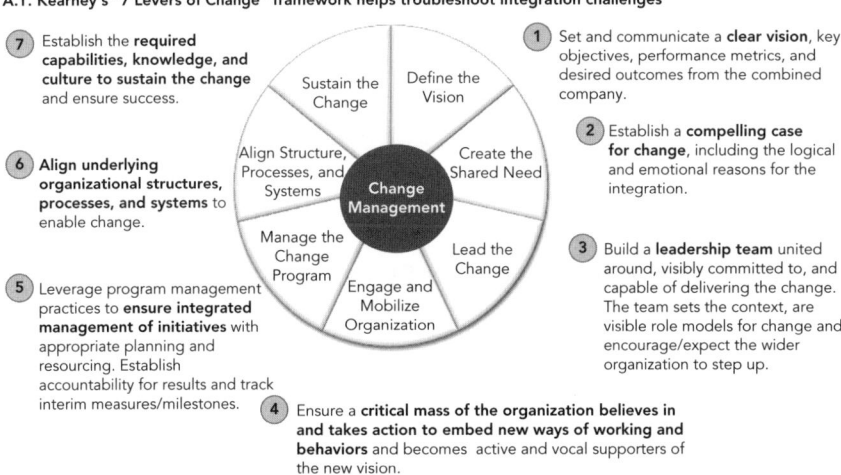

A.T. Kearney's "7 Levers of Change" framework helps troubleshoot integration challenges

(7) Establish the **required capabilities, knowledge, and culture to sustain the change** and ensure success.

(6) **Align underlying organizational structures, processes, and systems** to enable change.

(5) Leverage program management practices to **ensure integrated management of initiatives** with appropriate planning and resourcing. Establish accountability for results and track interim measures/milestones.

Sustain the Change · Define the Vision · Align Structure, Processes, and Systems · Create the Shared Need · Change Management · Manage the Change Program · Lead the Change · Engage and Mobilize Organization

(1) Set and communicate a **clear vision**, key objectives, performance metrics, and desired outcomes from the combined company.

(2) Establish a **compelling case for change**, including the logical and emotional reasons for the integration.

(3) Build a **leadership team** united around, visibly committed to, and capable of delivering the change. The team sets the context, are visible role models for change and encourage/expect the wider organization to step up.

(4) Ensure a **critical mass of the organization believes in and takes action to embed new ways of working and behaviors** and becomes active and vocal supporters of the new vision.

FIGURE 7.4 Seven Levers of Change
Source: A.T. Kearney analysis.

will spiral downward, and the newly enlarged company will fail to capture the full value of the merger exercise. Getting on top of these risks early—preferably before they crop up—is key. Prevention is the best cure.

Address Cultural Issues Proactively

Many differences in corporate culture and organizational culture can impact value creation: Some companies have flat structures, reward individual initiative, and focus strongly on staff, believing growth will follow the natural productivity of well-motivated employees; others are hierarchical, encourage process-oriented behavior, and focus strongly on customers. We'll get into this in more detail in Chapter 8, which is all about why culture matters in a merger or acquisition. Culture clashes—between companies with different corporate cultures or between staff of companies from different countries with different national cultures—can mire integration. Winning companies that have chalked up successful mergers conduct a cultural audit or assessment to understand the differences and create a strategy to bridge these gaps and harmonize the organization.

Establish Clear Goals and Manage Expectations

Setting clear, aggressive targets on where and how to capture synergy—including how much is expected and by when—takes you a long way toward achieving those goals. Integration teams and business managers can better focus if they have a clear map in hand and benchmarks to reach.

Create and Follow a Solid Merger Integration Plan

A.T. Kearney has a specific merger integration framework (see Figure 7.5) that helps establish a clear structure and plan for every step of the process. The three critical pieces to phase one of any integration are the following:

1. Merger management: This involves setting up the integration program structure, building integration capability, and beginning localized planning.
2. Synergy value capture: This involves assessing sources of value and creating an organizational strategy to capture that value.
3. Merger enablement: This focuses on integrating IT strategies and harmonizing HR policies, highly critical functions in any merger process.

Let's detail each one of these pieces.

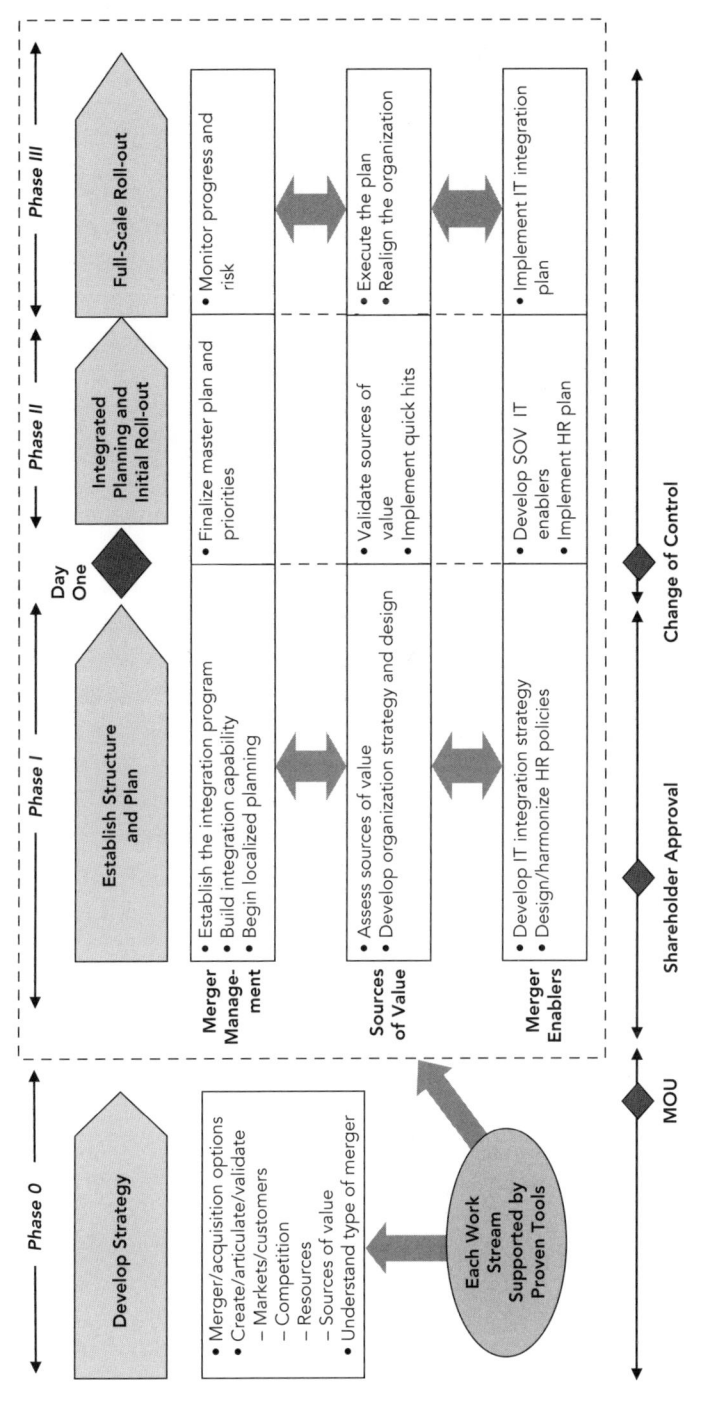

FIGURE 7.5 A.T. Kearney's Merger Integration Framework

Source: A.T. Kearney analysis.

MERGER MANAGEMENT: THE KEYS TO SUCCESS

Mastering the integration process is a critical success factor in capturing merger value. Most M&A fail because of the same set of consistent factors that relate to poor execution rather than strategic rationale. Almost all of the classic problems can be sidestepped with detailed planning. An integration exercise that's shaped by a clear set of guiding principles, backed by a solid merger-management structure, and run using tested tools and techniques will succeed.

Guiding Principles of Integration

A focused, organized, and well-run integration starts from the top. Before the ball gets rolling and the planning gets underway, the CEO needs to create a set of guiding principles to anchor the entire integration process.

As soon as a company starts building up toward an acquisition, the CEO should spell out the rationale and reasons for the deal. The CEO might argue, for example, that the industry is getting competitive and the company needs to build scale or might argue that the acquisition target brings a set of customers or technology that will benefit the organization. These drivers can be tapped to form the basis of the guiding principles for managing the integration.

The set of guiding principles usually comprises 10 or so central points that focus on the key goals of the integration exercise and the process of integration itself. These points help set broad boundaries and goals and ensure executives and their teams behave consistently throughout the merger process. Each of the guiding principles has implications for the integration process and should drive the behavior of the combined entity.

One consumer goods company we worked with, for example, created a set of guiding principles that focused in equal parts on customers, staff, and the merger (see Figure 7.6). The first principle on their list was "Customers are key." That had key implications for the company's post-merger strategy. Sales teams, for example, would need to be quickly combined to minimize customer disruption. The consumer goods company's guiding principles called for fairness and respect for all employees and went so far as to state, "We are in it together—the whole is greater than the sum of the parts." That helped drive home the point that everyone would benefit from the merger and had a part to play.

The consumer goods company's principles stated integration would be the platform for future company growth, and the integration office should be the focal point. This is a point many companies often miss: A well-organized integration leads to a successful merger, and winning companies create this house within a house to run the integration program. You must give the integration

Client Example in Consumer Goods	Client Example in Agribusiness Sector
• Customers are key • Fairness and mutual respect for all employees • We are in it together—the whole is greater than the sum of the parts • Working across boundaries is key to success • Relentless tracking and prioritization of risks and interdependencies • Effective teamwork and open communication are critical • The Integration Office is the focal point • Speed is essential—apply the 80% Rule • Build capabilities • Integration is a platform for future company growth	• Single corporate face to the farmers • Maintain functional specialization in the interim • All products manufactured and managed centrally • Minimize channel conflict • One culture in branch network • Consolidated financial reporting • Common HR procedures and policies • Drive economies of scale in corporate services • Leverage the relationship with grower network via branch network to achieve origination • Technology will be a key enabler to leverage customer information

Guiding Principles are key to "anchor" the integration and ensure all executives and their teams behave consistently

FIGURE 7.6   Guiding Principles
Source: A.T. Kearney client experience.

PMO the profile and authority it deserves; embedding this point in the principles that guide the exercise lends weight to that authority.

Some of the guiding principles could be operational in nature: The consumer goods company, for example, stated in its document that "speed is essential" and the PMO should "apply the 80 percent rule." Experience shows that 80 percent of the value of a merger comes in the first year, so a lot of heavy lifting must be done during the first 12 months. Stating this as a core goal helps set expectations and direct the pace of work, key milestones, and staffing requirements needed to make it happen.

Setting Up a Structure

If a company's leadership wants to achieve value out of a merger or acquisition, it has to recognize that integration is a full-time job. The CEO needs to set up an integration management office that operates as a house within the house, staff it with seasoned employees and bring in consultants with solid merger experience. This group of people holds everything together: It maps out the necessary changes, creates teams to put those changes into effect, and does what it takes to move the process.

The integration office, or PMO, should be composed of a mix of people from the acquiring and acquired companies. Below the PMO are the integration teams, which are divided into two streams: value capture SWAT teams and merger enablement teams. Value capture teams will pilot and implement initiatives to leverage synergies from the mergers; merger enablement teams—from groups such as IT, HR, legal and finance—will do the functional work needed to bring the two organizations together and support the synergy initiatives.

Some will work full-time in this role for a year or more until the integration is complete; others will pitch in part-time on top of their business-as-usual roles. The permanent program managers should be high-caliber people with a strong presence and excellent communication skills; they need to be able to unclog choke points, push integration teams that are behind schedule, get the attention of senior management, and escalate issues to the steering committee.

The foundation for this house is formed well before the deal's legal close, and we talked earlier about consultants who help companies set up a clean room and create a 100-day plan to jump-start the merger. Armed with the 100-day plan, the PMO can build integration capability and do more detailed, localized planning for an integration master plan. That detailed master plan identifies sources of value capture (be it top line, cost reduction, or productivity gains), identifies teams responsible for different parts of the implementation, and maps out a timeline for their deliverables. It is critical to create a framework early that establishes the structure and plan that will ensure an acceleration of integration, post-day one (see Figure 7.7).

The next job of the PMO is to put together the integration teams. On day one, the synergy SWAT teams pilot new ideas, implement quick hits to capture those gains, and move on to longer-term projects outlined in the master plan. Piloting each initiative helps determine which practice gives the best result and gives key staff a chance at a dry run before rolling it out to the entire company.

When we worked on Sime Darby's merger, for example, one of the key synergy initiatives was improving the yield of the palm oil trees (see sidebar at the end of this chapter). We put together a series of workshops with staff from all of the merged entities to share their processes and determine which was the best practice. The team picked a few hectares to test a range of initiatives, from the way they use fertilizers to how they harvest the fruit and maintain the fields around the trees. Team members had a chance to observe the results and familiarize their respective staff with the new processes before rolling it out companywide.

Each initiative is tracked. Each value capture team must document where the synergy will come from, how it will be measured, and what the baseline will be. Cost and revenue projections are worked into the master plan. The PMO creates a tracking system that maps when certain synergies will kick in and measures how much benefit and value it brings against what was expected. It is critical to be able to track and measure how much value has been captured as a result of the merger.

	Activities	Deliverables
Master Plan and Cross-Team Coordination	• Develop Integration "Guidelines"/"Vision" • Develop the initial "Master Plan" • Drive preparation for Day One with particular focus on HR and IT • Establish broad-level implementation responsibilities • Establish program management tools and processes	• Comprehensive Day One integration plan and checklists • Integration Guidelines • Program management infrastructure specifics • Integrated workplan for all teams • Initial perspectives on critical path items • Initial master plan quantifying synergies by initiative, team, timing, etc.
Baseline, Synergy Targets, and Benefit Tracking	• Establish the financial baseline and confirm synergy targets with the Value Creation teams for key areas of cost and revenue • Prepare synergy tracking tools and processes for roll-out	• Financial baseline of the companies involved just prior to Day One • Cost and revenue targets (as detailed as possible) • Customized synergy tracking tools—training materials, templates, roll-out plans
Communication Reporting and Risk Management	• Develop high-level communication plan • Conduct Steering Committee updates • Issue initial communications to stakeholders, as required • Prepare risk management tools and processes for roll-out	• Communications plan and content outlines for internal and external stakeholders • Information sharing guidelines • Appropriate Steering Committee reporting and update documents • Customized risk management tools—training materials, templates, and roll-out plans
Organization Design and Transition	• Review of organization structure of the companies involved • Development of preliminary organizational options and stages from Day One to Year One—likely end game • Define process, timing, and responsibilities to implement organizational options	• Preliminary organizational options for implementation post-Day One • Implementation plans and likely timings for organizational plan roll-out

FIGURE 7.7 Getting Ready for Post-Day One

Source: A.T. Kearney analysis.

The PMO also acts as a focal point for all merger-related communications. It reports regularly to the steering committee, which reports to the shareholders. The integration team works with the press office to communicate with media, investors, and the internal HR team to create a flow of messages to the merged company's employees. The PMO coordinates communication within the integration team and the value capture teams. Managing communication across multiple teams tasked with roles that are often interdependent is a critical job.

Another PMO role is risk management. During a merger, risks come from all sides: There's a tendency to lose track of the customer, key staff may depart, and there's the high-level risk that the merger may not deliver the originally anticipated value. Tensions are brought on by outside parties, such as labor unions, the government, or irate shareholders opposed to the deal. The press has its inevitable queries. The PMO has to deftly track and handle all of these issues without losing focus on integrating the two companies.

The other key role of the PMO is to help the HR department create a new organizational structure and map a transition strategy. The HR team typically takes ownership of this task and often works with an HR consulting firm. The PMO, however, will be a part of that team. The CEO and shareholders will quickly decide some of the big-picture issues, such as who will lead various functions and business units. Structuring the next layer down is a more detailed, complex piece of work that is one of the largest issues in any integration program. The HR integration team needs to map a new structure, including new functions and roles, and to decide who will fill each position.

Tools and Techniques for Merger Management

Coordinating the integration of two or more companies is an exercise in organization. The program managers need to coordinate a large number of integration teams whose projects are often interdependent while keeping all members on track and on time. A number of tools and techniques can keep all these teams focused and help senior executives understand what they need to do to clear any roadblocks along the way.

The first of these tools is the team charter, a one-page document written by each integration team to summarize its goals and initiatives. The charter outlines each team's key objectives and defines its mandate, scope, targets, deliverables, and timing. It should pinpoint the risks and issues that need to be addressed and identify the potential decision the steering committee must make to help the team cross hurdles and meet goals. The charter makes sure each team is on the same page, working toward a common goal, with the support it needs from the leadership.

Another important tool is the synergy blueprint. This one-page document prepared by each value capture team provides more detail about the benefit initiative they are pursuing. It outlines the rationale and assumptions of each initiative, provides detail on critical milestones, and lays out a time frame in which the expected benefit will materialize. If the team is focused on procurement, for example, the synergy blueprint will lay out items such as the total combined spend of the two merged entities and then break these out by categories. The document might state, for example, that the team plans to renegotiate a supplier contract within three months and expects to bring costs down by 5 percent. The target date for the new pricing will be stated in the document, along with an estimate for total savings.

A third critical tool is the flash report. This is usually a weekly or bi-weekly update prepared by each integration team on key activities, achievements, and issues that need to be escalated to the PMO or the steering committee. The PMO consolidates all the individual flash reports and creates a summary for the steering committee to review. Depending on how fast the merger is moving, the PMO may present a written consolidated report once a week or present the update in a face-to-face meeting every two weeks. That consolidated report will detail how many teams are on track, which teams are falling behind, what issues are miring the process, and what needs to be done to mitigate those problems. This reporting system allows the PMO to stay on top of each cost reduction initiative and do what it takes to remove any roadblocks along the way.

Another set of tools provides stakeholders with a bird's-eye view of the integration exercise and enables timely intervention to deal with issues as they arise. The first of these is the high-level master plan, a one-page high-level flight plan prepared by the PMO. It draws on each individual team charter and synergy blueprint and gives a snapshot of the entire integration program, including targets, milestones, major dates, decisions, and meetings required to facilitate these goals. It also delineates which projects are dependent on others and ensures those interdependencies are managed and communicated clearly.

The integrated master plan is a more detailed project plan that tracks the milestones and deliverables of all the integration teams. The individual integration plans put together by each team are rolled into this master plan, which tracks the totality of key tasks being pursued by all of the teams. This detailed map maintains the rigor and momentum of the program and ensures consistency in the overall integration plan. The master project plan is reconciled against the flash reports and is updated every two weeks.

Integration is nitty-gritty, detailed work. A good integration is backed by teams who execute against their charters and by a program management office that can track and manage the integration over a sustained period.

If a company sets up a dedicated team, gives it the appropriate authority and oversight, and brings in some experts to bring experience and discipline to the exercise, it's more likely to achieve the gains it anticipated at the start. If a merger is managed well, tangible numbers will come through the door.

 ## SYNERGY VALUE CAPTURE: HOW TO GET IT RIGHT

A number of core areas can be tapped to unlock value in almost any integration. We typically focus on ways to rationalize assets and capital investment, improve operations productivity, and boost top-line growth. Figure 7.8 illustrates the synergies that were captured, post-merger, by one high-tech company we assisted.

You have to move fast to get it. Research shows that companies who have pulled off successful M&A capture 85 percent of the deal's value in the first year. Setting the bar at the right level also helps. Shooting for targets you plan to exceed helps accelerate shareholder value creation. Be conservative about what you communicate to the market, but at the same time, set more aggressive internal targets. If a company states publicly that it plans to capture $500 million in synergies over two years but internally aims for $700 million in 18 months and meets that goal, it will win extra kudos from the market and investors. That scenario creates a strong upside for the company's stock price. It's always better to beat—not simply meet—what the street expects. The worst

FIGURE 7.8 Examples of Synergies
Source: A.T. Kearney Merger Integration framework.

thing is to promise merger targets that can't be met: The company's shares could take an unnecessary beating if you appear to fall short of your goals.

By the time legal day one arrives, consultants and senior line managers should have analyzed and identified how much value they can create and detailed how and when those goals can be achieved. Shortly after day one, value capture teams need to test out those synergy assumptions and incorporate those initiatives into their synergy blueprint.

We recommend our clients use a prioritization matrix that maps the likely impact in terms of value against the ease of implementation. The teams can focus on some quick hard hits that bring value in the door by moving first on high-value initiatives that are easy to carry off. The matrix maps contingencies and clarifies which efforts can be undertaken only after one or two other initiatives have been played. It will show the core synergy areas that typically deliver value in a well-structured integration.

Operational Synergies

When two competing companies merge, they often overlap in geography, production, or distribution. Frequently, production and distribution facilities can be rationalized, cutting costs dramatically. Consolidating production plants impacts costs around salaries, depreciation of manufacturing assets, maintenance costs, and even property tax and insurance.

Core production and distribution facilities can be expanded to build a better economy of scale; transferring a larger portion of production to the lowest cost of the two companies' facilities can add further value. Duplicate fixed assets, such as offices, branches, equipment, or trucks, can be reduced.

A merged company can find value by adopting the best practices of the two entities on everything from manufacturing and supply chain management to sales, IT, research and development (R&D), and accounting. A layperson might think that two competing companies in the same industry would operate similarly; the differences, however, are often surprising. Picking the most productive or cost-efficient method between the two and implementing it as the new standard can bring plenty of savings.

M&A often provide an opportunity to scale back future cash outlays for assets. Mergers typically create excess capacity that the company can grow into, reducing the need for much of the capital investment that either entity had previously planned.

Procurement is another area that offers value. The merged company can find quick cost savings by harmonizing prices, and the best price between two merging companies can be implemented for common purchases. The supplier base can be rationalized and consolidated, which increases purchase leverage.

When two competing companies come together, the new, larger organization with higher volumes and a higher spend has much more muscle to negotiate better deals from suppliers.

The newly formed entity can achieve savings by consolidating office space and redundant roles in areas such as accounting, finance, marketing, engineering, IT, and legal and public affairs.

We tend to focus on operational synergies early and repeatedly have wrung value in mergers in a wide range of industries. Figure 7.9 highlights a wide array of cases that we have worked on in recent years.

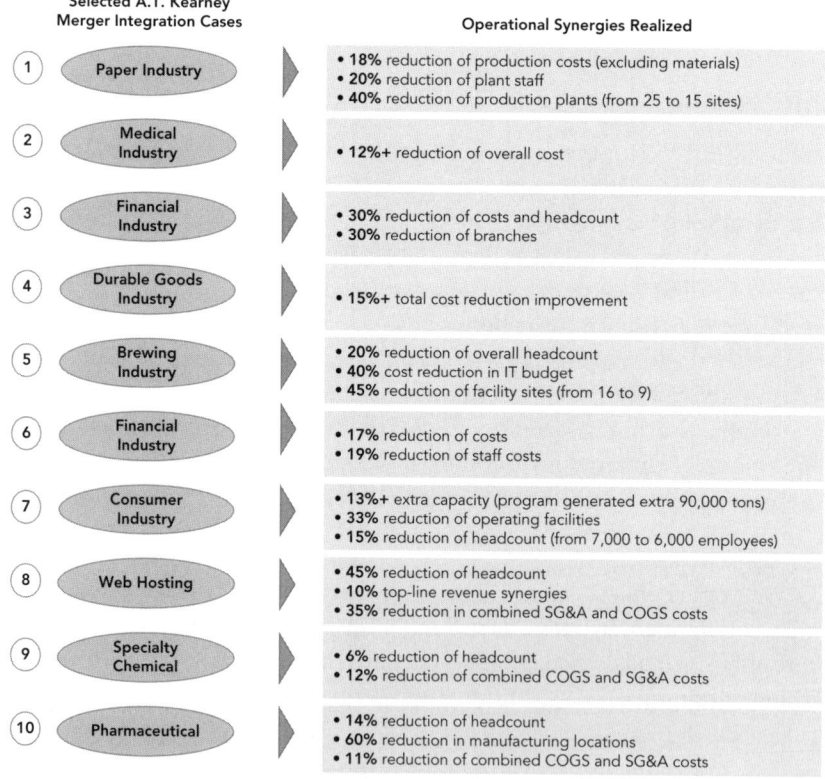

FIGURE 7.9 Our Merger Integration Experience Indicates That Substantial Operational Synergies Can Be Realized in Any Industry

Source: A.T. Kearney analysis.

Top-Line Synergies

Companies can drive revenue synergies by integrating branches or channels, leveraging the new depth and breadth of the expanded product line, and cross-selling to each other's customer base. A fuller product line will attract new customers who prefer to use fewer suppliers with a greater range of products. Brands can be bolstered by access to products that are superior or that weren't part of its stable.

To unlock this core revenue synergy, a newly merged company must sort out its organizational structure to support its sales and marketing teams and take steps to empower its sales force. In many cases, merging organizations are unprepared for this. All too often, these companies let the opportunity to empower the sales force and drive improved performance slip away.

The sales team typically faces multiple challenges in a merger situation: There's often a lack of systematic customer segmentation and a poor understanding of the needs of customers who are new to them. The sales force may have a limited understanding of the new product suites. Worse, the supporting systems and procedures to leverage leads for cross-selling are typically limited or lacking entirely.

These problems can be addressed by moving quickly to train sales staff to be conversationally competent across a broad range of product areas. A team of product specialists could be identified to offer assistance to sales staff during the early days, if the sales staff requires it. Creating financial incentives is important to motivate sales personnel to cross-sell the merged entity's full suite of products. If it is in their interest to tap clients and move products that are new to them, the sales staff will do it.

The leadership of the merged company must work quickly to educate its newly combined sales force about its recently acquired brands and the profile and details of the new set of customers. If sales staff from either organization knows little about the customers or products that have come from the other side, they can't do much to leverage new sales opportunities.

We worked on a merger in Singapore where one of the city-state's top four banks bought a government-owned retail savings bank that had a 95 percent share of basic retail deposit products but few other product offerings. Cross-selling and retraining were two of the core synergy initiatives. The merger brought in more than $40 million in annual cost savings, with no staff layoffs or customer attrition. More than 1,000 of the acquired bank's employees were offered specialized training and redeployed into productive jobs in the acquiring bank. It paid off: The acquiring bank enjoyed a strong upswing in profits after it began cross-selling its products to the retail savings bank's customers. What's more, the company's share price rose fivefold after A.T. Kearney came on board to implement the integration program. That sharp rise illustrates how a focused, well-organized PMI program delivers value to shareholders and the acquiring company.

Asset and Capital Investment Rationalization

In a merger, opportunities will arise to sell duplicate factories or move production to the lower-cost facilities in the company's newly broadened asset portfolio. As mentioned in Chapter 5, we often find, on closer inspection, that much can be done to improve productivity at existing facilities and postpone or cancel planned capital investment plans. All of this means significant savings to a merged entity.

Innovation Synergies

Product development and innovation is another area that offers value, provided key merger-related hurdles are removed. New R&D teams can crossbreed knowledge to create innovations and leverage competencies of the second entity to advance existing products. During a merger, it's often how two newly merged entities can leverage each other's product development capabilities. R&D can get bogged down by the absence of a budget, the approval process, and the governance structure in a merged entity: Product innovation may not be institutionalized, leaving research staff without funds, support, or direction. The combined companies may have yet to put the right incentives in place, such as key performance indicators (KPIs) or bonuses to motivate innovation.

A few key measures can unlock value from R&D. The heads of the respective research departments should be involved in merger planning and integration. If the research facility is located away from headquarters, leaders should bring key R&D people onsite as often as possible so they don't feel disassociated from the integration process. The heads of research from both companies need to connect early if any synergy is going to come from this unit. Products can take years to develop and test; this particular stream needs to come together and come online early in the merger process.

Integration program managers should establish a direct linkage between the customer-facing sales teams and the product and development teams from both entities. The R&D units need to work with their counterparts from the acquired company and need to create products for new customers who might have different needs. The final step needed to jump-start post-merger innovation is to remove any organizational barriers that might slow development. These often include lack of incentives, lack of clarity around organizational reporting lines, and lack of connectivity or support around the two former entities' IT systems.

MERGER ENABLEMENT: THE GLUE THAT HOLDS IT ALL TOGETHER

The HR and technology departments are the most critical levers for change in any merger or acquisition. HR and technology are high-risk, mission-critical areas that can facilitate a merger or wipe out value before the integration is complete. The ability of the leadership to provide HR and IT with the resources and mandate to transform their respective structures—and propel their constituents through a difficult transition—underpins the success of the entire venture.

Managing People

When a company sets out to buy another, it's not focused on bricks and mortar; it's acquiring human capital. People drive innovation, create brands, build client relationships, and push sales. A company's performance hinges on the skills, expertise, knowledge, and motivation of its employees. The success of any merger or acquisition largely depends on how effectively organizational issues and human capital are managed. Here's where an informed, organized, and merger-ready HR department comes in.

Before the merger occurs, HR needs to undertake a resources audit, figure out who adds value and where duplication exists, and map a new organizational structure. It needs to assemble a benefits package and retention strategy to ensure the most valuable resources stay on. One of the biggest risks in M&A is that the best employees will head for the door because they don't want to deal with uncertainty or they believe they're going to get a bad position in the new entity. To manage this risk, we provide a framework to our clients that identifies high-priority employees and categorizes each as a temporary or long-term asset to the company. Retention packages designed to keep these employees around ensures the merged companies capture the value of these key resources.

Employees might be classified as high-priority assets because they have a lot of retained knowledge about customers, the IT system, or the production process but aren't viewed as long term because someone from the acquiring company will take over their role. Employees should be apprised of the situation and offered an attractive package to stay on for 12 months to transfer their knowledge. High-priority employees with a long-term future should be assured they play an important role and should be offered a retention package.

About 5 percent of employees will fall into these two categories. The rest need to be reassured, and that should happen through the PMO's communication initiatives. Even if people are not losing their jobs, there's a huge amount of tension that builds before a major event like a merger or acquisition. The ability to keep employees engaged during a transition is critical. We advise our clients to make sure they do right by the organization and by the people. The notion of treating people fairly is at the core of the communications strategy we create for the companies we work with. We always advise our clients to be direct and honest. Never lie. Don't state the merger won't result in job loss. Even if layoffs aren't a major part of the value capture plan, some redundancies may occur. Be honest about job losses, if any are planned, or tell employees this issue is still being examined and state clearly when this announcement will be made.

A merger is a time of anxiety for employees, and HR plays a critical role in guiding people from both organizations through the inevitable roller coaster of emotions that accompany an integration exercise. Many staff will go through a cycle of denial, anger, and depression that can be pushed to acceptance and support by a responsive HR team. HR leaders must explain the benefits of the integration to staff from both entities, equip them with the training they need to succeed in the new organization, and provide the resources and incentives to reach new performance goals (see Figure 7.10).

The other major human capital issue that can rock a merger is a clash between the corporate or national cultures inherent in the two organizations. The HR department of an acquiring organization and the PMO need to measure and map cultural gaps and create a strategy to bridge those differences before the merger takes place. (For a more detailed discussion on this, see Chapter 8.) HR can do plenty to break down barriers that might impede a timely integration: Informing staff of what's going on, discussing problems,

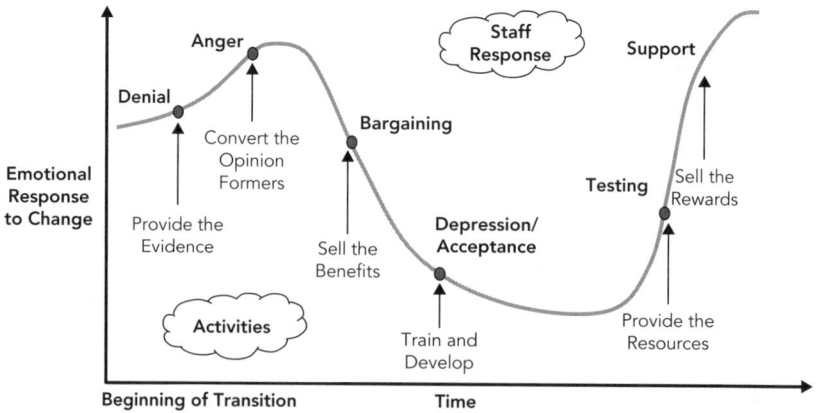

FIGURE 7.10 Managing Staff Emotion through a Merger
Source: A.T. Kearney analysis.

and involving staff in the process go a long way toward building acceptance, nurturing empowerment, and motivating employees.

Information Technology: The Anchor for Integration

IT plays a vital role in creating a smooth transition within merged companies and delivers quick, reliable value. A merger, however, could fail if poorly executed IT integrations bring sales and operations to a halt.

Merged firms will find they have similarities between their IT functions, even when few geographic, industry, or product overlaps exist. Reducing duplicate software applications and licenses, maintenance, and network contracts, and consolidating data centers can result in major savings. Organizational and support costs go down as duplicate applications and technologies are retired and as unneeded roles are eliminated and skills and competencies better defined. Companies can save 10–30 percent by reducing portfolios and outlining the skills and competencies needed for the future IT model.

PMI is the perfect time to save money by improving IT procurement contracts. A first post-merger step is to assess similar contracts within the new organization: Discrepancies in prices are a chance to reap concessions from vendors. The combination of existing contracts can lead to more volume savings, so reopening contract negotiations could be the right step. Figure 7.11 lays out several areas within IT that offer potential value during an integration.

IT enables other synergies. It's the glue that binds the business together, integrating major business functions, improving communications, enhancing

	Strategy	Potential Savings
Applications	• Rationalize applications and projects • Integrated enterprise resource planning systems • Reduce maintenance contract duplication	15–30%
Technology	• Consolidate data centers • Rationalize maintenance agreements and telecom and network contracts • Retire hardware	10–20%
IT Organization	• Reduce duplicate workers and roles • Rationalize development and support resources • Outline key skills and competencies	15–25%

Note: Savings for each category are based on incremental spending in the merger.

FIGURE 7.11 Value Categories in IT Integration

Source: A.T. Kearney analysis.

processes, and ensuring that customers receive uninterrupted service. This is vital: If customers walk out, the value of the merger evaporates into thin air.

The technology department builds the combined company's long-term capabilities and its operational model. Once the short-term integration work is complete, IT can devote its energy to support the new company's planned business growth. A cost-effective technology infrastructure is a prerequisite for success.

IT helps provide visibility during the merger integration, which is a period of uncertainty for those who work in the combining organizations. Reporting infrastructures, social networking, wikis, and dedicated portals can allow leadership to communicate plans and progress to the organization and halt the inevitable rumors. In this way, IT facilitates the integration of the companies, preserves employee morale, and ensures productivity in an otherwise turbulent environment.

An acquiring company can employ several different strategies when it comes to IT integration. Table 7.1 lays out five good options that work for

TABLE 7.1   Five Approaches to IT Integration

Approach	Description
1. Loosely coupled	Remain separate and fragmented, and modify reporting for consolidation purposes. This approach is appropriate when companies are independent entities within a larger conglomerate, and most viable when extreme time pressure exists.
2. Select one	From many IT setups, select the one that is most aligned with combined business strategy. This approach works best if there is significant discrepancy in sizes. It is the fastest method for reducing costs. The architecture direction defaults to Company X as a day one solution.
3. Best of breed	Choose the best of available setups with an eye on architectural direction. This is the best approach in a large-scale "merger of equals" or with entities with different business models across the combined organization. It can be time-consuming but functional.
4. Replace all	Phase out legacy systems and setups. This approach works best when point-specific solutions are poor in both companies and new software is easily integrated. It can be time-consuming in selection and implementation.
5. Outsource	Spin out systems issues to a third party that is aligned with architectural direction. This approach is advantageous in mergers where there are large size discrepancies, repeated acquisitions, and poor internal IT skills. Here, "economies of learning" from several mergers reduce integration time.

Source: A.T. Kearney analysis.

different companies, depending on the style of management, financial position, and other circumstances.

Our approach to integrating IT requires aligning IT with the merged company's business strategy. We used this approach to help several companies save millions of dollars in IT costs while smoothing out often rocky post-merger transitions. The four key steps include the following:

1. Launching day one activities: The goal on day one is to minimize near-term disruptions, a particularly big concern for any company with customers and transactions. At the start, the long-term vision of the company's IT function and the business's short-term viability are woven together as potential risks, and risk mitigation strategies are assessed.

   The implementation plan examines immediate IT requirements and initiatives to offer interim guidance for the merger before undertaking deeper analysis of the merger plan. This phase is an opportunity to take stock of each merging entity's current IT systems and organizations and set the baselines that will form the foundation of the future IT organization. An analysis of current costs will allow the merged company to estimate potential savings and desired results of the integration, which can be shared with and approved by major stakeholders.

2. Evaluating integration approaches: Determining the merger approach most applicable to your company is essential to a successful IT merger integration. Detailed maps and evaluations of the state of the merging IT functions—applications, organizations, regions, footprints, and infrastructure—along with an assessment of the merging organizations' preparedness for change may answer this question. The goal is to list current IT capabilities and to develop an understanding of the major business capabilities of the combined IT setup, augmented by a plan for migrating and integrating applications.

3. Enabling synergies: By reviewing and prioritizing IT initiatives before day one, the combined IT organization can get a leg up on generating expected revenue and cost synergies. While examining the major opportunities of the merged IT functions, we can identify and address the associated risks, offering guidance in designing the combined IT setup.

4. Developing the IT road map: In this final phase, integration begins with a transition plan that estimates the investments needed and potential cost savings, taking into account data, application, infrastructure, and staffing needs and identifying negotiation opportunities with suppliers and partners. This will identify the quick wins that can generate great savings.

Program management is a major part of this phase, including outlining communication plans and risk management strategies that can mitigate threats and manage stakeholder behavior.

Several companies have used our IT integration approach to generate great benefits from a merger or acquisition. After one global food and beverage company made its largest acquisition, its first move was to absorb more than 20 different IT operations into three regional IT setups. The company jump-started the integration by examining infrastructure, data center, and applications to design a new IT organization and find cost-cutting opportunities. It placed new governance structures to manage all ongoing IT integration efforts and created a two-year IT plan that outlined the organization, technology platforms, and budget for the department. IT operations costs were cut by 10–30 percent, leaving the company free to pursue its longer-term growth agenda. Another large European utility, which owned majority stakes in several utilities, had to combine diverse IT functions into a single IT organization. When the firm evaluated its options, including analyzing its current IT infrastructure and broader IT trends, it found it could save $135 million by standardizing its application portfolio, harmonizing business processes, improving service levels, and minimizing running costs.

THE POST-MERGER MUST-DO LIST

1. Set up a central PMO that has the backing of top management and the authority to drive change.
2. Create value SWAT teams dedicated to deriving synergies from the merger. Each team creates a list of priority initiatives, puts together a team charter, and reports to the PMO on a weekly basis.
3. Create a weekly reporting system that allows each team to flag issues that are holding up value-creation initiatives, and put in place a system to track and measure the success of each synergy plan.
4. Make sure the key enablers, including IT and HR, are on track to support the structural and technological change needed to support the merged entity and its customer-facing staff.
5. Identify which business managers will continue to drive these value initiatives once the integration is complete, and create a set of KPIs to ensure they maintain momentum.
6. Communicate more: Senior management and leadership tend to communicate less than they need to in a merger situation.

SIME DARBY MERGER SHOWS HOW POST-MERGER INTEGRATION, DONE WELL, CAN DELIVER QUICK VALUE

In 2007, Sime Darby, Golden Hope, and Kumpulan Guthrie merged to form the world's largest palm oil plantation company. The merger helped consolidate Malaysia's fragmented industry and delivered unprecedented value to the company's shareholders.

Integrating these three large, publicly listed companies was a mammoth task, and A.T. Kearney was brought in to drive the synergy initiatives in the plantation business. According to briefings to analysts the enlarged company managed to implement 10 large-scale plantation synergy initiatives that delivered 160 million ringgit (RM) ($51 million) in earnings before interest and tax (EBIT) in 9M FY08. That figure was higher than the RM28 million ($9 million) boost that had been originally forecast. This merger illustrates how a well-planned and executed post-merger integration (PMI) program can unlock value quickly.

Malaysia's agricultural sector was initially dominated by rubber plantations, which produced 50 percent of the world's rubber output by 1921. Stiff competition prompted the government to look for ways to diversify its economy, and it settled on palm oil. Malaysia's landscape and climate are perfectly suited to palm oil trees, which produce more oil for every hectare planted than any other competing vegetable oil crop. It's one of the cheapest edible oils, and, by 1966, exports to Europe, India, and China turned Malaysia into the world's largest palm oil producer. Palm oil is used as a cooking oil and as an ingredient in a wide range of downstream products, from chocolates to cosmetics to biofuel. By 2007, however, land-rich, lower-cost Indonesia surpassed Malaysia's output and took the number one spot.

The government decided consolidation would give its highly fragmented palm sector a badly needed boost, and in 2007, three government-linked palm oil companies—Sime Darby, Kumpulan Guthrie, and Golden Hope—agreed to merge.

Guthrie was set up as a rubber plantation company in 1821; Golden Hope was set up in 1905 and Sime Darby in 1910. All three were taken over by the Malaysian government after independence. Despite their rich histories, each of these companies had gone into a slump and become somewhat bureaucratic.

Merging companies that had such storied legacies meant a lot of work had to be done to drive every joint decision. People who have worked for a lifetime in a historical company tend to feel that their way is the right way. Deciding which of the varied planting, fertilizing, and

(continued)

(continued)

harvesting methods the new entity should adopt, for example, gave rise to emotional debates and heated exchanges. The decision to take Sime Darby's name for the merged entity was painful for many employees of the other two companies.

We set up a joint A.T. Kearney-Sime Darby PMO, working with another external firm, which quickly created a day one action plan, created an integration structure below the office, including a set of synergy capture teams, compiled a set of team charters, and put together an integration master plan. The PMO put a set of synergy benefits tracking and reporting processes in place and set up a risk management program and a communication plan, targeting internal and external stakeholders.

Our first job was to validate some of the synergy targets that had been mapped before the merger. We created synergy capture teams to pilot these initiatives and drive consensus among the merged management about how best to reach these goals.

Leadership of the synergy capture teams was jointly held by the three merging companies, with each team led by a leader and supported by two sub-leaders from the other two companies. Care was taken to ensure team leadership was spread across the three companies, and that the team members respected the new team leaders.

One of our synergy initiatives was to adopt a standardized best-practice approach to estate management. Each company had its own agronomical and estate management practices, and each was determined to keep them. We went into minute detail to extract synergies: Dozens of policies ranging from how to prepare the land, how far apart to plant the trees, and when the fruit is ripe enough to harvest had to be aligned to smooth operations and deliver value. We even tested new ways to get workers to pick up loose fruit that drops off the palm bunches during harvesting.

Palm fruits, which are about five times the size of a peanut, grow in bunches slightly bigger than a basketball that weigh around 20 kilograms. These are cut by harvesters and fall up to 30 meters to the ground. Often, the super-ripe fruits, which are richest in oil, fall off the bunch before harvesting or break off the bunch and scatter as they hit the ground during the harvesting. The collection team, which typically gets paid by weight, often passes over the loose fruit because collecting the individual fruits is tedious, backbreaking work. Focusing on the fruit bunches is easier. Palm oil goes into everything from chocolate to shoe polish, and the best grade oil commands a higher price and, therefore, higher margins. The ripe loose fruit produces the most valuable oil, and the synergy capture team piloted a number of ideas to ensure these gems weren't left on the forest floor. One idea was to make it easier for workers to collect loose fruit by giving them a long-handled tool for grabbing small kernels without bending over. Another initiative was to pay collectors based on the grade of fruit they brought in, not just on the weight.

Some of the meetings to decide on best practices for the merged company became heated and wound up in arbitration. A workshop run to determine the type of seeds the new enterprise should use, for example, ended in a deadlock. Most plantation companies produce their own seeds, which take years of R&D to develop. Selecting the winning seed was a touchy topic for these planters. Data-driven records were needed to decipher which firm's seeds had proved the most productive after normalizing factors like soil quality, rainfall, etc.

Another big initiative was to consolidate over 20 different estates into 12 estates. By reducing the number of administrative staff, office expenses, and estate supervisors, the merged company saved money. We created a team to figure how to optimize mill capacity and routing. The new, larger network of mills and estates created an opportunity to re-route freshly picked fruit, reduce transit times, and get the palm fruits processed more quickly, which would lead to better quality oil. The teams leveraged the new scale of the company to renegotiate lower external transport costs.

Some of the other synergy initiatives the teams helped put in place included reducing fertilizer costs by moving to the lowest-cost suppliers and garnering discounts for higher volumes. The capture teams also reckoned they could leverage the scale of the combined company to reduce the cost of spare parts for its mills.

A.T. Kearney helped create clear implementation plans and identify which managers were accountable for each synergy initiative. We helped define KPIs, responsibilities, and targets for management's top level to support the process. Finally, we helped design the incentive structure at all levels of the organization to motivate the employees to implement the improvement plans and back up the business strategy.

Investors got their money's worth out of this integration. The shares of all three companies were trading around RM8.90 when they were delisted in November 2007, halfway through our transformation program. The shares of the expanded Sime Darby were relisted at RM11.20 less than one month later.

ACKNOWLEDGMENTS

The following A.T. Kearney white paper was used as background material in writing this chapter: "Make or Break: The Critical Role of IT in Post-Merger Integration," by Sumit Chandra, Christian Hagen, Jason Miller, Tejal Thakkar, and Abha Thakker.

CHAPTER EIGHT

Culture Matters

Many executives understand that culture matters in mergers and acquisitions (M&A) but fail to address it sufficiently. Culture will be an important consideration given the diversity of Asia, and the inevitable increase in "West-East" deals. Cultural differences are not just at the national level; corporate cultures as well as local cultures will need to be dealt with. We have an eight-pronged approach to tackling culture: conducting a culture audit, putting a label to differences, maintaining communication, leveraging the 100-day plan, understanding the web of relationships, looking for hidden costs, addressing the talent challenge, and managing local expectations.

THE TANTALIZING PROSPECT OF forming the world's fifth-largest food and beverage company brought Japan's Kirin Holdings and its smaller rival, Suntory Holdings, to the table in 2009. The merger talks fell apart when the discussion turned to integration. In early 2010, both parties walked away from the deal, citing a clash in corporate culture.

Publicly listed Kirin, a well-structured organization run by a professional management team, didn't see eye to eye with the privately held Suntory, which is still controlled by the family of its original founder. Kirin wanted the merged entity to be run by an independent, professional executive team, and accused Suntory of wanting to structure the shareholding of the merged entity so the family members could retain control. After going round in circles, the companies abandoned the plan. "The two sides could not agree on how the merged firm would be run," Kirin President Kazuyasu Kato told reporters.[1]

Cultural clashes can sink a merger or mire integration. One A.T. Kearney survey cited cultural differences as the number one reason for merger failure, outstripping more obvious stumbling blocks such as poor planning, unrealistic expectations, or inadequate due diligence. A culture clash can lead to poor communication, misunderstanding, uncertainty, loss of motivation among employees, and loss of key talent.

In Asia, executives working on cross-border deals have to navigate multiple cultural minefields: gaps in national culture, clashes in corporate culture, and differences in the local business culture and norms, which sometimes condone practices that can take foreign acquirers by surprise.

Managing national culture gaps is no longer just about understanding Asia. The direction of deal flow is reversing, putting a new spin on cultural integration. As Asian outbound M&A continue to rise, a growing number of Asian executives find themselves struggling to manage this "soft" side of an acquisition in the West, where American or European staff may be wary of their new foreign managers or resistant to change.

Troubleshooting these cultural gaps comes down to foresight. Planning early, doing your pre-merger legwork, and creating a road map to guide the way can bridge almost any divide.

 ## IT'S NOT A SMALL WORLD, AFTER ALL

The growing number of acquisitions of targets in developed markets by companies from emerging Asia is putting an increasing number of Asian executives in the cultural hot seat. The stakes, in some cases, are high. Many cash-rich Asian companies are buying bigger, better-known Western companies in a bid to leapfrog to the next level by acquiring a brand, a technology, or marketing know-how. That big-bang effort could self-combust if a culture clash were to demoralize staff at the value-added target company and the key talent walked away.

To understand the challenges faced by Asian acquirers, consider the case of a large, publicly listed Indian pharmaceutical and biotechnology company that stumbled, then found its footing, early in its European acquisition spree.

The Indian company, which has a market capitalization of around $1 billion, develops and manufactures pharmaceuticals, and employs some 9,000 staff worldwide. The company, which declined to be named, and which is referred to as "Ganga" in this case study, has spent more than £11 million acquiring pharmaceutical companies in the United States, Ireland, France, and the United Kingdom.[2]

In 2003, Ganga bought a loss-making British drug manufacturer, dubbed C-Pharma, to get a leg up on technology and better access to markets, notes Aston Business School Professor Pawan Budhwar, co-author of the case study on the takeover, published by the *Multinational Business Review*. The British company had licenses to market drugs in Africa, the Middle East, and the United Kingdom. The Indian acquirer's plan was to move the bulk drug manufacturing to India, while continuing to develop and manufacture pharmaceuticals that required more extensive research and development (R&D) in the United Kingdom. By doing this, it could improve the cost structure at the ailing British company and acquire new technologies and markets at the same time.

C-Pharma had an estimated excess labor force of about 300 employees, which hurt productivity, and the company faced high pension costs as well. It had a small portfolio of drugs and relied on sales of its animal insulin for the bulk of its revenue. Lower-cost competing products had hit sales of that core drug hard, which ultimately led to its sale to Ganga.

When Ganga took over the company, executives attempted to wipe out the existing operation and corporate culture and replace it, wholesale, with its own. Numerous leadership positions at C-Pharma were replaced by expatriate staff from India. Ganga imposed the HR policies it used in India, including a performance appraisal system that linked performance to pay, and a competency base framework for recruitment, selection, and training. Ganga's HR staff proceeded to use its appraisal system to weed out the unproductive labor and identify the people it wanted to keep. The HR team made a conscious effort to change the culture and values of C-Pharma employees by focusing everything on productivity, quality, cost, and speed. One thing Ganga did not do was conduct a cultural audit or give its Indian managers any form of cross-cultural training during the pre-merger or integration stage.

The acquisition hit a cultural wall from the beginning. The system of performance-linked pay was alien to the British employees at C-Pharma, and they refused to accept it.[3] Ganga's Indian managers at C-Pharma demanded long hours and extra effort, which led to further tension with the British staff. In India, Ganga commanded a competitive workforce that was willing to put in extra hours, typical of much of Asia, where people routinely work late and often come in on weekends. In Europe, staff is more used to working a nine-to-five day. C-Pharma's British staff chafed under the management style of their new Indian bosses, who were used to deference from the staff back home.

Indian companies do tend to be hierarchical, and an executive who oversees a team or a function is used to getting full compliance from staff: The boss says what needs to be done and how it needs to be done and the staff make it so. An enormous level of respect is shown to the boss and reflected through all manner of interactions and behavior. On the flip side, Indian companies tend to have a strong "family" feel that Western companies often lack. Those in charge take a personal interest in their employees and typically know and care about what's going on in their life at home. If they need help or assistance, the manager does what he or she can to provide it. In many respects, work relationships are like family relationships: The younger, more junior people unquestioningly obey the older, more senior folk, who, in turn, take care of them personally and professionally. That can be an unusual or unwelcome dynamic in a Western corporate setting, which tends to promote a more "flat" power structure, encourage individual expression and opinion—even if it's at odds with the boss—and respect individual privacy.

Either way, the managerial style of their new Indian bosses meshed badly with C-Pharma's employees, who were unsettled by job losses and disgruntled at the new performance-linked pay.

Ganga U.K.'s Indian CEO described the fallout as a classic outbreak of merger syndrome: Morale plummeted, unrest spread, and C-Pharma staff started quitting. He attributed the exodus to the rapid downsizing of 300 staff, the sudden change in the management ranks, and the poor communication around the performance management policy.

The HR team, he reflected later, should have done more to educate staff on the need for change and prepare them for the changes. The employees had preconceived notions about the Indian style of management and assumed their Indian managers were going to be directive, bureaucratic, and unsympathetic to employee welfare.

After the acquisition, the new CEO changed tack. He began building personal relationships with employees, and involving them in his decision making. The HR team began "selling" the logic for change to employees and explaining the benefits they would derive from the new performance management scheme. HR staff and managers provided training for staff to equip them for their new roles and set clear goals and objectives. The HR team provided counseling sessions for stress management and cross-cultural training. Although the late start had left wounds that took time to heal and it took nearly a year of intense

HR efforts before Ganga felt the acquisition would succeed, the efforts paid off. Employees who initially railed against the acquisition felt proud to be part of the Ganga family. Ganga applied the lessons it learned at C-Pharma to a string of future acquisitions in Europe, which went far more smoothly.

Other Indian companies have taken more of a go-slow or "do nothing" approach to their European acquisitions. Tata, for example, made few changes—and sent few Indian staff—to Corus Steel, Tetley Tea, and Jaguar Land Rover after it bought those companies. Instead, Tata was primarily looking to learn from its acquisitions to help launch its own global expansion, using the brands' existing management and employees.[4]

Although these brands were plagued by high costs and other problems, Tata was more concerned with reaping big-picture benefits than about short-term losses. This hands-off strategy allowed the company to sidestep cultural gaps. "It's always about talking to the shareholders, to stakeholders, to the board, to management," Syed Anwar Hasan, managing director of Tata Limited, the European arm of Tata Sons, told *The Sunday Times* in April 2011. "So, when we had the Tetley acquisition (in 2000), we did not have a planeload of Indians descending on Greenford (West London) saying, 'Okay, now it's goodbye to the chief financial officer, goodbye to the chief technical officer.'"[5]

Likewise, when Tata Steel bought Corus, Ratan Tata stated that "our intention is that Corus will retain its identity for the foreseeable future, will remain an Anglo Dutch company."[6]

Instead, Tata Steel created an umbrella management team, or a "group center," that consisted of senior Corus Group and Tata Steel executives, co-chaired by Tata Steel's managing director B. Muthuraman and Corus CEO Philippe Varin. The group center was set up to ensure a common approach across all key functions: technology, integration, finance, strategy, corporate relations, communications, and global markets.

Still, both parties had concerns. A few months after the 2007 acquisition, Corus hired Communicaid, a European culture and communications skills consultancy, to run a series of courses on understanding Indian business culture for senior Corus management in London. "We aim to minimize the impact culture can have on the relationships between Corus and Tata Steel," Corus' head of communications said in a statement at the time.[7]

Despite Tata's relatively hands-off approach, and Corus's bid to understand Tata, cultural differences have caused strain and frustration. In May 2011, Tata Group Chairman Ratan Tata lashed out at the work culture of British managers, citing poor performance at Corus and Jaguar Land Rover (JLR) as prime examples. Mr. Tata said managers at the two firms were unwilling to work hard in critical situations, but their Indian counterparts would work till midnight in "a war-like situation."[8]

"It's a work ethic issue. In my experience, in both Corus and Jaguar Land Rover, nobody is willing to go the extra mile," he said in an interview with the *Times Daily.* "The entire engineering group at JLR would be empty on Friday evening, and you have got delays in product introduction. That's the thing that doesn't happen in China or in Indonesia or in Thailand or in Singapore," he said.

Like the case of "Ganga," the Indian pharmaceutical company that bought the ailing British drug maker, the difference in work culture between the go-go East and the more mature Western markets has emerged as a major thorn. In Asia, employees work longer hours than people in the West and, in some countries, would never dream of leaving the office before their boss does, even if it's 7 or 8 p.m.

Whether Mr. Tata's complaints are valid is unclear. *Economic Times* columnist Sudeshna Sen, who took issue with Mr. Tata's diatribe, noted that Europeans strive to achieve a work-life balance that doesn't exist in much of Asia. People in the West also don't have cheap, live-in domestic help, which is common among many middle-class Asians. "If you don't leave work by 5 p.m. to pick up your kids, chances are they'll be left at the gates of the crèche waiting in sub-zero weather," wrote Ms. Sen. It's an issue more Asian companies will need to grapple with as they head West. As for Tata, the recent outburst by the company's chairman indicates that gaps in culture, outlook, and expectations plague the company's European operations even though years have passed since those acquisitions took place.

The challenges faced by these two Indian acquirers illustrate the pitfalls that differences in corporate culture, business norms, and national culture, which impact how people communicate, can create in a merger or acquisition. Executives can avoid these pitfalls if they know what to look for and expect the unexpected.

 ## NATIONAL CULTURE AND COMMUNICATION: WHAT THE INTERPRETER WON'T TELL YOU

The first 100 days of a merger can set the tone of relationships and lay the groundwork for capturing synergies. Communication is everything during this critical point, yet it's the time when cultural gaps can create the biggest pitfalls.

As discussed, many Asian cultures encourage deference to the boss, so employees don't like to contradict their superiors or offer their opinion unless it's solicited. That's a bad thing when executives from an acquiring company want to understand issues at the target company and figure out what to fix and where they can wring the most synergies. Executives who have worked on mergers in Asia say they have sometimes had to get the boss to leave the room to have a productive conversation in a meeting situation.

Some Asians also don't like giving bad news, partly because they don't want to stick their own neck on the line or appear to come up short and partly because they want to "save face." When Renault sent Carlos Ghosn to Japan to turn Nissan around after the two companies merged, he ran into this issue: Middle managers tried to cover up problems and reported that everything in their unit was fine. Mr. Ghosn, speaking at a private seminar, described the situation as a "garden full of hundreds of stones" that he had to turn over, one by one. He had to win each manager over and slowly wring the truth out before he could find out what the company's myriad problems were.

Cultural differences can affect the timing and pace of mergers as well. In 2002, a Japanese technology manufacturing company and an American competitor agreed to transfer their manufacturing operations to a new stand-alone company. The Japanese company was to run the new entity. When the merger team sat down together to map out the transition, the cultural differences became apparent: Japanese people are conservative and like to move slowly during M&A, to better accommodate the unknown. Americans, on the other hand, accomplish multiple tasks in the shortest possible time. Indeed, executives from the American technology company felt "Day One," the formal transaction target date, should take place within three months or so. The deal had been announced, and the American company wanted to move as quickly as possible to complete the merger to assure clients that it was business as usual. The Japanese, however, wanted a horizon of six or seven months to study the American company's operations and acquire sufficient confidence about merging the two operations and operating it as one entity. "It took ages to get an agreement on anything," says one executive involved in the deal.

People from different cultures often communicate in starkly different ways. Consider the differences between how people in China and the United States highlight the key points in a discussion. In a meeting, a U.S. executive will typically state his or her main point right away, then follow it up with supporting evidence. A Chinese executive tends to talk in a more roundabout fashion, starting off with anecdotes and illustrations, and saving the big point for the end.

Japanese people tend not to say "no" even though they disagree; in Japan, if someone hasn't given a resounding "yes," it's understood by other Japanese that they don't agree at all. Needless to say, that can be confusing to a foreign executive. During the merger talks between the Japanese technology manufacturing company and its American competitor, for example, discussions over which production line would be closed were mired by this kind of confusion. Each party wanted to maintain its own production line and wanted the other company to take the hit. The American executives argued that the Japanese company's facility was smaller and didn't have the same economical scale as theirs and should, therefore, be the one to be shuttered. The Japanese executives said that yes, they understood. In their minds, however, they hadn't agreed to close the line, but the American executives thought they had.

In cross-border mergers there is "phenomenal scope for misunderstanding," says Stuart Chambers, former chief executive of Nippon Sheet Glass. Nippon Sheet Glass bought U.K. glass manufacturer Pilkington Plc, which Mr. Chambers used to head, in 2006, and made him the CEO of the enlarged entity. Confusion over what people had said or agreed to during the merger meetings was a major problem.

"For example, at meetings during integration with various heads of departments—with professional translators, and some of the staff were proficient in English—we would agree on something and go our separate ways. Every time I would write down in an email exactly what I felt we had agreed, but about half the time it came back that that was not what we had agreed at all. If I had executed what I thought was understood, imagine the mistrust and frustration that would generate," says Mr. Chambers.[9]

"It's not a question of the words, these are translated and understood, but what is meant by those words and goals is different according to different cultures. When meeting with people from different cultures, go back and check that everyone has understood what has been agreed upon." Some of these complexities may have played out in Mr. Chambers' experience at the company; he resigned one year after taking on the role, citing a desire to move back home and focus on his family. He acknowledged that the decision went against the social norms in Japan, where workers often put their company first. "In that process I have learned I am not Japanese," he told reporters in 2009.[10]

LOCAL BUSINESS CULTURE CAN SHAPE THE FOCUS OF A COMPANY

The amount of time that boards spend on different stakeholders varies between countries, which can further confound companies pursuing cross-border deals.

Japanese boards, for example, spend around 70 percent of their energy and commitments on customers, 25 percent on employees, and 5 percent on shareholders, said Stuart Chambers, former chief executive of Nippon Sheet Glass. Nippon Sheet Glass bought U.K. glass manufacturer Pilkington Plc and acquired Mr. Chambers, then head of Pilkington, in the process.

British and American firms, on the other hand, spend 50 percent of their time worrying about shareholders, 25 percent on employees, and another 25 percent on customers. The difference in focus can impact corporate culture, strategy, and outlook in myriad ways. Striking a compromise may be the best way forward. In the case of Nippon Sheet Glass, Mr. Chambers noted during his tenure: "I have amended my attitude to some extent, and my Japanese colleagues have done that as well."*

*Tor Ching Li, "Nippon Sheet Glass CEO Stresses Need for Clarity—Ensuring Understanding Is Key for a Company With Different Cultures," *Wall Street Journal*–Managing in Asia, April 6, 2009, page 20.

CORPORATE CULTURE MATTERS: MAKING MIXED MARRIAGES WORK

The failed merger talks between Kirin and Suntory illustrate how wide the gap can be when two different corporate cultures clash, particularly when neither party wants to give up its way of doing things. The corporate culture of a company is reflected in a multitude of ways: how decisions are made, how staff work together, how customers are approached, and how deftly the company handles and adapts to change. When companies consider a merger, they need to ask key questions: Is the other organization flat or hierarchical, is decision making decentralized or top-down, is the organization team-based, or do superstars rule the day? The issues that killed the merger of Kirin and Suntory are common in Asia and raise more questions: Is the company family-run, controlled by its founder, or run by independent professionals?

Even two companies that are publicly owned and share the same nationality can have key cultural differences.

Consider the merger of Bank of Tokyo Mitsubishi Ltd and UFJ Bank Ltd: The two banks merged at the holding company level in 2004, creating Japan's largest bank. In the typical Japanese go-slow approach to mergers, the actual banking entities continued to operate separately for another two years. In 2006, the units were finally combined into the Bank of Tokyo-Mitsubishi UFJ, Ltd.

The two banks had markedly different corporate cultures. UFJ had a market-driven culture fostered by aggressive, outspoken leaders. Mitsubishi, which was highly structured and organized, was viewed as stuffy and elitist.[11] The slow pace of integration did nothing to bridge the gap; rather, it allowed the different camps to hunker in their silos, awaiting the next, slow move. When the banks finally became one, discontent set in. The hierarchical culture of Mitsubishi, the larger bank, dominated, and many good UFJ staff, unable or unwilling to adapt, left the organization. The bank continues to hold on to its number one spot, but loss of talent during any merger can only erode optimum value creation.

Failure to forge a common corporate culture during a merger can haunt a company for many years after the deal is signed.

Consider the case of Mizuho Financial Group. The Japanese financial giant was formed in 2002 by the three-way merger of Dai-Ichi Kangyo Bank, Fuji Bank, and the Industrial Bank of Japan. The merged entity sought to cater to the leadership of each founding bank by creating a delicate balance of power: The top slots at the new group were parceled out among executives from the three founding banks, who continued to operate their own silos much as before. The awkward balancing act was criticized as inefficient and was widely seen to have weakened competitiveness and hurt earnings growth.[12]

It also kept the banks from forming a common culture. A survey conducted a year after the merger took place showed that many employees were dissatisfied and could not "rid themselves of the awareness of which bank they came from," according to a *Nikkei* article in October 2003.

The situation came to a head during the March 2011 earthquake in Japan: Massive donation transfer requests overwhelmed Mizuho's computer system, causing a breakdown in the bank's network of automated teller machines (ATMs). The infighting and finger pointing that ensued shone a spotlight on the lack of cohesiveness of the bank's deeply divided executive team. The bank announced it would shake up its executive line-up and restructure operations to regain trustworthiness after the staggering system failure.

Yasuhiro Sato, who became the bank's new chief executive as part of the restructuring, pledged to change the corporate culture of the bank and expedite integration. "We'll speed up working toward becoming one entity," said Mr. Sato, who was, and will remain, head of Mizuho's wholesale banking unit. "Earlier, it was kind of hard to tell who was really in charge of the company."[13]

Mr. Sato said that cultural differences between the bank's units represented the biggest hurdle to integrating operations. "Building a new corporate culture swiftly is my task," Mr. Sato said at a June press conference.

EXPECT THE UNEXPECTED: LOCAL BUSINESS CULTURE AND NORMS CAN BE COSTLY AND SURPRISING

Business practices that are considered unusual at home may be entirely acceptable in another country, and compliance standards vary. Both can result in hidden costs and complexities during an acquisition. This kind of business culture gap made the purchase of a Chinese freight company by a Western multinational logistics operator more complicated that anyone had anticipated.

The Chinese freight company had a strong "Clan" culture (see "Put a label on it" later in this chapter), and the founder served as something of a patriarch. A large part of his management team even came from his own home village. He demanded unflinching support on the one hand, yet "took care" of his own, handing out perks and favors to people who needed it and supported him. Many of his team members, for example, owned several of the line-haul trucks the freight company used, a status quo that the owner condoned, partly because fringe benefits such as this allowed salaries to stay low.

This practice is typical of many Chinese transportation companies. A common result, though, is that employees will delay the loading of certain line-haul trucks and wait for their own trucks to arrive or will load their own trucks with lighter freight to save on gas, allocating heavier loads to somebody else's vehicles to maximize personal profit. Of course, this is a cause of poor performance and unreliability.

This fringe benefit approach created operational performance issues, and it posed a major post-merger problem for the multinational buyer, which followed a structured set of compliance rules, ethical guidelines, and procurement standards. It took more than a year for the acquiring company to unravel the network of side deals and impose a more merit-based corporate culture.

Poor understanding and bad management of cultural gaps and business practices has killed several cross-border mergers in China. One high-profile M&A failure involved the joint venture between food conglomerate Danone and Chinese beverage giant Wahaha. Danone, which owns a 51 percent stake in 39 Danone-Wahaha joint ventures, accused Wahaha of defrauding it by setting up its own companies to make products identical to those produced by their joint ventures, and selling branded drinks without Danone's permission. Another example is the merger between Ernst & Young and Shanghai Dahua, which resulted in lost employees and customers due to inadequate management of different cultures and business practices.

HOW TO BRIDGE THE CULTURE GAP

Executives heading into a merger or acquisition can troubleshoot almost any cultural gap if they know what to look for, and have an action plan. Here are eight strategies to help smooth over differences and make any kind of mixed marriage work.

Do a Cultural Audit

Culture is a key determinant in the success of mergers, but a limited time frame exists at the start of an integration exercise in which cultural differences can be managed before rifts and resistance set in. The program office or integration team needs to appreciate and anticipate the differences between cultures of the merging organizations and build the appropriate contingency plans into the merger plan (see Figure 8.1).

The key tool for this kind of pre-planning is a cultural audit. Typically conducted by an internal HR team or an HR consulting company, the cultural audit is designed to highlight the key differences in the organizations. These will include the culture inherent in the structure, systems, and processes, the prevailing management style and skills, and even the staff's background. It should identify possible "pain points" and establish actions that can improve the situation.

Consider the audit conducted on two merging banks with different corporate cultures: The audit found that Bank A was product-centric, with a comparatively flat structure and strong internal focus on co-workers; Bank B, in contrast, was customer-centric, with a hierarchical structure and a strong external focus on customers.

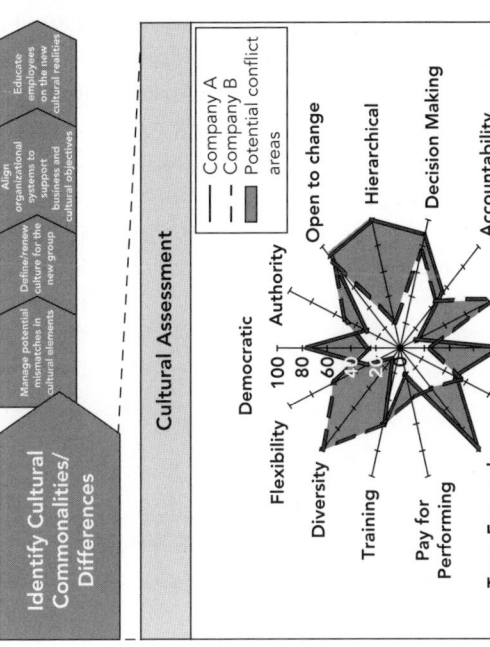

What (and How Much) to Harmonize?

- **What elements of the new business must be integrated to release value?**
  – What decisions need to be made together?
  – Who needs to work together, and how?
- **What kinds of behavior are critical to competitive advantage? How well do the current cultures perform?**
  – Today's business?
  – Tomorrow's business?

How (and How Fast) to Harmonize?

- Is the main rationale for the merger to grow revenues or to improve efficiency by cutting costs or assets?
- How similar or different are the beliefs and behaviors of the two organizations to begin with?
- What are the relative sizes of the organizations?
- What are the regulatory (or other) constraints?

Identify Cultural Commonalities/Differences | Manage potential mismatches in cultural elements | Define/renew culture for the new group | Align organizational systems to support business and cultural objectives | Educate employees on the new cultural realities

Cultural Assessment

Legend:
— Company A
– – Company B
▓ Potential conflict areas

Chart axes: Open to change, Hierarchical, Decision Making, Accountability, Customer Focus, Conflict Management, Aggressiveness, Team Focused, Pay for Performing, Training, Diversity, Flexibility, Democratic, Authority
Scale: 100, 80, 60, 40, 20

FIGURE 8.1 Identify and Proactively Address Cultural Issues That Impact the Value Capture Program
Source: A.T. Kearney analysis.

The audit concluded that the management styles of the banks were different: In one, key decisions were centralized, and in the other, they were devolved to divisions. The key takeaway for the merger program office was clear: During the transition period, managers had to be aware of their precise roles and responsibilities in decision making. Any ambiguity could lead to confusion and potentially destabilize the integration.

Some audits specifically focus on differences in corporate culture and management style. Cultural audits can cover a broader range of issues, such as differences in communication style and local culture. A cultural audit can troubleshoot poor post-merger morale by helping parties on both sides understand who is acquiring them and what that will mean for individual employees since misperceptions can do more to derail morale than gaps between two company's cultures.

One strategy is to assemble a group of key individuals from both companies to generate a consensual view of each organization's culture. The next step is to ask that group to create a shared vision of the desired, shared culture of the merged organization (see Figure 8.2). A good cultural audit, or assessment, can drive this exercise.

When GE Capital's Japan (GE Japan) unit bought Sanyo Electric Credit, GE's in-house team conducted a cultural audit to help get staff from both units on board a few days after the legal merger. Sanyo Electric Credit was an established company with a major reach in the Japanese market, and GE Japan was

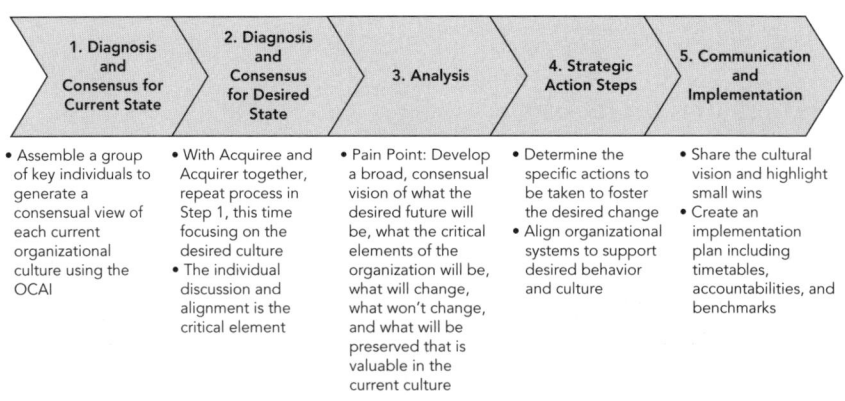

FIGURE 8.2 An Organization Culture Assessment Instrument Is a Tested Methodology for Designing Cultural Harmonization

Source: A.T. Kearney, Cameron, K., and Quinn, R. Note: OCAI—Adapted from *Diagnosing and Changing Organisational Culture* (1999).

a world-beating company with a strong brand. The HR team put together two groups from both companies, and asked the GE Japan people their perceptions of Sanyo Credit's culture, their perception of their own corporate culture, and what they, the GE Japan staff, imagined GE Japan might look like to Sanyo. They asked the same three questions of the Sanyo team.

It became quickly apparent that both teams felt the other party had strengths they couldn't compete with and were apprehensive about working together as a merged entity. The emphasis was on the differences between the two organizations and not the similarities. The Sanyo people, for example, felt that GE Japan had a performance-oriented corporate culture, where only top performers would flourish and be happy, and everyone else would flounder. They saw GE Japan as this global powerhouse that could back its staff with all kinds of gun power, including magic bullet strategies and tools to generate new business. The truth was that GE Japan was the result of an earlier takeover of another Japanese company, and though some of that GE Japan culture was there, it was still largely a Japanese organization. No magic bullets existed. Instead, the top performers reached their goals through hard work, the same way as Sanyo Credit's staff had always done.

During the course of the cultural audit, staff discovered more similarities than differences between the two organizations. This realization made it easier to set common goals, create mixed teams, and get staff working together during the early days of the merger. The exercise reduced merger anxiety and moderated expectations, equally important in maintaining staff morale in the post-merger period.

Put a Label on It

Most corporations can be categorized into one of four widely recognized organizational cultures: Clan, Adhocracy, Hierarchy, and Market (see Figure 8.3). A Clan culture is characterized by a friendly, consensus-driven environment and a strong sense of loyalty, tradition, and commitment, and it is run by leaders who are viewed as mentors. In an Adhocracy, leaders are typically risk takers who value individual initiative and foster a dynamic, innovative environment. In a Hierarchy, leaders are strong coordinators and operate in a formal, structured environment that relies on procedure and values predictability, stability, and security. A Market corporate culture promotes a result-oriented, competitive environment, meaning it's all about getting the job done. Leaders are demanding and goal-oriented, and they drive their staff hard.

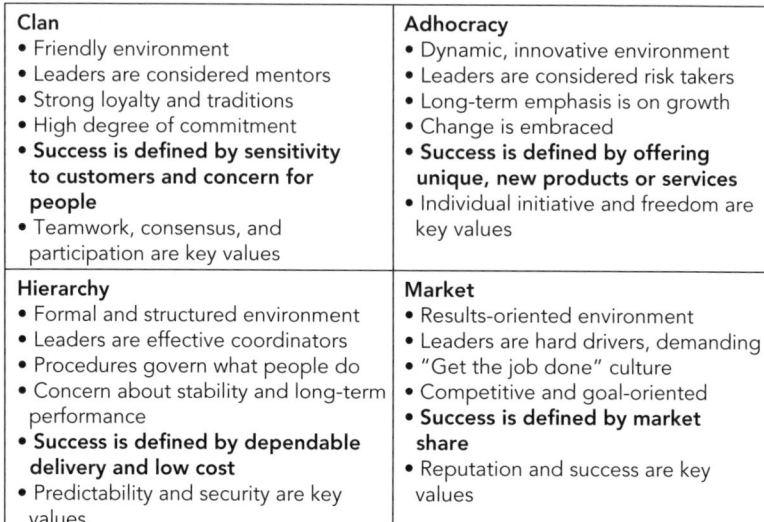

Clan	Adhocracy
• Friendly environment	• Dynamic, innovative environment
• Leaders are considered mentors	• Leaders are considered risk takers
• Strong loyalty and traditions	• Long-term emphasis is on growth
• High degree of commitment	• Change is embraced
• **Success is defined by sensitivity to customers and concern for people**	• **Success is defined by offering unique, new products or services**
• Teamwork, consensus, and participation are key values	• Individual initiative and freedom are key values
Hierarchy	Market
• Formal and structured environment	• Results-oriented environment
• Leaders are effective coordinators	• Leaders are hard drivers, demanding
• Procedures govern what people do	• "Get the job done" culture
• Concern about stability and long-term performance	• Competitive and goal-oriented
• **Success is defined by dependable delivery and low cost**	• **Success is defined by market share**
• Predictability and security are key values	• Reputation and success are key values

FIGURE 8.3 The Four Organizational Cultures

Source: K.S. Cameron and R.E. Quinn, Organization Culture Assessment Instrument (OCAI) (1999); A.T. Kearney analysis.

When companies enter merger talks or conduct a cultural audit, figuring out which category each company slots into is a good idea when it comes to corporate culture. Categorizing the company by culture can help the program office understand, before the ball gets rolling, how each party might approach things and allow merger parties to anticipate potential challenges. Two companies with different corporate cultures will mesh poorly unless the integration is handled carefully, and the program office takes those differences into account when mapping its strategy.

Consider the merger of Bank of Tokyo Mitsubishi Ltd and UFJ Bank Ltd we talked about earlier. UFJ, which was run by leaders who were risk takers, belonged to the Adhocracy camp; larger Mitsubishi had more of a Hierarchy-driven corporate culture. The leaders failed to address the differences early on, and as a result, the dissimilarities festered during the slow integration. Mitsubishi's hierarchical culture became the norm, and many UFJ staff, clinging to their identity years after the merger, resigned. If the bank's leadership had identified the differences in corporate culture at the outset and taken steps to forge some common bonds, it could have defused the onset of merger syndrome before it became entrenched.

Communication Is Key

Failure to communicate with employees—particularly those who work for the company that's being acquired—creates tensions and heightens cultural differences. Companies that succeed in mergers that span corporate or national cultures tend to communicate with employees from the first stages of the acquisition. To create an atmosphere that supports cultural change, companies should understand each other's culture and people should be willing to work together after the merger. That can only be achieved with clear and regular communication between employees of the two organizations.[14]

The story of the Indian pharmaceutical company, Ganga, that bought the ailing British drug maker, C-Pharma, underscores the need to conduct a cultural due diligence before integration and make use of communication levers to bring about successful change. Executives interviewed after the merger conceded that many post-merger problems could have been circumvented if they had involved and communicated with employees at every stage of the process. Employees resisted change because of lack of communication, and explaining how the changes would benefit them could have brought staff on board much earlier.

When Standard Chartered Bank for South Korea bought Korea First Bank in 2005, winning over Korean employees was at the top of the agenda from day one, and communication was the key pillar of the company's strategy. "It was a question of meeting several times a week on how are we doing, what are we communicating, what else do we need to communicate, what needs to be done?" Tom McCabe, who was chief executive officer of Standard Chartered at the time, told the *Wall Street Journal*. "A lot of feedback groups of employees walked the floor several times a day and would meet with different groups of staff."

McCabe was keenly aware that a lot of uncertainty existed among employees. Several banks had merged shortly before Standard Chartered's acquisition, resulting in significant job losses. There were differences in both organizational and national cultures that had to be bridged, as well. "People want to be dealt with as individuals, they want to be dealt with in a respectful way. So, you need to make sure you approach everything with what's going to be the payoff, what's in it for the employees, what's in it for the customer, the other stakeholders, the community," said Mr. McCabe. "So you start finding common bonds and common goals, and you work from there."

Out of meetings with the staff came the idea for what Mr. McCabe calls the Korea Day Concept, which was designed to showcase Standard Chartered as an attractive employer. The bank sent around 100 employees from Korea to 40 markets in Asia and the Middle East, where they learned about the bank's operations and what it was like to work there. Upon return, those employees held a series of meetings to share what they had learned with other staff. This program defused many anxieties and misperceptions about working for the bank and led to the success of the acquisition, according to McCabe.[15]

Leverage Your 100-Day Plan to Foster Team Spirit

A good 100-day plan can help the leadership teams from the two merged entities get organized and focused on the goals at hand. It can bring people together. In Chapter 6, we describe how a 100-day plan is a critical tool during the pre-merger and early post-merger phase. Under a typical 100-day plan, executives create joint teams and assign responsibility and goals those teams must deliver on during the first 100 days of a merger. This means the people in both entities must get to know each other and work together from the outset; the spirit of cooperation that arises naturally nips the cultural clashes in the bud that can derail a merger. A good 100-day plan delineates and times internal communications, one of the most important tools in heading off potential cultural clashes.

Consider the case of an Asian semiconductor test and assembly company that bought a U.S. competitor: Its 100-day plan, which was originally designed to focus on areas where they could capture synergies, integrate operations, and address overlapping customers, eased many concerns staff from both sides had about working for and with each other.

Going into meetings of the joint team charged with executing the 100-day plan, the Asian managers were concerned that their more assertive counterparts would dominate or resist working with them; the American employees were worried their jobs would be impacted by the acquisition. During the meetings, however, consultants facilitated discussions between the Asian managers, who spoke less, and the Americans, who expressed their views and spoke more directly and assertively. This approach helped defuse many preconceived notions and apprehensions on both sides.

Creating the joint teams, which were staffed by operational managers and their direct reports, helped convey the message that the Asian acquirer wasn't going to come in and wipe out the entire management, and that both sides had a role in the new organization. It created a space for both sides to articulate their concerns and priorities and raise any key issues in an open manner. The acquisition and integration went smoothly, thanks in large part to the importance placed on team building under the 100-day plan.

Understand the Web of Relationships

Global companies who do M&A in places such as China need to understand the web of relationships behind local target companies. Complicated relationships often exist between suppliers, internal employees, customers, and local government officials. The initial due diligence may not uncover unethical practices that are often costly to untangle.

New entrants must navigate these relationships carefully, since they often form the basis of employees' steady incomes. Before closing a deal, companies should seek to discover hidden incentives within the company's relationships. After a deal, change that is too sudden or abrasive could lead to widespread dissatisfaction and sabotage. Savvy managers with an awareness of company culture and protocol are essential for building relationships. An assessment of the complex relationships and power bases will help identify "change agents" in the company, which can offer these individuals incentives to align their interests with those of the company.

That's how A.T. Kearney helped the Western multinational logistics company troubleshoot some of the integration issues with the Chinese freight company it had acquired from its Clan-style owner. During the owner's tenure, the web of relationships extended to relatives who supplied trucking services to the company. Moving quickly to end the system of outsourcing trucking contracts to employees' families would have angered many; it was deemed better to take a slow approach to this sensitive issue. Regional managers ran their units like a fiefdom; so, we went to each location to explain the benefits of a more transparent, merit-driven tendering system. The company put a performance management system in place that rewarded profitability, and once regional managers realized that bringing on more efficient truckers would improve operational capacity and allow the unit to take on more business, they began to come on board. The new owner was able to find enough key stakeholders among the regional management ranks to support the move to an open, transparent tender system.

Watch for Hidden Costs

In countries such as China, compliance-related costs for a foreign company acquiring a domestic target often increase post-acquisition, sometimes as much as 30 percent. This is because foreign companies typically have stronger compliance and responsibility policies than domestic companies, which focus on expediency. Because there is reluctance to explore gray areas in tax, labor, health, and safety due to fear of corporate liability, compliance costs tend to arise after the deal is closed (see Figure 8.4 for other potential areas).

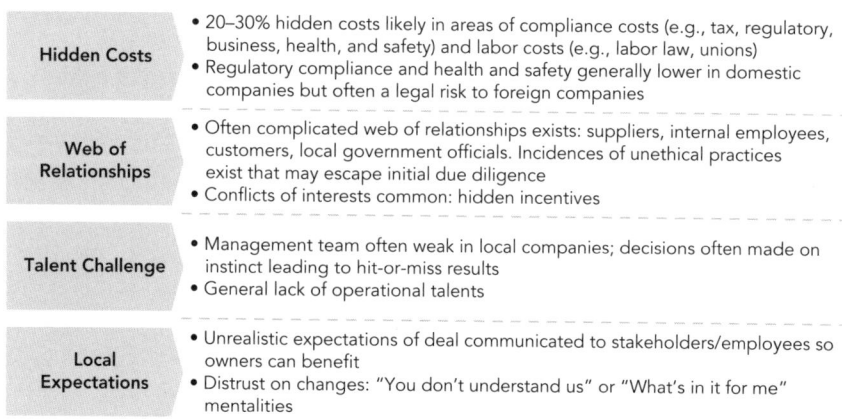

FIGURE 8.4   Potential Areas of Hidden Costs—China Logistics M&A Example
Source: A.T. Kearney analysis.

Let's focus on a few key areas where compliance costs often shoot up (see Figure 8.5). Labor costs in China, for example, tend to rise by as much as 8 to 15 percent when companies move to fulfill the letter of the labor law. Many Chinese companies don't offer all the benefits required under law, and enforcement is typically lax. When foreign companies, who must adhere to the local law to meet their own internal conduct codes, step in, costs often rise. Local companies tend to evade anywhere from 25 to 50 percent of business and income taxes. When we add all that up, the net margin could decrease by 3 to 5 percent, which can have a 2 to 4 percent negative impact on overall profitability.

Among the benefits that many companies do not offer are, for example, employee health benefits and safety programs. However, foreign entities usually cannot sustain these cost savings, as the legal and corporate risks are much higher. Imagine the ramifications if a newspaper reported the number of annual deaths caused by a lack of health and safety programs.

China has a new labor law, which may be another challenge for foreign companies struggling to control incremental costs. The law requires compliance with labor-related issues, emphasizes formal contracts, and mandates a minimum wage and social benefits. But many local companies fail to follow strictly or enforce the law. So, when a foreign buyer acquires a local company, it may face unexpected costs getting the company into compliance. Profits may appear higher because the target has not been following the labor law, an approach that's not available to international companies, which typically have strict ethical and legal compliance guidelines.

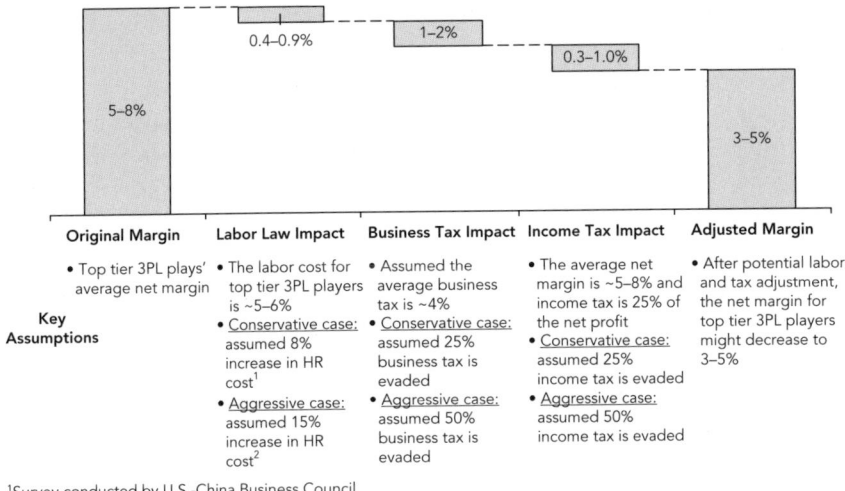

FIGURE 8.5 Potential Profit Impact from Compliance
Source: A.T. Kearney analysis.

The new law may benefit international firms, as most have such corporate labor guidelines in place, a state of affairs that levels the playing field for foreign and domestic firms and creates room for competition.

During the pre-close phase, it is nonetheless wise to conduct due diligence to understand the hidden costs that may arise after the acquisition and build this knowledge into the business case. Once the deal is done, it is important to manage incremental costs by understanding local regulations and practices.

Address the Talent Challenge

There is often a lack of educated, experienced operational talent in developing countries. Important decisions are often based on instinct rather than information and analysis, leading to hit-or-miss results.

Though acquiring companies often send finance or human resources teams to the target company, they rarely do so for operations, as they assume the new acquisition has enough capability to be successful. Yet operations are often the toughest nut to crack. Acquired companies, proud of their operations and past success, can become defensive and resistant to change. Rigorous due diligence is essential for assessing the target company's true operational and human capabilities before a deal is agreed and ensuring the acquiring company gets what it pays for.

According to research by executive search firm Korn/Ferry International, the talent shortage in Asia is severe. Asia's economies, once driven by manufacturing, have moved on from their role as the workshop to the world in the past few years: Domestic consumption is driving growth, and Asia's economies, which recovered fastest from the 2008–2009 global financial crisis, are driving global growth. The kind of talent needed to succeed in this era is thin on the ground. Korn/Ferry estimates that 4 percent of managers and 5 percent of executives in Asia have the skills needed by companies today. The figure is worse in China: Just 1 percent of managers and 1 percent of executives have the competencies needed for the future.[16]

An acquiring company might do well to take a page from SingTel's book. The company, which has stakes in regional mobile companies all over Asia, transfers senior-level and operational-level staff for one-year or two-year stints. This practice helps transfer learning and skill and is a key prong in the company's bid to strengthen the local talent pool.

Providing full-time, on-site operations leadership or support with a focus on winning the trust of the local operations team can improve operational performance after a deal.

Manage Local Expectations

It is important to communicate with local workers during the acquisition process rather than leave it to the target company's management. Many employees in domestic companies in Asia, for example, think that working for foreign companies means better salaries and an easier workload. The owner of the target company may promise employees huge salary increases or improved benefits to generate approval for a sale. When such promises go unfulfilled, the resulting distrust and low morale will hurt production. In China's domestic logistics sector, where the companies are usually decentralized with strong local power bases, there will be resistance to top-down changes that jeopardize local interests. An effective employee communication program implemented early in the process can mitigate false and unrealistic expectations. Revamping the incentives system, building up trust and credibility, and engaging in honest communication can counteract resistance. A strong leader with first-rate people skills can help bridge cultural differences and close the talent gap.

IT'S NOT AS HARD AS IT SEEMS

Managing cultural differences in a merger or acquisition is not about erasing one culture or building a new culture from scratch. Instead, it's about doing your research, being aware, and communicating well.

It is an ongoing challenge to cope with various cultural differences, such as regional or business-specific cultures versus corporate values and beliefs. From our experience, acknowledging cultural differences and stimulating awareness and acceptance through extensive, timely, and well-coordinated communication and the exchange of key people is more effective than designing a theoretically ideal culture from scratch.

Why? Because the target company's people want to know their culture and heritage are not going to be discarded even as the acquirer's staff is concerned about its culture being diluted. Failure to address these two constituencies' concerns can lead to low morale and retention issues. The point isn't so much to create a hybrid culture as to address these softer issues head-on before resentment and misunderstanding set in.

CULTURE CHECKLIST

1. **Never assume:** Don't head into an integration thinking that staff from other companies, countries, or cultures will approach issues or communicate the way you do. It's probably safer to assume they won't.
2. **When in Rome, investigate:** Take the time to learn about the local business norms and practices. International companies with global standards and codes of conduct can't always do what the Romans do.
3. **Create a road map:** Do a cultural audit to map and address culture differences. Building bridges should be a priority.
4. **Brace yourself for added costs:** Assume hidden costs will appear when doing business in developing countries.
5. **Turn the tables:** The growing number of Asian acquirers snapping up companies in the West face a new host of cultural challenges. Address the West-East gaps early and defuse stereotypes before they become a problem.

ACKNOWLEDGMENTS

The following A.T. Kearney white papers were used as background material in writing this chapter: "Making Your Chinese Merger 'Marriage' Work," by Mui-Fong Goh, Chee Wee Gan, Jian Li, and Tammy Ku; "Three Years After the Marriage: Merger Integration Revisited," by Jürgen Rothenbücher, Sebastien Declercq, Phil Dunne, Simon Mezger, Pablo Moliner, and Sandra Niewiem; "The Offshore Culture Class," by Marcy Beitle, Arjun Sethi, Jessica Milesko, and Alyson Potenza.

9

Conclusion

A S WE WRITE THIS, the world has entered its second major economic crisis in four years. Europe is gripped by a series of sovereign debt crises, and the United States is facing the prospect of a double-dip recession. Last year, 2011, started off strong but finished with a seemingly endless parade of economic, stock, and earnings downgrades. Analysts agree that the United States and Europe will face several years of slow growth.

Amid all the volatility and uncertainty that's racked the global economy in recent years, one thing is certain: Asia's star is rising. Asia is no longer a workshop to the world, and the region's economies are starting to decouple from the West. Asian consumers are driving domestic growth, and that shift is happening at a critical time. Western consumers are struggling, and it will be years before those economies get back to normal.

Companies across the world were homing in on Asia's consumers before the current crises set in. Asia's middle class is growing at a frenetic pace, and over the next two decades, the bulge of the world's middle class will shift from the West to Asia, according to the Brookings Institution. That agency reckons Asia will be home to 66 percent of the world's middle class by 2030, up from just 28 percent in 2007.

Multinational companies recognize this and are making moves to capitalize on the shift. They're moving research centers to this region and scaling up investment in Asia-driven research and development (R&D): Novartis, Abbott, Cisco Systems, IBM, and General Electric (GE), to name a few, are pouring millions of dollars into R&D facilities in Asia, bringing innovation closer to tomorrow's customer base. They're putting global heads of key divisions, like finance, marketing, and strategy, in Asia, another sign this region will increasingly pilot global growth for many companies. Cisco, for example, created a new position of "chief globalization officer" in 2006 and sited that role in Bangalore. The ongoing global economic crises will add momentum to this trend. Bank of America relocated its global marketing head from Boston to Hong Kong in late 2011. In February 2012, ad agency DDB Worldwide announced it was moving its global creative headquarters to Shanghai. More will follow.

 ## NOW IS THE TIME TO GO ON THE OFFENSIVE

The message is clear: Asia is where it's at. Asian companies must recognize they don't need to be on the defensive during this volatile period. To be sure, Asia's economies are linked to the West and an incidental effect of a global slowdown will occur. The fundamentals in Asia, however, remain strong. We have one message for Asian companies: This is your time. If you want to track Asia's trajectory, you need to think about inorganic growth.

M&A has not traditionally been part of the corporate mindset of many Asian companies. Multinationals have been the predators in almost every sector, and Asian companies have been too fragmented or too focused on creaming the easy profits from the natural, steady organic growth this region has delivered. Now is the time to turn that around and think about regional or global opportunities. Markets are down, the stock prices of multinationals have been hammered, and valuations are low. Asian executives who put inorganic growth on the annual planning agenda can leverage this opportunity and catapult their organization onto the global stage.

 ## M&A THE ASIAN WAY

Asian companies don't need to look to the West for signals or lessons on consolidation. Asia is rewriting the M&A rules. Historically, consolidation happens within the country first, and the big players buy other big players and the smaller guys get the squeeze. That doesn't apply here. It's fine to pursue cross-border deals before you buy domestically. Asian companies have embraced this strategy because they have to: The heavy weight of the public sector in many local economies and the large presence of family-run firms mean certain industries or companies won't consolidate in line with free market forces. That's given rise to a notably higher rate of cross-border activity than you'd theoretically expect, given the state of development of local industries or economies. It's worked fine so far. We think Asian companies should continue to pursue cross-border deals, rather than wait for the public sector or family companies to ponder the benefit of free market forces.

That said, the public sector would do well to add M&A to its own agenda. Public companies owe it to their shareholders and taxpayers to transform themselves into competitive front-runners. M&A is one of the best tools for the job. Governments can use M&A to help create a more competitive domestic industry that can survive and thrive under the inevitable wave of liberalization that's sweeping through the region.

Markets or industries don't need to consolidate fully, in the Western sense. We believe that Asia's fragmented consumer markets will give rise to local optima, which will derive value from different sub-segments. Asian companies with strong local insights are positioned to emerge as champions in this scenario.

Those champions don't need to be big to triumph in the ring. That's another rule that Asia has thrown out the door. Smaller companies can buy bigger rivals, even dominant, global brands. Look at Tetley Tea or Geely. Your company might be small, but your balance sheet may be healthier, and your leverage lower, than bigger, better-known Western brands. That can help aspiring Asian companies move sharply up the value chain by acquiring a better technology or brand or gaining access to new markets.

Global multinational corporations (MNCs) are getting cheaper as their stock prices fall, and they're realizing they've grown too big. That's going to create a "starburst" effect, as companies start selling off bits and pieces that aren't their core business. In 2011, Kraft Foods, ConocoPhillips, Tyco International, and McGraw-Hill announced they would break up their companies to focus on their core operations and maximize shareholder value.[1] The pickings will be plentiful for Asian companies that want to grab a business unit or two and extend their reach westward. The ongoing volatility will continue to foster an environment ripe for spin-offs and divestments.

Asian companies should consider entering markets where global players fear to tread. Indian and Chinese oil and gas companies have made bold acquisitions in countries that multinationals have struggled in, like Vietnam, or can't enter, like Iran. More will follow, sensing opportunity. When the world was gripped by news of Greece's possible default in October 2011, Japan's Mizuho Financial Group quietly took a 15 percent stake in Vietnam's largest listed bank, Vietcombank, for $567 million. The strategic move gives Mizuho a leg up in a fast-growing emerging market that's opening its financial services sectors to foreign companies.

THE KEY TO SUCCESS: PLANNING AHEAD

There are risks en route. The majority of M&A fail to deliver value, largely due to bad planning. All too often, executives make snap decisions without doing proper due diligence, or they fail to understand the cultural differences between the staff or organizations.

Clashes in corporate culture have mired many post-merger integrations, and Asian companies will increasingly need to navigate the complexities of national culture clashes, too. The business culture, management style, and work-life balance differ around the region and differ between East and West. As more Asian companies buy Western competitors, Asian executives will need to build expertise in bridging these cultural gaps.

They need to build, buy, or hire expertise in the fundamentals of M&A. Asian companies don't typically build M&A into their annual planning cycle, but they should. Companies need to understand where their industry is on the consolidation curve, and map a strategy to ensure they come out on top. Companies who are successful at M&A plan and execute their acquisitions with an attention to detail. They use a framework to identify and track potential targets for several quarters or years. They buy companies that fit and can deliver value; they don't buy on impulse.

We are strong advocates of conducting a deep and thorough operational due diligence (ODD) that helps a buyer understand the local subtleties and opportunities for value creation that can be made through operational improvements. M&A are not simply adding a competitor's revenue to your balance sheet; they mean capturing synergies and finding ways to unlock hidden value.

Planning is as critical as execution. The bulk of failed mergers fall apart during integration. The bankers who made the match have taken their fees and departed. This is where the real work begins. Many Asian companies lack the experience in merging two operations and fail to understand the complexity and detail behind this critical part of the job. An integration program team, composed of top-tier, in-house resources and outside experts, should be put in place and empowered to get the job done. We advocate the use of specific tools to identify, test, execute, and track initiatives to unlock synergies, and techniques to equip and motivate line managers, sales staff, HR teams, and IT departments to support and drive value creation.

THINK GLOBALLY, ACT GLOBALLY

Asian companies have gained stature and prominence over the last 15 years, but by and large, the bulk still run export-oriented operations. Only a few have made moves to become global champions. Now is the time to do that. Asia is at an economic tipping point; not only will Asian consumers drive domestic growth, but Asia will become the engine of growth for the world. A structural shift in the economy has occurred, and a corresponding structural shift needs to occur in the mindset and ambitions of Asian companies if they want to become global champions.

Not every company needs to undertake M&A. Still, inorganic growth should be part of each company's planning cycle and long-term strategy.

Everyone wants a piece of Asia. Local players will have plenty of competition going forward from multinationals, but for now, those companies face weakness at home, in terms of their stock price if not earnings growth. The odds are stacked in favor of Asian contenders. This is Asia's time. Make it yours, too.

Appendix
PMI Tools

B ASED ON A.T. KEARNEY'S experience performing numerous post-merger integration (PMI) engagements, we have developed a set of PMI tools that can facilitate project management throughout the merger integration process.

PREPARE FOR AND EXECUTE A PERFECT DAY ONE

Day One Checklist by Function

Description: The checklist contains a consolidated list of actions that each function will need to perform prior to day one.

Objective: This allows each function to prepare to ensure a seamless execution and transition on day one.

Tip: Checklist can include due dates, prioritization of activities, activity interdependencies, and activity owners to promote accountability and task management.

Day One Action Plan

Description: The action plan provides details of all activities to be executed on day one, grouped by key integration categories.

Objective: The project management office uses the action plan to organize the various work streams and to ensure all critical steps are completed on day one.

Tip: Similar to the day one checklist, the day one action plan outlines timing, prioritization of activities, interdependencies, and activity owners.

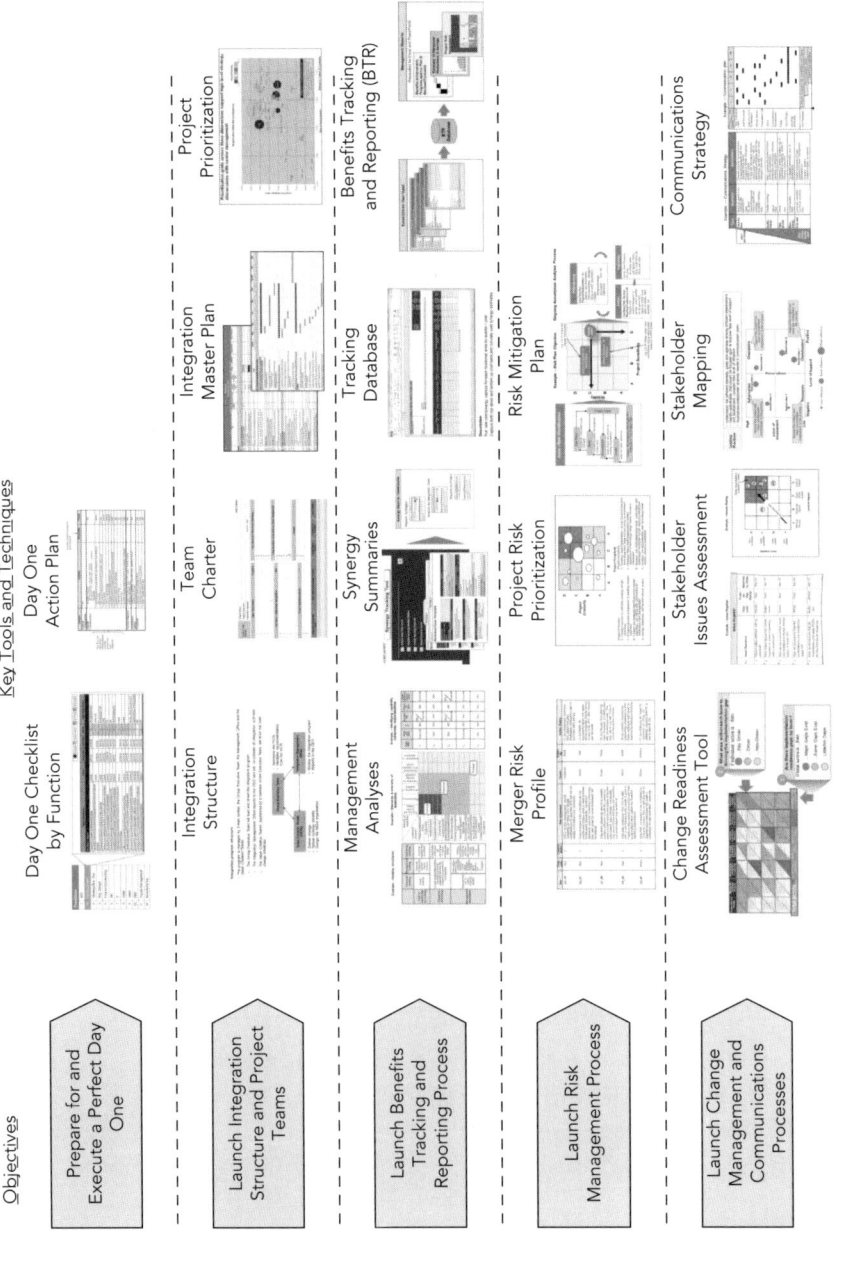

FIGURE A.1 Post-Merger Integration Tools Overview

Detailed Checklist by Function

Example

Functions							
1	IMO						
2	Communication						
3	Strategy/Bus. Dev.						
4	Org. Design						
5	Finance/Connecting						
6	HR						
7	IT						
8	Legal						
9	Sales						
10	R&D						
11	Supply Management						
12	Manufacturing						

					D Delayed · Y Needs Action · G On Track · C Completed		
Major Initiatives		**Owner**	**Start Date**	**End Date**	**Status**	**Interdependency**	
Pre Day 1 / Day 1							
Develop a master communication plan		Joe B.	8/7/10	9/19/10	G	All workstreams	
Develop a Q&A process and messaging for internal and external queries		Joe B.	8/19/10	9/7/10	C	GTM, HR	
Develop and launch revised corporate web site		Joe B.	8/11/10	10/1/10	C	Finance & IT (IT)	
Develop and distribute Pre-Day 1 communication for customers		Joe B.	8/23/10	10/1/10	C	GTM	
Develop Pre-Day 1 communication for all stakeholders		Ann H.	10/30/10	10/1/10	C	HR	
Develop key messages for Works Council presentation (NS)		Ann H.	8/11/10	10/1/10	C	HR	
Develop and launch Pre-Day 1 communication for employees		Ann H.	8/2/10	10/1/10	C	All Workstreams	
Distribute policies on business conduct to NS employees and hotline information		Ann H.	8/18/10	10/1/10	C	Legal	
Notify and support Board of Directors communication		Ann H.	8/11/10	10/1/10	C	Legal	
Develop and support Pre-Day 1 investor communication		Carole B.	8/11/10	10/1/10	C		
Develop Pre-Day 1 Media and External Stakeholder Notification		Carole B.	8/11/10	10/1/10	G	Media, GNO, Finance & IT	
Develop Pre-Day 1 communication plan for vendors		Carole B.	8/11/10	10/1/10	G	Agribusiness, Procurement	
Develop Pre-Day 1 communication for union/hourly employees		Carole B.	8/11/10	10/1/10	Y	HR	
Develop and support benefit communications		Henry Y.	8/31/10	10/1/10	G	HR	

FIGURE A.2 Example of a Day One Checklist by Function

LAUNCH INTEGRATION STRUCTURE AND PROJECT TEAMS

Integration Structure

Description: The integration structure provides an organizational overview of the merger integration process, listing the team members and their roles and responsibilities in executing integration activities.

Objective: This tool allows the project management office to track the groups driving the integration activities and their roles, identify any gaps in responsibilities, and assign resources accordingly.

Team Charter

Description: The team charter is a summary of the initiatives undertaken by each integration team. Most team charters contain three major sections:
1. Description of the team's broad mission and the team's structure and staffing.
2. Key deliverables, potential risks, and project interdependencies.
3. Resources and capabilities required.

Objective: This gives the project management office easy reference to the activities, deliverables, and composition of each team to track initiative progress.

An owner must be assigned to each milestone →

Category	Activities	Responsible	Priority
External Communication	☐ N/A		
Internal Communication	☐ Information sessions • New Hire Session – U.S. and EMEA: Benefits • Exit Session – U.S.: Outplacement, severance, IT equipment coordination		☐ High
	☐ Welcome boxes for all stars, keepers, and integration keys staying 60 days or more		☐ Medium
	☐ New hire and exit packets with information on benefits, rollover, etc.		☐ High
	☐ Buddy system		☐ Medium
	☐ CEO 1:1 with stars begin		☐ Medium
	☐ Corporate communication at buyer's HQ		☐ Medium
	☐ E-mail from CEO to all employees (buyer and seller combined)		☐ High
	☐ Acquisition target site visits worldwide		☐ High
	☐ Leadership briefing		☐ High
	☐ All Hands call		☐ High
	☐ Bi-weekly company update from CEO to all employees (combined)		☐ High
Systems Migration	☐ Transfer HR data into buyer's HR systems (benefits tracking, employee information, etc.)		☐ High
Organization Roll-out	☐ Publish new organization chart with clearly understood lines of reporting and structure		☐ High
Functional	☐ Coordinate retention package roll-out		☐ High
	☐ Coordinate severance payments to transitions		☐ High
	☐ Finalize benefits rollover plan		☐ High

Each Day One Plan should include detailed activities grouped into major categories

FIGURE A.3 Example of a Day One Action Plan

Integration Program Structure

- The program is managed by three main bodies: the Group Executive Team, the Management Office, and the Integration Teams
  - The Group Executive Team will lead and direct the integration program.
  - The Integration Management Office reports to the CEO and will coordinate all integration activities.
  - The Integration Teams, sponsored by a member of the Executive Team, will drive the main change initiatives.

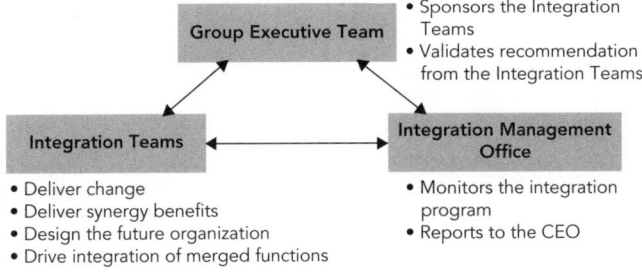

FIGURE A.4 Integration Structure

Integration Master Plan

Description: The integration master plan is the essential operational flight plan of activities, milestones, owners, dependencies, and timelines for all activities in the integration process. The master plan compiles all the initiatives undertaken by each team (in the team charter) into a master schedule.

Objective: The integration master plan:

- Provides an overview of the activities being carried out by each team.
- Allows the project management office to track initiative progress.
- Highlights interdependencies between initiatives.

Tip: The master plan may be subject to ongoing updates as activities are carried out and unexpected changes occur. However, critical milestones and deliverable deadlines should be highlighted to ensure these are not delayed. Highlighting owners of initiatives and prioritizing activities is a good practice.

Project Prioritization

Description: Prioritization of projects is derived from assessing each project's long-term strategic value, its ease of implementation, and financial attractiveness.

Team Charter

Project Team Charter	Project Name:	
	Project Objective:	
	Executive Sponsor:	Revision Date:

Major Deliverables	Deadlines
• X	...
• X	...
• X	...
• X	...
• X	...
• X	...

Key Issues and Risks to Be Addressed

- • X
- • X
- • X
- • X
- • X
- • X

Key Dates—Stakeholder Management	Date
• X	...
• X	...
• X	...
• X	...
• X	...

Likely Decisions to Be Made by Senior Management

- • X
- • X
- • X
- • X
- • X
- • XX

Project Interdependencies

- • X
- • X
- • X

Budget

- • X
- • X
- • X

Resource Functional Area	Skill Sets or Knowledge Needed	Organization Source	Number of People	Estimated Timing

FIGURE A.5 Sample Team Charter

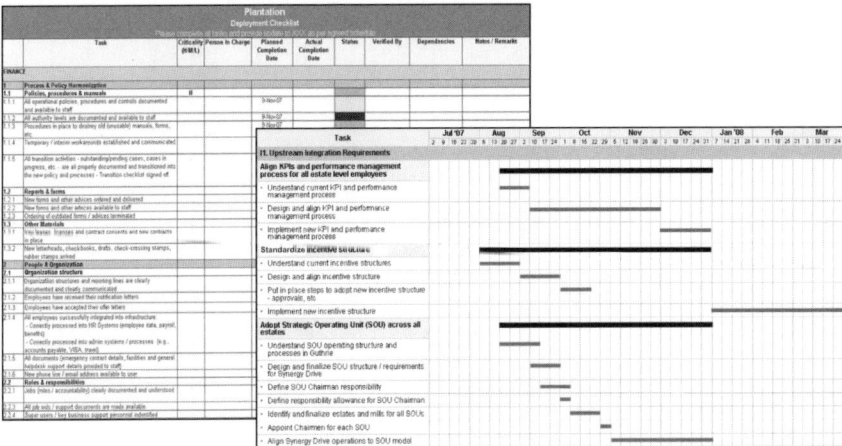

FIGURE A.6 Integrated Work Plan

Objective: This is a strategic assessment of each initiative in the overall integration program. Prioritization is critical in discussions with senior management about making trade-offs or when allocating resources among competing initiatives.

 ## LAUNCH BENEFITS TRACKING AND REPORTING (BTR) PROCESS

Management Analyses

Description: Management analyses target topics that are critical to the goals of the integration process. Such analyses can include the following:
- Characteristics and relationship of the acquiring vs. acquired company.
- Organizational models of the companies.
- Major levers (financial, functional, and strategic) for realizing the value of the merger.
- Capability portfolio analyses of corporate functions.

Objective: Management analyses are performed on information gained from the companies involved to give management a second-level insight into the integration synergies and obstacles. These analyses may throw light on decisions that management needs to resolve during the integration and trade-offs that need to be made (e.g., functions with weak capabilities may be candidates for outsourcing).

174

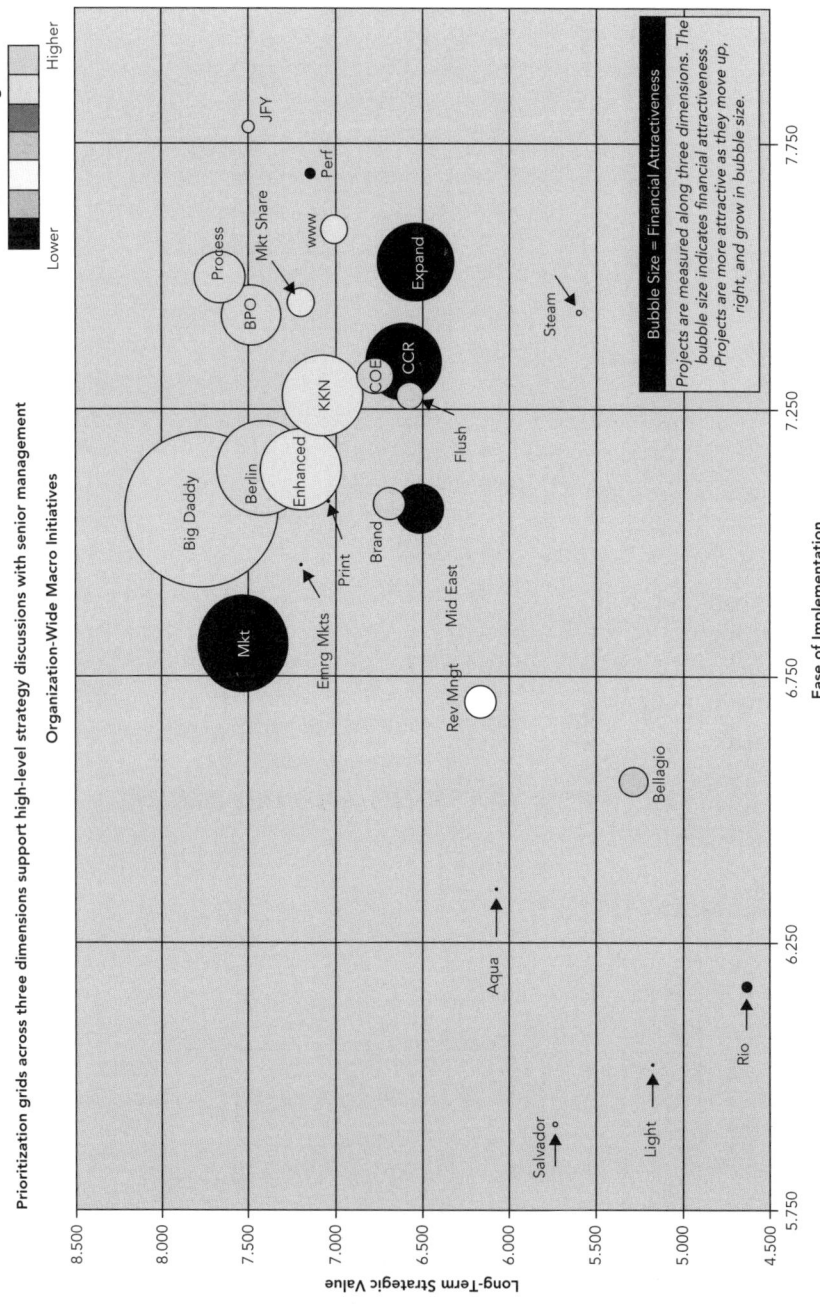

FIGURE A.7 Prioritization Grids

Example—Holding structures

	Financial holding	Management holding	Operating holding
Kind of leadership by holding	Purely financial	Financial, strategic, and specific central functions	Financial, strategic, and functional
Character of holding	Legally independent entities are at the same time organizational units with independent operational management		Organization units need not correspond to legally independent entities
Management orientation	Management only by setting financial targets	The holding carries out: • Leadership functions • Coordination • Strategic orientation • Central tasks • Realization of synergies	Holding dominates in operations: functional link between holding company and subsidiaries

Example—Elements & intensity of leadership

Intensity of leadership / Leadership elements	Finance and liquidity linkage	Risk balancing	Homogeneity of reporting	Utilization of synergy potentials	Development of a corporate culture	Involvement in operations
Financial planning and control						
Credit control						
Investment policy						
Budgeting/budget policy						
Group reporting						
Involvement in the strategic planning process of companies/department						
Internal group auditing						
Working groups on group level						
Personnel, law, and tax department						
Combined group purchase (e.g., accounting, EDP)						
Combined group activities (e.g., materials, finance)						
Common standards of business						
Limiting of the operative competencies						

(Labels within the matrix: Financial, Functional, Strategic)

Example—Identifying capability ownership responsibilities

Capability	Product R&D	HR	Budgeting	Process R&D	Acquisition or Divestment
C_1	Corporate	SBU	SBU / Corporate	SBU	Corporate
C_2	SBU	SBU	SBU	SBU	SBU
C_3	SBU	SBU	SBU / Corporate	SBU	SBU / Corporate
C_4	Corporate	SBU	SBU	SBU	Corporate
C_5	SBU	SBU	SBU	SBU	SBU

FIGURE A.8A Examples of Management Analyses

175

Leadership elements \ Intensity of leadership	Finance and liquidity linkage	Risk balancing	Homogeneity of reporting	Coordination of overlapping corporate interests	Utilization of synergy potentials	Common service departments	Compatibility of business principles	Compatibility of management systems	Common personnel and development policies	Development of a corporate culture	Involvement in operations
Financial planning and control											
Credit control	Financial										
Investment policy											
Budgeting/budget policy											
Group reporting											
Involvement in the strategic planning process of companies/department					Functional						
Internal group auditing											
Working groups on group level											
Personnel, law, and tax department											
Combined group purchase (e.g., accounting, EDP)											
Combined group activities (e.g., materials, finance)											
Common standards of business								Strategic			
Limiting of the operative competencies											

FIGURE A.8B Examples of Management Analyses

Synergy Summaries

Description: Synergy summaries provide details on the expected integration benefits identified during the M&A process prior to day one.

Objective: These summaries provide the project management office with an overview of the synergies expected, the initiatives that need to be executed to achieve the plan, and the resources required.

Tracking Database

Description: The tracking database is a financial summary of the expected benefits of each initiative, derived from the synergy summaries.

Objective: The tracking database provides a quantitative view of the benefits expected from the integration and the targets for each initiative.

Benefits Tracking and Reporting (BTR)

Description: The BTR is a toolset that allows users to input and update key project data easily, quickly, and frequently via Excel-based input documents. This allows management quick access to obtain information on the

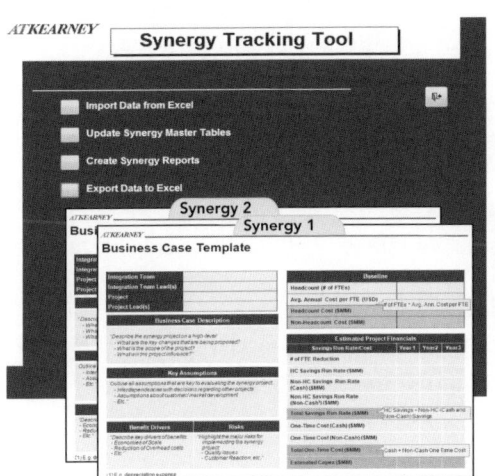
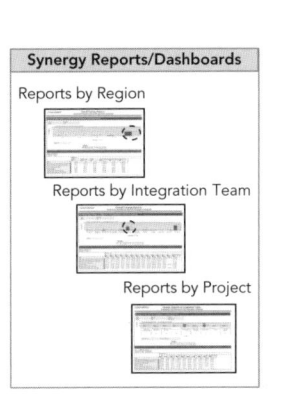

FIGURE A.9   Synergy Summaries Tool and Reports

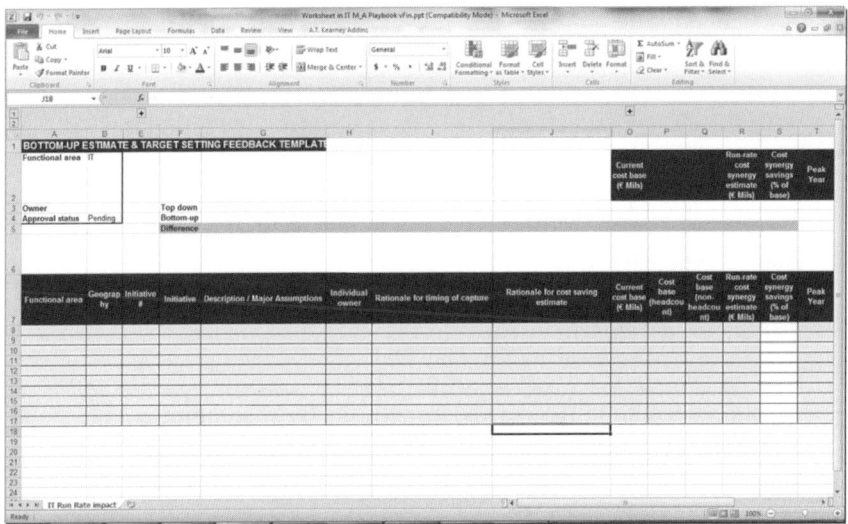

Description

Run-rate cost synergy capture for each functional area by quarter/year

Capture both top-down and bottom-up cost base and run-rate cost synergy estimates

FIGURE A.10   Example of a Tracking Database

progress of each initiative. This key tool establishes a BTR process in the integration program.

Objective: The BTR's ability to provide information to management in a customizable format achieves multiple goals:

- Provides leaders with critical information to manage risks, acknowledge wins, close gaps, and allocate resources accordingly.
- Provides a forward-looking view on the risks and milestones expected in the near term to alert key stakeholders on upcoming deadlines and potential risks.
- Tracks and charts benefit delivery across multiple initiatives. Financially, this helps to reconcile benefits delivered vs. underlying business performance and maps these benefits against the integration plan.

LAUNCH RISK MANAGEMENT PROCESS

Merger Risk Profile

Description: The merger risk profile is a comprehensive list of risks expected from M&A and during the PMI process. The risk profile should contain the following information:

- Risk owner: The team member who has the most interest in resolving the risk and is best placed to assess that it has been managed successfully.
- Risk action manager: The team member tasked to action the risk plan under the supervision of the risk owner.
- Risk status update.

Objective: Provides the project management office with an overview of the risks expected in the PMI process.

Project Risk Prioritization

Description: Project risk prioritization is a strategic assessment of the risks highlighted in the merger risk profile. Inputs on the prioritization are derived from interviews with project managers and validated with the relevant sponsors and champions. These are reviewed and rated based on criticality and complexity in resolving.

Objective: Project risk prioritization is a critical activity in the risk management process to identify risks and allocate resources in managing these risks. The project risk prioritization allows management a visual representation of these risks.

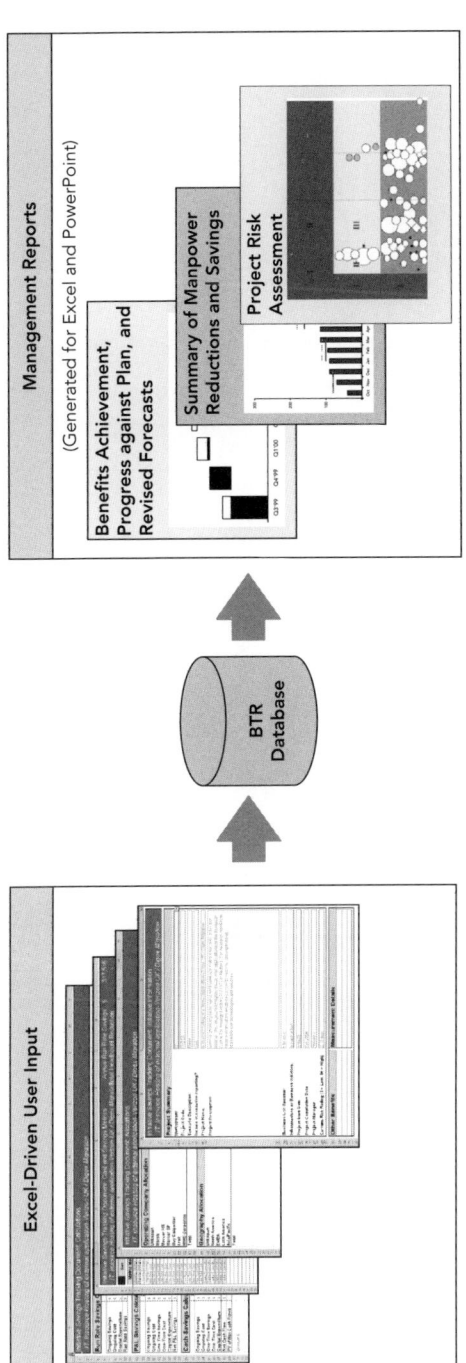

FIGURE A.11 Benefits Tracking and Reporting (BTR) Framework

179

Example—Risk register

Ref.	Criti-cality	Control-ability	Risk Statement	Owner	Action By	Action Status
LO_19	Red	D	• If MTS on-line developments are not completed to relieve XYZ storage constraints by 21 Aug, then MTS will not run reliably in Frankfurt post-conversion.	Anderson	Smith	• June 21 (Anderson): Additional Unix expert recruited. Developing contingency plan to purchase extra storage.
LO_21	Red	C	• If any business units or locations do not provide end of days (EOD) to meet timelines for the dress rehearsals, conversion weekends, and post-conversion processing, then start of day for some businesses will be delayed.	Jones	Holt	• June 15 (Holt): All business/locations unit heads will be contacted directly by end of July. Units XYZ, ABC missed EOD last week
LO_29	Red	B	• If the dress rehearsals are not a complete and true reflection of both the conversion week's end and end-to-end testing of the live environment, then untested functionality may be run for the first-time post-conversion and reconciliation may be difficult.	Burge	Stone	• June 20 (Burge): Test data have been developed in collaboration with the business units. The tests will be run with 150 percent of normal transaction volumes
FR_29	Red	C	• If the data conversion from XYZ to ABC UAT is not finished by the middle of June in Frankfurt, then manual procedures will have to be in place that satisfy the Frankfurt reporting requirements.	Jones	Smith	• June 20 (Jones): Considering outsourcing conversion to XYZ. Three additional staff would be required for manual processing.
LO_47	Amber	A	• If the PQR conversion is not completed by 12 Aug for London, then re-planning will be required since conversion will create a contention for key controllers' resources.	Wilson	Simpson	• June 15 (Willson): On target for conversion on 5 Aug. An additional resource from NY is due to start 29 Jun.

FIGURE A.12 Merger Risk Profile

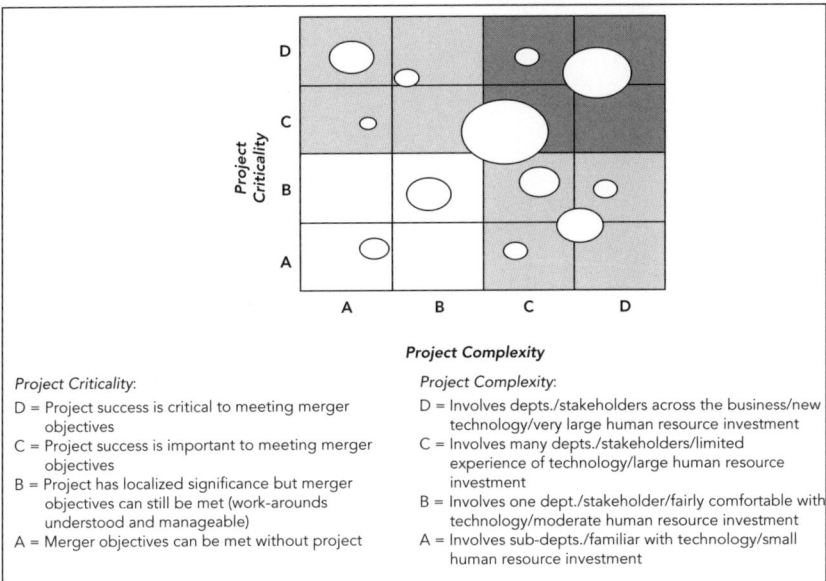

Project Criticality:

D = Project success is critical to meeting merger objectives

C = Project success is important to meeting merger objectives

B = Project has localized significance but merger objectives can still be met (work-arounds understood and manageable)

A = Merger objectives can be met without project

Project Complexity:

D = Involves depts./stakeholders across the business/new technology/very large human resource investment

C = Involves many depts./stakeholders/limited experience of technology/large human resource investment

B = Involves one dept./stakeholder/fairly comfortable with technology/moderate human resource investment

A = Involves sub-depts./familiar with technology/small human resource investment

FIGURE A.13 Project Risk Prioritization

Risk Mitigation Plan

Description: Once risks have been documented and prioritized, a risk mitigation plan is formulated by the team to be executed.

Objective: Risk mitigation should be a formal process that helps the team anticipate and plan for risks expected in the integration process. The risk mitigation plan is the output of this planning process with specific action steps to be implemented.

Tip: Actions from the risk mitigation plan should be incorporated into the main project plans. Risk mitigation plans are often dynamic as the integration process moves forward and should be regularly updated.

LAUNCH CHANGE MANAGEMENT AND COMMUNICATIONS PROCESSES

Change Readiness Assessment Tool

Description: The change readiness assessment tool helps evaluate each function's level of willingness and ability to execute and prepare for the integration.

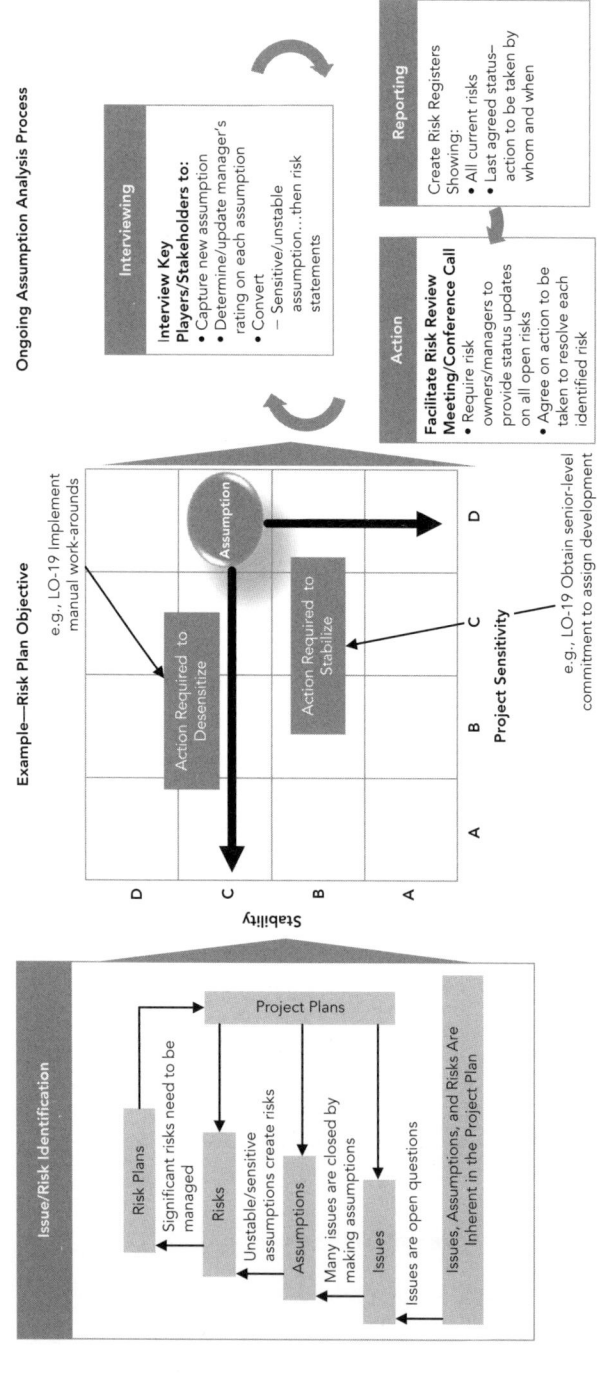

Ongoing Assumption Analysis Process

Interviewing

Interview Key Players/Stakeholders to:
- Capture new assumption
- Determine/update manager's rating on each assumption
- Convert
  - Sensitive/unstable assumption…then risk statements

Reporting

Create Risk Registers Showing:
- All current risks
- Last agreed status—action to be taken by whom and when

Action

Facilitate Risk Review Meeting/Conference Call
- Require risk owners/managers to provide status updates on all open risks
- Agree on action to be taken to resolve each identified risk

Example—Risk Plan Objective

e.g., LO-19 Implement manual work-arounds

Action Required to Desensitize

Action Required to Stabilize

Assumption

Stability

Project Sensitivity

A B C D

D C B A

e.g., LO-19 Obtain senior-level commitment to assign development resources to MTS project

Issue/Risk Identification

Project Plans

Risk Plans

Significant risks need to be managed

Risks

Unstable/sensitive assumptions create risks

Assumptions

Many issues are closed by making assumptions

Issues

Issues are open questions

Issues, Assumptions, and Risks Are Inherent in the Project Plan

FIGURE A.14 Mitigation Planning Process

Objective: The tool provides management with an overview of where each function stands in regard to the changes anticipated in the integration process. This will allow management to anticipate resistance, identify roadblocks, and direct resources, or develop a mitigation plan to resolve any issues.

Stakeholder Issues Assessment

Description: Stakeholder issues assessment is a comprehensive analysis of the issues raised by key stakeholders regarding the integration. Inputs from each key stakeholder are first consolidated in an issue register and rated according to their associated risk and level of impact to the organization and the integration process.

Objective: The stakeholder issues assessment is an important process to anticipate and understand any issues in the merger and plan for any possible risk. This helps to provide early resolutions aimed at addressing the needs of stakeholders.

Stakeholder Mapping

Description: Stakeholder mapping identifies the key stakeholders and their impact on the integration. Stakeholders are typically grouped into four main categories:

1. Adversaries: Oppose the project and have considerable involvement.
2. Naysayers: Oppose the project but have low involvement.

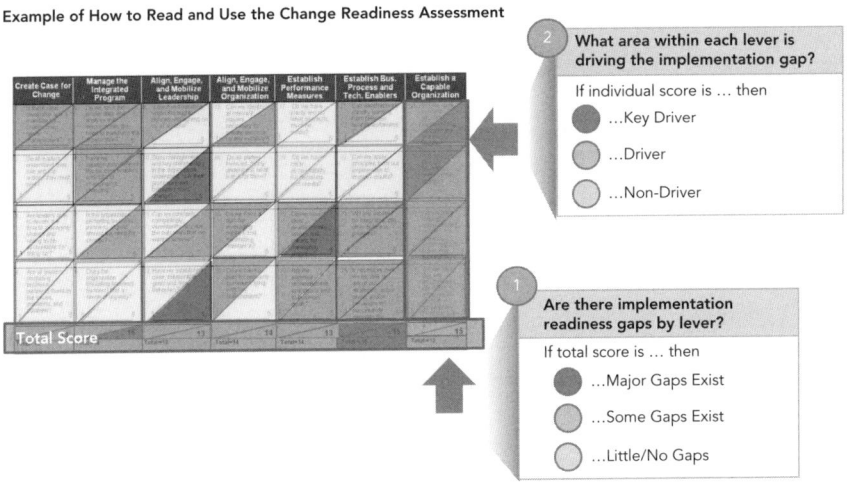

Example of How to Read and Use the Change Readiness Assessment

FIGURE A.15 *Change Readiness Assessment Tool*

Example—Issues Rating

Risky assumptions (convert to risks)

Issue Stability

				Risky assumptions (convert to risks)
D — Very unstable			A1 A2	A12 A3
C — Fairly unstable	A6		A4	A5
B — Fairly stable				
A — Very stable				

Increasing risk

Level of impact

A — Minimal impact · B — Moderate impact · C — Significant impact · D — Critical impact

Example—Issue Register

	Issue Register			
No.	Issue (Question)	Origi-nator	Poten-tial Risk Rating	Resolved by (date)
1	Which sales platform will be adopted?	Squire	Red	March 31
2	How many resources will be required to cover marketing data conversion?	Wake-mann	Red	April 15
3	How do we ensure that users are available to review design specs in week 24?	Howe	Red	April 15
4	How do we ensure that the workstations are installed by week 19?	White	Red	April 30
5	How do we ensure that all businesses complete EODs for the first dress rehearsal?	Ander-son	Amber	April 15

FIGURE A.16 Stakeholder Issues Assessment

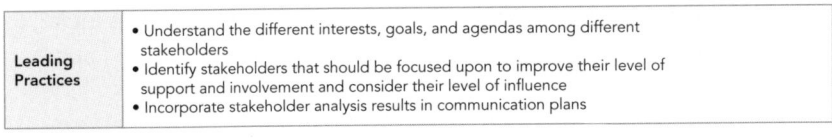

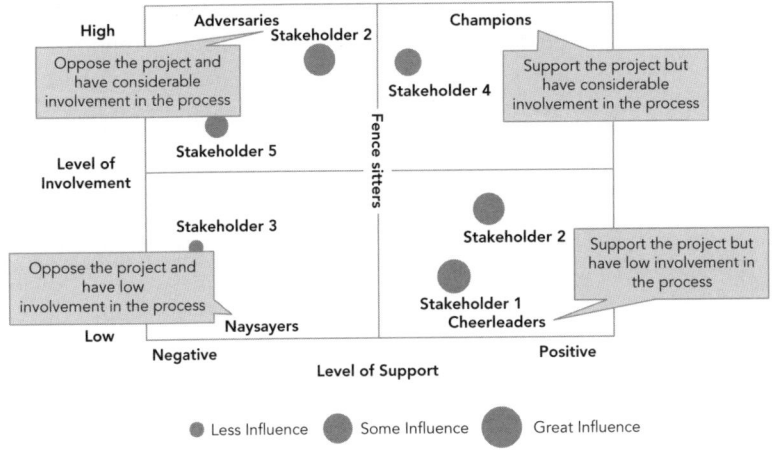

FIGURE A.17 Stakeholder Mapping

3. Cheerleaders: Support the project but have low involvement.
4. Champions: Support the project and have high involvement in the project.

Objective: Stakeholder mapping is crucial to ensure support continues to drive the change. Mapping the stakeholders on a matrix allows the PMI team to understand the different interests, goals, and agendas among various stakeholders and understand which stakeholders need to be managed and which can be leveraged.

Communications Strategy and Plan

Description: The communications strategy matrix identifies how information should be delivered throughout the integration process. It considers key factors such as the importance of the message, the audience's likely reactions, credibility and appropriateness of the delivery method, timing of the message, and availability of the individual deliverers.

Objective: The communications strategy should be a formal process in mapping the different types of communications required, the stakeholders to which they should be delivered, and the timing of these communications. The communications strategy matrix is a deliverable from this planning process.

Tip: A communications plan should be developed after creating the strategy matrix. In this plan, activities are scheduled to coincide with specific initiative development progress. The schedule establishes overall ownership and control responsibility. A senior level manager should be responsible for coordinating the control and consistency of communication activities.

Example—Communications Strategy

	Type	Example	Description
Inter-personal	**Face-to-face**	Divisional department meetings Site visitors/tours Q&As HR Q&As Senior management visits to department meetings Breakfast meetings Other	• Cascade used for some messages • To promote familiarity with new sites and to help break the ice • Designed to identify and answer problem issues • To deal with job-related questions • Opportunistic "drop-in" visits to departments to facilitate face-to-face • Opportunity for staff to meet senior managers informally
	Audio-visual	Satellite briefings Videos Other	• Major announcements/face-to-face across the organization • Introduction to company; executive interviews on integration
	Tele-phone	Hotline Other	• Designed to answer questions such as who is responsible for what; organization charts of emerging organization
	Elec-tronic	E-mail updates Other	• For detailed information (e.g., on appointments)
Electronic/ mechanical	**Printed**	Corporate newsletter Functional newsletter Other	• Weekly summaries of major issues/recent senior management statements, etc. • Integration updates • Weekly/every two weeks as required

Example—Communication Plan

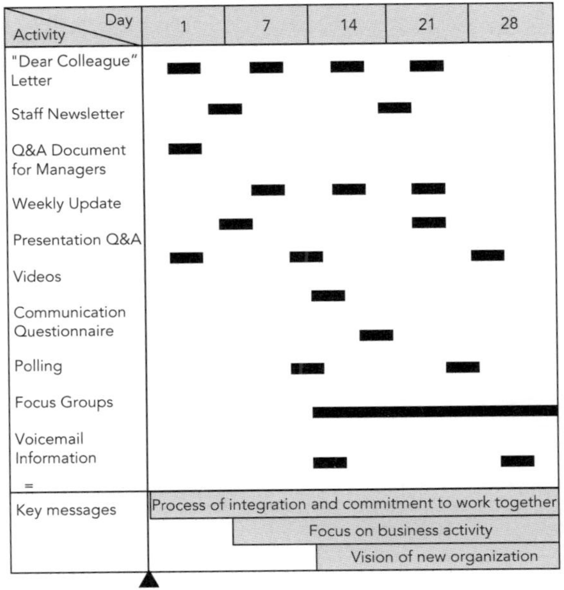

FIGURE A.18 Communications Strategy and Plan

Notes

CHAPTER 2

1. *CIA World Factbook.*
2. Euromonitor International, *Retailing in China,* January 2011, 12.
3. "Retail Global Expansion: A Portfolio of Opportunities," The 2011 A.T. Kearney Global Retail Development Index, www.atkearney.com/index .php/Publications/retail-global-expansion-a-portfolio-of-opportunities2011 -global-retail-development-index.html.
4. "China Resources Could Buy Jiangxi Retail Asset, Accelerates Development of Retail Business," *Business China,* March 30, 2011, http://en.21cbh.com/ HTML/2011–3–30/3MMjUwXzIwOTc3Mg.html.
5. "CR Snow Breweries Buys Henan-Based Brewer for 3rd Time, Gearing Up for Local Market," *Business China,* July 23, 2011, http://en.21cbh.com/ HTML/2011–7–23/xMMjUwXzIxMDYxMA.html.
6. "Henan's Last Independent Brewer Waging Lonely Battle," *Want China Times,* March 10, 2011, www.wantchinatimes.com/news-subclass-cnt.aspx?cid=12 02&MainCatID=12&id=20110310000080.
7. Michael Shari, "Asia's Banks on the Fast Track," *Global Finance,* June 2011, 23.
8. "China's Hebei to Launch Steel Consolidation Drive," *Reuters,* November 4, 2010, www.reuters.com/article/2010/11/05/china-steel-consolidation -idUSTOE6A401K20101105.

CHAPTER 3

1. Ann Graham, "Too Good To Fail," *Strategy + Business* (strategy-business.com), February 23, 2010, www.strategy-business.com/article/10106?gko=74e5d.
2. "Tetley Bagged by India's Tata," *BBC.com,* February 27, 2000, http://news.bbc .co.uk/2/hi/business/658724.stm.
3. Shankkar Aiyar, "2000 Tata Tea-Tetley Merger: The Cup That Cheered," *India Today* (Indiatoday.in), December 28, 2009, http://indiatoday.intoday.in/site/story/ 2000-Tata+Tea-Tetley+merger:+The+cup+that+cheered/1/76481.html.

4. Ibid.

5. Robert Clark, "Strait Crossing Sees SingTel Take Telkomsel Stake," *Telecom Asia*, December 1, 2001.

6. Loizos Heracleous, "SingTel: Venturing into the Region," *Asian Case Research Journal* 9, no. 1 (2005): 37–60.

7. Adeline Paul Raj, "CIMB Aims for Top 3 Spot in Asean by 2015," *The Business Times* (Malaysia), April 9, 2011, 1.

8. "CIMB Looking to Acquire Banks in the Region," *The Star/Asia News Network*, April 10, 2011, www.asiaone.com/Business/News/Story/A1Story20110410–272739.html.

9. Effie Chew and Patrick Barta, "Malaysia's CIMB Takes Aim at Southeast Asia," *The Wall Street Journal*—Asia, March 31, 2010, 33.

10. Ibid.

11. Ibid.

12. SingTel press release, February 2003.

13. Alvin Chua, "Singapore Telecommunications," *National Library Board Singapore Infopedia*, March 21, 2011, http://infopedia.nl.sg/articles/SIP_1610_2011–03–21.html.

14. Lynn Lee, "Antitrust Case: Temasek Loses Final Appeal," *The Straits Times*, May 25, 2010.

15. Dhanya Ann Thoppil, "Infosys Wants U.S. Acquisitions," *Wall Street Journal* (WSJ.com), February 24, 2011, http://online.wsj.com/article/SB10001424052748703408604576163704059394880.html.

16. Bharghavi Nagaraju, "Infosys Eyes Buys in Europe, Japan, and Healthcare Sector," Reuters, May 1, 2011, www.reuters.com/article/2011/05/01/us-india-infosys-acquisition-idUSTRE7400OQ20110501.

17. Naazneen Karmali, "Sunil Mittal Seals Zain Deal," *Forbes.com*, March 30, 2010, www.forbes.com/2010/03/30/bharti-india-telecom-mittal-africa-zain.html.

18. Devidutta Tripathy and Eman Goma, "Bharti Closes $9 Billion Zain Africa Deal," *Reuters*, June 8, 2010, www.reuters.com/article/2010/06/08/us-zain-bharti-idUSTRE6570VJ20100608.

19. Ibid.

20. Devidutta Tripath and Sumeet Chatterjee, "Why Is Bharti Chasing Zain's Africa Assets?" *Reuters.com*, February 16, 2010, http://in.reuters.com/article/2010/02/16/idINIndia-46194820100216.

21. Peter S. Goodman, "IBM Deal Puts Lenovo on Global Stage: Buyout of the U.S. Company's PC Divisions Highlights China's Emergence," *The Washington Post*, December 8, 2004.

22. Ibid.

23. Sharon Silke Carty, "Tata Motors to Buy Jaguar, Land Rover for $2.3B," *USA Today*, March 26, 2008, www.usatoday.com/money/autos/2008–03–25-ford-sells-jaguar-land-rover-tata_N.htm.

24. Steven Rothwell and Vipin V. Nair, "Tata Motors Plans to Build Jaguar, Land Rover Models in China," *Bloomberg*, May 28, 2010.

25. Anirban Chowdhury and Nikhil Gulati, "Tata Motors Profit Zooms as Jaguar, Land Rover Sales Rise," *Dow Jones Newswires*, February 11, 2011, http://online .wsj.com/article/BT-CO-20110211–705738.html.

26. "Kirin Eyeing Synergy Among Group Firms in Asia-Oceana," *Nikkei report*, August 19, 2010.

27. Michiyo Nakamoto, "Kirin Buys F&N Stake from Temasek," *FT.com*, July 26, 2010, www.ft.com/cms/s/0/8f84a796–98bb-11df-a0b7–00144feab49a .html#axzz1Lui1VUaK.

28. Dr. Krishna Kumar and Dr. Kishore Kumar Morya, "Tata-Corus: Spearheading India's Global Drive to Growth," 2008, www.london.edu/assets/documents/ facultyandresearch/Tata_Corus_Spearheading_Indias_Global_Drive_to_ Growth.pdf.

29. Matt Chambers, "China Heads Local Mining Merger and Acquisition Deals," *The Australian*, February 16, 2010, www.theaustralian.com .au/business/china-heads-local-mining-merger-and-acquisition-deals/ story-e6frg8zx-1225830682572.

30. Rita Nazareth, Christopher Donville, and Elisabeth Berhmann, "China's Need to Acquire Africa Means Bid for Equinox Increases 18 Percent: Real M&A," *Bloomberg*, April 5, 2011, www.bloomberg.com/news/2011 –04–05/china-need-to-acquire-africa-means-bid-for-equinox-increases -18-real-m-a.html.

31. Lwazi Bam, director of corporate finance at Deloitte, "Africa Poised for Growth," April 14, 2011, *Deloitte SA blog*, http://deloittesa.wordpress.com/2011/04/14/ africa-poised-for-growth/.

32. "Tata Taps Equity Markets to Repay Jaguar Debt," *Euroweek* 1126, October 16, 2009.

33. Jamil Anderlini, "China to Deploy Forex Reserves," *Financial Times* (FT.com), July 21, 2009.

34. Chris V. Nicholson, "Chinese Oil Company Gets $30 Billion Loan for Acquisitions," *New York Times*, September 9, 2009, www.nytimes .com/2009/09/10/business/global/10oil.html.

35. Daisuke Wakabayashi, "NTT to Buy African Firm," *Wall Street Journal Asia*, July 16, 2010, B6.

36. Kana Inagaki and Juro Osawa, "Takeda, Toshiba Make $16 Billion M&A Push," *Wall Street Journal Asia*, May 20, 2011, 1.

37. Chris V. Nicholson, "Thai Union to Buy MWB in $884 Million Deal," *New York Times* (NYT.com), July 28, 2010, http://dealbook.nytimes.com/2010/07/28/ thai-union-to-buy-mwb-in-884-million-deal/.

38. Kathrin Hille, "Sinopac Rebuffs Taishin Bid and Opts for Merger," *Financial Times*, March 29, 2005.

39. Mark Scott, "Controversy Swirls Around Rio Tinto-Chinalco Deal," *Businessweek.com*, March 17, 2009.

40. Eric Johnston, "Singapore Finally Walks from ASX Bid," *Sydney Morning Herald* (SMH.com), April 8, 2011, www.smh.com.au/business/singapore-finally -walks-from-asx-bid-20110408–1d6o4.html.

CHAPTER 4

1. Carlos D. Ramirez and Ling Hui Tan, "Singapore Inc. Versus the Private Sector: Are Government-Linked Companies Different?" International Monetary Fund Working Paper WP/03/156, July 2003, www.imf.org/external/pubs/ft/ wp/2003/wp03156.pdf.

2. John Burton, "Malaysia's CIMB to be Delisted in Bank Revamp," *Financial Times*, June 6, 2005, www.ft.com.

3. Anand P. Raman and Peter J. Williamson, "How China Reset Its Global Acquisition Agenda," *Harvard Business Review*, April 2011, 109.

4. Ibid.

5. M. Jegathesan, "Malaysian Airline Tie-Up Hailed as a Win Win," *Agence France Presse*, August 10, 2011.

6. S. Jayasankaran and Cris Prystay, "Fare Fight: Discount Airlines Proliferate Across Asia, Despite Red Tape — Former Malaysia Music Man Leads Parade of Carriers Offering Low-Cost Tickets," *Wall Street Journal Asia*, July 20, 2004, 1.

7. Leslie Lopez, "Major Overhaul of Malaysia's Airline Sector," *The Straits Times*, August 10, 2011.

8. Joseph P. Manguno, "India Considers a Proposal to Combine its Growing Domestic, Overseas Airlines," *Wall Street Journal*, August 13, 1986.

9. Ravi Velloor, "India's National Airline Flying on Empty," *The Straits Times*, August 13, 2011.

10. Ibid.

11. Ibid.

CHAPTER 5

1. Keith Wallis, "Mainland Mega-Carrier Could Emerge Amid Consolidation," *The South China Morning Post*, March 11, 2011, 1.

2. Margot Patrick and Fiona Law, "HSBC To Cut Costs, Sell Businesses in New Strategy," *Wall Street Journal*, May 11, 2011, http://online.wsj.com/article/ BT-CO-20110511–708804.html.

3. Anthony F. Buono, "Consulting to Integrate Mergers and Acquisitions," in L. Greiner & F. Poulfelt, *The Contemporary Consultant: Insights from World Experts* (Mason, OH: Thomson/South-Western, 2005), 229–249.

CHAPTER 8

1. Taiga Uranaka and Mayumi Negishi, "Japan Brewers Kirin, Suntory End Merger Talks," *Reuters*, February 8, 2010.
2. Pawan S. Budhwar, Arup Varma, Anastasia A. Katou, and Deepa Narayan, "The Role of HR in Cross-Border Mergers and Acquisitions: The Case of Indian Pharmaceutical Firms," *Multinational Business Review* 17, no. 2 (July 1, 2009).
3. Ibid.
4. Eric Bellman and Jackie Range, "Merger, Indian Style: Buy a Brand, Leave It Alone," *Wall Street Journal*–Europe, March 22, 2008, A9.
5. Carly Chynoweth, "Dare to Try, the Indian Way: The Takeover of British Companies by Tata, the Asian Conglomerate, Provides Useful Lessons for Both Sides," *The Sunday Times*, April 17, 2011, 1.
6. Ruth David, "Tata Acquires Euro Steelmaker Corus," *Forbes.com*, October 22, 2006, www.forbes.com/2006/10/22/tata-corus-mna-biz-cx_rd_1022corus .html.
7. Communicaid Press Release, 2007, www.communicaid.com/news .php?newsId=76.
8. "Ratan Tata Hits Out at Corus, JLR Managers for Not Walking Extra Mile," *The Economic Times*, May 21, 2011, http://articles.economictimes.indiatimes .com/2011–05–21/news/29568738_1_jlr-scunthorpe-corus.
9. Tor Ching Li, "Nippon Sheet Glass CEO Stresses Need for Clarity—Ensuring Understanding Is Key for a Company with Different Cultures," *Wall Street Journal*–Managing in Asia, April 6, 2009, 20.
10. Josephine Moulds, "Stuart Chambers Quits Nippon Sheet Glass on Finding He's 'Not Japanese'," *The Telegraph*, August 26, 2009, www.telegraph.co.uk/ finance/newsbysector/industry/6094612/Stuart-Chambers-quits-Nippon -Sheet-Glass-on-finding-hes-not-Japanese.html.
11. Martin Fackler, "Japanese Bank Merger Plan Draws Support—UFJ-Mitsubishi Tokyo Deal Is Expected to Break Mold By Making Business Sense," *Wall Street Journal*–Europe, July 15, 2004, M1.
12. Makoto Miyazaki, "Mizuho's Balancing Act: Megabank's Shakeup Could Hinge on Personnel Issues," *Yomiuri Shimbun*, May 25, 2011, www.yomiuri.co.jp/dy/ business/T110524005737.htm.
13. Atsuko Fukase, "New CEO, New Mizuho Culture," *Wall Street Journal*–Asia, June 23, 2011, 22, http://online.wsj.com/article/SB1000142405270230465 7804576401482167239952.html.

14. P. C. Haspeslagh and D. B. Jemison, *Managing Acquisitions: Creating Value through Corporate Renewal* (New York: Free Press, 1991).

15. Ven Ram, "Managing Asia: Former Standard Chartered Executive's Credo—Acquisition Taught Lessons in Bridging Bank Cultures," *Wall Street Journal—Asia*, May 4, 2009, 24.

16. Indranil Roy and George S. Hallenbeck, "Asia 2.0: Leading the Next Wave of Growth in Asia," The Korn/Ferry Institute, December 2010, 8, www.kornferryinstitute.com/files/pdf1/Asia2.0.pdf.

CHAPTER 9

1. Ryan Dezember, "Mergers, Acquisitions Fall by the Wayside," *Wall Street Journal—Asia*, October 3, 2011, 25.

About the Authors

 **Vikram Chakravarty** is a partner with A.T. Kearney's Singapore office and heads the strategy and corporate finance practice in Asia. He has over 15 years of consulting experience and has advised leading corporations across Asia on strategy and competitiveness issues.

Vikram has led over 60 projects in private equity, commodities, energy, industrials, consumer products, logistics, and financial industries. Prior to joining A.T. Kearney, Vikram was Monitor Co.'s Regional Director of Strategy and Competitiveness.

 **Chua Soon Ghee** is a partner with A.T. Kearney's Singapore office, and is a core practitioner of both the firm's strategy practice and its communications/high-tech practice. He has over 14 years of consulting and industry experience across Asia, and is focused on advising global and Asian corporations on how to grow in Asia and run their operations efficiently.

Besides the telecommunications and electronics industry, where he spends most of his time, Soon Ghee also has experience in the automotive, logistics, and agriculture industries.

Index